ADVANCE PRAISE

"Very few of us can claim to have been raised by the ideal mother. . . .
The information that Dr. Poulter provides here will help the reader attain
the self-knowledge and understanding to remove these impediments."

   —Dr. Barry Weichman, Dentist

"I'm giving this book to every one of my clients. Why? Because every
person's life is on these pages! It's amazing. Dr. Poulter captures how *The
Mother Factor* affects your life, how to change it, and how to heal the old
hurts to help you reach your dreams. Enjoy reading your story. . . . You'll
laugh, you'll cry, you'll smile. Enjoy the journey."

   —Kathleen Hellmers, CEO, InvestmentGoals

"Dr. Poulter is a genius! This book has helped me solve lifelong mys-
teries about my own behavioral patterns and gain much insight into my
own mother. . . . This book is going to help me lead a better and more fulfilling life from this point on. I urge all ages and genders to read it."

   —Amy Hackman, Real Estate Broker

"Poulter offers a unique look at the profound effect our mothers have on
our emotional well-being and happiness. Its easy-to-comprehend
approach first helps us identify the type of connection we have with our
mothers and then suggests how we can finally break free from those
often painful ties that bind. . . . *The Mother Factor* left me with a smile
on my face and feeling closer to my mother than ever before."

   —John Ehrenfeld, Writer/Producer

"Dr. Poulter's book resonates with clarity for me. . . . His sound, straightforward analysis and suggestions should be appreciated and taken to
heart by all of us moms and daughters. They also suggest [how] a little
bit of the 'mother' in all of us can be applied in our relationships with our
family, friends, and the world at large."

   —Jean M. Clark, Institutional Investment Manager

"Dr. Poulter perfectly captures what it is like to grow up with an unpredictable mother, but more importantly how to work through the issues it presents in your life."
—Evan Carter, Consultant

"Dr. Poulter provides us with the tools to examine our emotional legacy and explore how our past relationships impact our current relationships and functioning. His valuable words give us the ability to recognize emotional strengths, examine our emotional liabilities, and ultimately empower us to develop our highest potential."
—Mary Klem, Marriage and Family Therapist

"Stephan Poulter empowers adult children by revealing the many ways in which mothers' parenting styles influence our own style of relating to others. *The Mother Factor* illustrates that it is possible to transform and enhance our lives by incorporating only the most positive aspects gained from our first love relationship."
—Danica Thornberry, LAc
Licensed Acupuncturist and
Founder of Well Women Acupuncture

"I feel like Dr. Poulter wrote 'The Unpredictable Mother' . . . for me! So much of it rang true. I only wish I had more time with my mom, just in case there was the chance that things 'could be different.'"
—Sally Levine
Cofounder and President, Memory Lane Sports Collections

"Having spent most of my adult life concentrating on personal growth, I am no stranger to the subject of parental impact on children, and how that impact influences adulthood. Stephan Poulter's book brings the subject 'down to life size' like no other I've read, without ever sacrificing substance or oversimplifying it. I learned a lot from this book."
—William Malin, President, Historic Masquers Club

THE MOTHER FACTOR

Stephan B. Poulter, PhD

THE MOTHER FACTOR

How Your Mother's Emotional Legacy Impacts Your Life

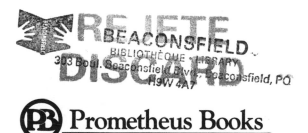

Prometheus Books

59 John Glenn Drive
Amherst, New York 14228-2119

Published 2008 by Prometheus Books

Inquiries should be addressed to
Prometheus Books
59 John Glenn Drive
Amherst, New York 14228–2119
VOICE: 716–691–0133, ext. 210
FAX: 716–691–0137
WWW.PROMETHEUSBOOKS.COM

12 11 10 09 08   5 4 3 2 1

Library of Congress Cataloging-in-Publication Data

Poulter, Stephan B.
The mother factor : how your mother's emotional legacy impacts your life
/ by Stephan B. Poulter.
    p. cm.
Includes bibliographical references.
ISBN 978–1–59102–607–5
1. Mother and child. I. Title.

HQ759.P68 2008
155.9'24—dc22

2007051920

Printed in the United States of America on acid-free paper

To

Madison and Jonathan, who never stop inspiring me.
Charlotte, Debbie, and Pete, you are always in my heart.

All the women and men who have struggled to find,
understand, and grasp their mother factor.

OTHER BOOKS BY THE AUTHOR

Mending the Broken Bough:
Restoring the Promise of the Mother-Daughter Relationship

Father Your Son:
How to Become the Father You Have Always Wanted to Be

The Father Factor:
How Your Father's Legacy Impacts Your Career

CONTENTS

SECTION II: FIVE MOTHERING STYLES OF THE MOTHER FACTOR

SECTION III: MOTHER FACTOR POTENTIAL— CREATING YOUR LIFE

AUTHOR'S NOTE

All the stories, examples, and voices in this book are derived in part from over twenty-five years of work experience, my clinical experience, research, law enforcement career, and ministry experience. However, the names, places, and other details contained in this book have been altered to protect the privacy and anonymity of all the individuals to whom they refer. Therefore, any similarities between the names and stories of the individuals and families described in this book and those individuals known to readers is inadvertent and purely coincidental.

The use of feminine pronouns and specific references to only mothers in this book are for the sole purpose of explaining the issues of mothers to their daughters and sons. The apparent exclusion of masculine pronouns is for the purpose of writing, educating, and illustrating the subject matter only. The importance and relevance of fathers to this topic is also covered.

ACKNOWLEDGMENTS

I could write a complete manuscript for all the people who have contributed to the creation of this book. The people past and present have been countless and vitally important to assisting in creating *The Mother Factor*. Special thanks to the late Celia Rocks, Kevin Dirth, Jennifer Hung, Mike Bloomberg, and Peter Brett Poulter. I want to especially thank Linda Greenspan Regan for again giving me the opportunity to create a book; Julia Wolfe, who lent me her hand, wisdom, and unconditional timeless support; Kye Hellmers, for the endless discussions about being "perfectly imperfect"; and all the daughters, sons, and fathers who shared their stories with me. Finally, all the wonderful people at Prometheus Books for their support and guidance.

I want to thank my extended support network and *Mother Factor* contributors: Kye and Kathleen Hellmers, William and Mary Klem, Barry Weichman, Bill Malen, Kalila Shapiro, Winston Gooden, Bruce Wexler, Evan Carter, Sandra Vasquez, Mike Jones, Ed Vanderflet, and B. Zax. Without these types of people in my life (past and present) and in my career, I could have never ventured out of my personal, professional, and family box and sat down in front of my laptop to put this all together. Sometimes life has a way of putting things in place, and you know it is all coming together perfectly. *The Mother Factor* is example of that. I owe so many people a "thank-you" and I know my gratitude is because of the people involved.

Section I

THE BASICS OF THE MOTHER FACTOR LEGACY

INTRODUCTION
We Are All Sons and Daughters

I am living my mother's life. She said to be single, I am single. She said live alone, be happy and don't allow anyone to control you.

I have done everything my mother wanted. She died twenty years ago but she is still very alive in my life today. I have just the life she wanted.

—Betty Lou, age fifty-eight

Even though I had a close relationship with my father, my mother has been my emotional guide. I am very similar to her in how I express my thoughts and feelings. My mother has influenced all my relationships. I can hear myself at home and at work, handling situations, talking to people in the way my mother did/does.

—Edward, age thirty-nine

People typically are more apt to talk about their mother than their father. The role of mothers with daughters and mothers with sons is a timeless relationship. The two quotes above clearly illustrate the ongoing emotional impact that mothers have on their children regardless of age, distance, or death. This impact isn't limited to simply a positive or negative parent-child dynamic. It's based on an emotional legacy—the mother factor. The mother factor, in essence, incorporates all the different types of emotional functioning, mothering styles, communication patterns, individuation processes (separating from mom), and the ongoing psychology of the mother-daughter, mother-son relationship. The mother and adult child relationship (regardless of age—we are all sons and daughters), in all its different facets, emotional states, life circumstances, and everyday situations helps create the fabric and substance of our lives.

No one argues with the truth that mothers matter. Yet most of us will spend a lifetime not understanding this very complex legacy/relationship and its far-reaching impact. Mothers have historically been the center of heated discussion, research, debate, and mystery. The wealth and depth of psychological research into the mother-daughter and mother-son relationship have never been fully exhausted nor completely understood. We all know that our relationship with our mother has shaped our sense of self as nothing else has. This fact doesn't diminish or reduce the timeless influence that a father's legacy has on his children. Our mother and father are the bookends of our life, and our relationship with each is unique to us all. Each parent needs to be fully understood and appreciated in the special context of that relationship. Many times the most problematic parent becomes the sole focus of a child's life, while the other parent is dismissed as inconsequential. This is a very common family dynamic and can be a potential blind spot for that child in his or her adult life.

To avoid this very widespread mistake of ignoring a parent—the mother and her emotional imprint on her children—we will explore the wide-reaching influence mothers have on our lives. These pages will create a deeper appreciation of the enormous impact that your mother's emotional legacy has had on shaping and directing your life.

Let's first agree that your mother handed you her emotional

legacy, whether she did it consciously or unconsciously. The development of your emotional legacy started with you and your mother during pregnancy and continues on to this day, regardless of her age, death, or geographical distance. What constitutes that legacy is the focus of this book. For the purpose of clarity, the mother factor is defined as the following: *Your emotional development, functioning, and ability to form meaningful relationships in your family life, in your social life, and with your intimate partners; an emotional template started with your mother-child relationship that influences your feelings of frustration, love, fear, and hope; your mother's style of parenting as the template for your emotional disposition and your core sense of who and what you are in the world; your emotional functioning as consciously and unconsciously shaped by your mother.*

Your spoken and unspoken rules, behaviors, attitudes, relationship styles, communication patterns, and emotional functioning are all pieces of your mother factor. Since we all are sons and daughters, it would serve us well to intimately know the different pieces and facets of this powerful ongoing influence. There are very few issues or topics that will automatically elicit a daughter's or son's anger, frustration, sympathy, or love as quickly as a discussion of their mother. Remember that no one is neutral about one's mother or the emotional bond with her.

If you're still wondering about the existence of the mother factor, try an experiment. Think about a conflict you recently had with a friend, partner, boss, child, or a customer/client. Perhaps your close friend didn't call you as promised, a co-worker disappointed you, your child ignored your twenty cell phone calls, or your partner completely misunderstood something you did and the incident became a big conflict. Whatever the episode, summarize it in a paragraph, focusing on how you felt emotionally and the words and actions that you chose at that time.

Todd's paragraph, forty-four years old: I told Linda [his exclusive girlfriend of four months] that I couldn't meet her for a Sunday night dinner as we had planned. I became very defensive when I heard the disappointment and anger in her voice. I accused her of being selfish and only interested in her agenda, not my life. My gut feeling was shame and embarrassment. I feel this way every time I have to say no to a woman. What is difficult for me is the feeling that I am disappointing someone and especially my romantic partner now and in the past. The only thing that runs through my head when I am explaining myself is my mother's being mad at me. Linda was very mad at me for canceling dinner and I didn't speak to her for almost a week after the incident. She had a right to be mad, I just always "freak" out. Then I feel like I have to find a way to fix the problem. I have no way of fixing the problem, which becomes this frustrating continuous cycle. I do fine in other areas of my life but I can't tolerate conflict with my girlfriend. I have this random gut feeling when these situations occur, which is frequently. I feel as if I'm being scolded by my mother for disappointing her. I know that letting people down or upsetting them is part of a relationship, but for me it is a very big problem. I think one of the reasons that I am not married is I hate when a woman is upset with me or is disapproving of me. I feel absolutely pained when it happens and then I avoid the relationship.

Alexandra's paragraph, forty-one years old: I got off the phone with my mother the other day and was completely furious with myself. I know not to ask for her opinion or tell her anything that is remotely personal or important about my life. My mother always finds a way to criticize me or put me down. No matter what the topic is, it will always become a discussion about her. Then I start to yell the way she does and it becomes an awful discussion. I then feel like I am thirteen years old again, fighting for my personal independence from her control. I still find myself at times looking to my mother as my emotional guide. Then I spend at least the next two hours after these encounters really upset that I have had such a pointless emotionally heated argument with my mother. I never feel good about myself after speaking with her or seeing her. This tension evolved since I developed my own opinions. Now it seems that the problem is worse because I feel insecure about myself after any type of conflict with friends, co-workers, my kids, and my husband. I tend to overreact like my mother when I get upset and think I am being misunderstood. My mother's style of communicating is to get very emotional and become verbally aggressive. I am becoming like my mother.

After writing your paragraph or thinking about it, answer the following questions:

1. Did what you say in the encounter remind you in any way of how your mother spoke to you when you were a child?
2. Was there anything you said that was either the exact opposite of or identical to the tone and substance of your mother's conversations with you?
3. Were your feelings in this emotional encounter similar to or the exact opposite of those you experienced when you had a conflict with your mother as a child or now as an adult?
4. How do you or did you (if she is deceased) communicate with your mother as an adult?
5. How would you like to handle future emotional encounters in both your personal and professional relationships?

The odds are that, even without going through this formal exercise, you've experienced situations in which your words, thoughts, or feelings in a given situation remind you of an encounter with your mother. People commonly report talking to a friend or partner exactly as their mother spoke to them, even to the extent of using the same gestures, emotional tone, and expressions. They also frequently recall relating to a close friend in the same way that they related to their mother. In other instances, the impact of a mother on an adult child's emotional life can be less obvious but equally as powerful. In the examples of Todd and Alexandra, they have a very powerful emotional legacy from their mothers and are attempting to figure out how to channel it into a more positive factor rather than a stumbling block.

The most important issue at this point is to begin to recognize that there is an impact. The mother factor is only a negative in your life if it goes unrecognized, dismissed, and misunderstood. When you're more aware of the many different facets of it and learn to manage it, this factor can become a positive, life-changing force for you. Therefore, let's look at some issues that should begin to raise your awareness of the profound emotional impact your mother has on your life today. Feeling good about yourself and where your life is going starts with your mother and you.

OUR FIRST LOVE RELATIONSHIP

The first woman we ever loved was our mother! We may love many women later in life (girlfriends, lovers, sisters, friends, aunts, and daughters), but our mother was the first woman we've ever loved. This fact makes this relationship the most prominent factor in your emotional development. You were literally a part of your mother during her pregnancy. The wiring in your brain naturally makes you want to emotionally bond and connect with her. Babies want to be held, fed, and cared for by their mother. This initial bond becomes the seedbed and foundation from which all future emotional development, communication styles, personality types, and self-esteem formations evolve. No other relationship in your life has the potential to shape you like this one. The more you understand the emotional components of it, the more choices and opportunities will be available to you for relationship change and personal growth.

The mother-child bond can be likened to the sturdiness and operation of a car. You don't know what's really under the hood and how it will perform on the road until it leaves the factory—as when a child reaches adulthood and sets out on his own. The factory is the mother-child relationship that builds (develops) and installs the motor and all the necessary functioning parts. Knowing what's under the hood, your internal components, gives you the personal power and choices to further develop and create your own legacy. Whatever life circumstances you find yourself in require that you use your intelligence and emotional stability to properly navigate the conflicts and relationships on a personal, family, and professional level to create your own legacy. It is your ability to emotionally function in different settings that becomes the strongest and most accurate indicator of your potential for personal, professional achievement—your legacy. Your ability to function in adult relationships, whether personal or professional, is directly connected to your mother factor legacy. The foundation of your emotional life, personality, and self-esteem started developing when you were a very young child.[1]

It is the lack of bonding and unhealthy development that creates the early fractures (lack of trust, paranoia) in a person's psychological development and emotional foundation. These early fractures can be healed and resolved—but how? In order to heal and empower ourselves, we first must understand how our mother factor was constructed and formed. For all sons this is the first woman that we ever loved. For all daughters, this is also the first woman you ever loved and your first same-sex identification relationship. These naturally occurring bonds and early interactions create the powerful dynamic between a mother and son and mother and daughter. For a mother, the birth of her son or daughter arouses memories of her emotional connection with her own mother. As we move through these pages, we will repeatedly see how the power of this "first love relationship" has an enormous impact on our personal and professional life.

Some would think that the one thing that both mothers and children have in common—their time together from birth *onward*—would automatically create a positive emotional bond and a healthy, productive mother factor. Unfortunately, it doesn't always work out that way. The collective emotional experience of being in this relationship can create ripples and sometimes tidal waves in subsequent relationships that is felt for the duration of an adult child's life. It is this turmoil that can erupt in our emotional interactions and feelings, through our communication style and intimate relationships.

The wealth of literature on the power of our first love has been a topic of popular psychological mainstream discussion since Sigmund Freud, Carl Jung, and Melanie Klein described the lifelong influence and power that mothers have on their children.[2] Since that time, it has become widely accepted that a child's emotional disposition is dramatically influenced, impacted, and shaped by the day-to-day interactions with his or her mother. *The typical "blind spot" of this relationship is not understanding the legacy of these interactions where we assume that emotional stumbling blocks are random and inevitable.* This type of narrow belief tends to be shortsighted and one of the biggest hurdles to fully comprehending the mother factor and using it productively. One of the primary goals here is to expand your understanding so that your mother factor legacy becomes a source of strength and power, both personally and professionally.

MOTHER FACTOR ISSUES

Some common beliefs, concerns, experiences, frustrations, and comments that sons and daughters make about their mother factor are listed below. When the topic of mothers is raised, hardly anyone is without an opinion. (Saying that you have no opinion about your mother or feeling numb toward her are very serious anger issues that will be discussed later.) Consider the following questions and statements and how they relate to your mother-child relationship in the past and present:

- Why does my girlfriend get along fabulously with her mother and I can hardly stand to be in the same room with mine?
- I wish I was close to my mother.
- I am very irritable with people when they don't follow through on things for me. My mother is the same way with me.
- My mother always told me, "No one will ever be good enough for you." I have never had a relationship last longer than six months (a forty-nine-year-old son revealed).
- Every time I talk to my mother, why does the discussion always focus on her?
- I felt invisible to my mother while I was growing up. She still doesn't know what I do every day.
- I don't trust women (a daughter admits).
- I never get very close (emotionally) to my girlfriends (a son speaking).
- I have no close girlfriends; all my friends are men (a daughter confides).
- My mother's opinions, emotions, and communication style are a huge problem in my marriage: my wife hates my mother.
- My partner says I act just like my mother when I get angry or frustrated with people.
- I yell at people when I get upset.
- I have always felt insecure in relationships. I have this uneasy feeling that I am not good enough.
- While growing up, I found it impossible to speak with my mother about my feelings or emotions. Now I rarely express my thoughts or feelings to anyone.
- I avoid calling or talking to my mother, and she makes me feel guilty for not calling more (a son speaking).

- While growing up I felt that all roads led to my mother. She was the emotional commander in our house. My father never spoke unless my mother asked him a question.
- My mother always told me to never let anyone know when you were angry or upset. You are too vulnerable if you tell others your true feelings.
- Caring for my mother has caused me to always focus on others first and myself second. This pattern has made me very dependent on others and their opinion of me.
- I got along better with my father than with my mother, while growing up.
- I am forty-five-year-old woman and I still hear my mother's voice in my head whenever I go against her rules or beliefs. Her voice is very critical and angry.

The admissions listed above are just a few of the issues that underlie a son's and daughter's emotional legacy. It is clear from this short list of concerns expressed by both adult men and adult women that the mother-child emotional relationship is a force that has a lifelong, residual impact that is not easily measured or understood. The more you understand your mother-child relationship, however, regardless of your age or life circumstances, the more choices, options, and positive changes will be available to you.

It is important to mention that this entire investigation into your mother factor is for the sole purpose of your gaining new, valuable insight and clarity, which will open more options to your life. Too often this type of discussion can go in the direction of blame, resentment, and anger. We will discuss at length the need to move beyond blame and finger-pointing (removing your stumbling blocks) and instead to heal old wounds. There is an old saying in psychology: *you can't let go of what you don't know you're holding.* We are going to focus on your mother factor from many different angles and perspectives to give you a more complete view of your own legacy. Once you have these new and crucial insights, you will have the personal power to make different choices, to let go of old self-defeating patterns, to take new and positive action, and to have a deeper sense of fulfillment.

THE MOTHER FACTOR—TRANSCENDS TIME, DEATH, GENDER, AND INTIMACY

A very common obstacle to appreciating the profound effect of the mother factor is to rationalize away its significance. For example:

- My mother has been dead for ten years: how could she still have an impact on my relationships or the way I act now?
- I'm a man, so it makes more sense that my father, rather than my mother, would affect my emotional choices and relationships.
- I was never particularly close to my mother. I don't think she has much of an impact on my personal life today.
- My mother was a 1950s–1960s stay-at-home mom and she never had a professional paying job. How can she influence my professional choices and feelings?
- I never respected my mother's handling of emotional issues or her psychological maturity. I am completely different.
- My mother allowed my father to make all the decisions in the family, and I learned to follow my dad's lead, not my mothers.

Let's look at why each of these rationalizations is a very common blind spot and potential stumbling block to your future.

If your mother has died, that doesn't mean that the feelings from that relationship are dead too. Your unresolved feelings about your mother may be dormant or buried. Your mother's passing doesn't imply that the value or influence of her is at all diminished. Many of the most important relationships we will have in our lifetime are timeless and not confined to a particular stage of our life. We carry the residual impact of these relationships in our minds, emotions, and hearts for the duration of our existence. When women and men of all ages talk to me about the death of their mothers, even those who maintain that they didn't have a close relationship with their mom say they were surprised by how much they were affected by her death. People routinely use terms such as feeling "devastated" and "overwhelming loss" to describe their reaction. It is not unusual for daughters and sons to suffer from depression and hopelessness and/or to begin to question their life's meaning and purpose after their mother's death.

Years later, this death/loss still has tremendous power and influence. When some consider leaving a relationship or a business partnership, long after their mother has passed away, a number of them note that they can hear their mother's voice in their head, "I didn't raise my children to be quitters," and they heed that voice. When others decide to make a significant relationship or personal change, they often explain it by saying, "I didn't want to end up dying like my mom did, never having had the chance to do what I really wanted to do." Therefore, don't underestimate the impact of your mother on your personal life and relationships. If your mother is dead, recall the enormity of your feelings for her at the time of her death. If she's alive, talk to a trusted friend whose mother has passed away and ask him whether his personal life is affected by the memory of his mother. The meaning and power of your mother factor is in how you have incorporated her legacy into your everyday life. That impact transcends time, place, and death.

Many men—in fact, some women—believe that their father had more of an influence than their mother did over their personality and communication and relationship style. No one (particularly me—I wrote *The Father Factor*!) would argue the commonsense logic that fathers are invaluable to their children's development.[3] In fact, in the world of stay-at-home mothers and emotionally and physically absent fathers (in which many of us were raised), mothers had the greatest daily impact on our lives, simply because they were there, dealing with us day-to-day. Regardless of who made the financial decisions in the house, your mother was an emotional force in your life. Mothers, by virtue of their position in the home as the emotional caretaker, were and are the role models for their children and their interpersonal relationships. This primary relationship becomes the template for a child's adult emotional life. And because of the typical emotionally distant relationship between fathers and daughters/sons, a wound develops between father and child that often becomes the focal point of a child's life. Typically, mothers are mistakenly discounted in terms of importance and long-term emotional influence.

Adults tend to focus on the "problem parent," which in many cases is the absent, distant, or passive father. In such cases, mothers tend to get lost in the other parent's neglect, abandonment, or irresponsibility. If your relationship with your father was problematic, it is essential to understand the role that your mother had in your life. Mothers many times play the peacekeeper role between children and their fathers. This is the woman who taught you valuable skills; you were taught diplomatic methods and emotional intelligence (how to understand people's actions and raise questions without alienating them) by watching your mother manage family ("personnel") conflicts. You learned an incredible amount about relationship skills from your mother by observing her function every day.

Despite all of this, most of you from the baby boom generation were probably raised with a man as the primary breadwinner in your family. In the prototypical nuclear family or some variation of it, mothers were responsible for the everyday functioning of the family. This role hasn't been viewed—implicitly or explicitly—until very recently as being nearly as valuable as that of the primary breadwinner role. Unfortunately, mothering for some time has been considered a second-class position within the family. This perspective about mothering, which only recently has become outdated as women's rights and roles have expanded, is problematic and very misleading. The value of mothers can't be limited to their economic contribution, but rather should be based on the bigger picture of their emotional contribution, despite the fact that some women today earn more than their husbands. The influence on an abstract emotional level rather than a monetary one is where a mother's full influence on her son or daughter can be properly understood. It is imperative to look at your mother from a symbolic perspective, not a monetary one. Your emotional life and personality were shaped by this relationship, not your mother's yearly income or credit rating.

It is an all-too-common mistake to minimize your mother's influence if she didn't work outside the home or provide the entire economic support for the family. Even if your mother worked in the stereotypical helping professions (teacher, nurse, social worker), it is a blind spot to consider her influence on your current relationships, professionally and personally, as minimal. Most of our mothers were given the nonverbal social and family message that the then masculine professions (lawyer, doctor, business executive) weren't the proper place for a woman. Assessing her influence by the male model yardstick of position, title, and wealth will tend to yield very little information or new insight. Your mother's impact on your life and career functioning supersedes these artificial walls of separation based on finances and power.

Women have been defined for thousands of years by how they functioned at home. Now women are not only being defined in the home but by their profession and career. Still, the home has been women's sanctuary and place of nurturing and healing for generations. It is impossible to minimize the impact that your "mother's home" had on your entire development and personality. *Your home was the place where you learned how "life" worked.* School, friendships, and work were and are the places that the home lessons were applied and used, and still are to this day. It is counterintuitive and a mistake to think that your home life with your mother didn't erect a cornerstone in your life. For thousands of years, a child's development was the sole responsibility of the mother. This was based in part on the fact that men/fathers had to leave the house, children, and wife to find food, work, and later a career. Now these very entrenched social roles are becoming more adaptable to change and the needs of each individual family (blended families, second marriages, adoption, and other limitless combinations). The role that mothers play in their adult children's everyday choices—mate selection, professional relationships, emotional fulfillment, parenting style, sexuality, and communication—cannot be overstated.

Whether their mother was a homemaker or a college professor, many people dismiss the magnitude of their mother's influence on their life because the relationship was strained, emotionally painful, distant, or highly conflicted. They should consider these two vignettes:

Christina's story, thirty-seven years old: When I was growing up, my mother was an alcoholic who went to work everyday as a bookkeeper for a car dealership in town. When I was fifteen years old, I moved out of the house because I couldn't stand my mother. We didn't talk for seven years. I realized one day while driving that I spent most of my time consciously or unconsciously trying to prove my mother wrong and prove myself right. I realized that in this way I was really just as close to her as when I lived with her. I just didn't talk to her for seven years. Once I stopped fighting my mother in my head, I began to understand her much better. Now we get along better too and I appreciate her and her ability to focus at work everyday. I thought my anger was what kept me away from my mother, but it really kept me right next to her. I was completely shocked to realize how emotionally close I was to her, when I thought we were really very distant. Her drinking was her way of dealing with life and my anger was my way of dealing with her.

Danny's story, twenty-eight years old: I will never forget the day I heard about my mother's death. All my disappointments and frustration with her vanished in a second. I couldn't believe how my feelings immediately changed toward my mom and have never gone backwards. I always told people that we weren't close or anything alike. Now, five years after her death, I am more like my mother than I ever suspected or thought was possible. I wasn't aware growing up how much she shaped my attitudes, my personality, my emotional reactions, my parenting, my marriage, and my life. I feel bad that I spent so many years and precious time fighting with her about ridiculous stuff. Now I hear myself talking and know it is still my mother's voice in my head and heart.

Christina's and Danny's stories are far more the rule than the exception in regard to the emotional legacy of mothers. It is impossible for a child with as highly a conflicted relationship as Christina and Danny had with their mothers not to be emotionally bonded with their mother.

On the surface it may appear that you and your mother have nothing in common. Usually it is quite the opposite, and the truth is you have many things in common with your mother. The problem is that the extensive and murky overlap of thoughts and feelings between you and your mother may be unclear, and you need to sort these out. Remember, you are creating your own emotional legacy for the people in your life.

Finally, your mother may not have been the career role model, relationship model, or parenting model, or even the type of person you care to emulate. Given that, the slippery slope of anger, resentment, and bitterness may build to the point that many daughters and sons, regardless of age, fall into the trap of desperately trying to become the person their mother never was. This relationship approach is an understandable reaction to the family trauma that many children experienced growing up. There is often an edge of aggressiveness and cold-heartedness to adults who have never resolved or come to terms with who and what their mother was. In addition, they may never reconcile themselves with what happened positively and negatively in the relationship. The driving force in these sons' and daughters' lives is the complete rejection of who and what their mother was as a parent. The challenge for these adult children is overcoming the painful disappointment and disillusionment of their memories of their mother. The ability to trust others and form meaningful long-term relationships are difficult tasks for adults who have had this type of mother-child relationship.

HOW THE MOTHER FACTOR WORKS: THE MANY POWER SOURCES

The mother factor can work *for* you or *against* you; it all depends on whether you understand and appreciate it or ignore it. Let's assume you prefer the former, or you wouldn't be exploring this topic. The key to understanding and comprehending your legacy depends on looking at the mother-child relationship from the following perspectives:

1. *The four different types of attachment/nurturing (the emotional bond) you had with your mother.* The four types—intermittent, avoidant, depressed, and secure—provide insight on how you connect emotionally in all of your relationships. (They are described in detail in chapter 1.) Those adult children who when younger formed secure nurturing relationships with their mother usually have sound work relationships and faithful intimate relationships as adults. A secure attachment means that the child and her mother bonded early in the relationship and maintained that bond, giving that child a strong sense of security and a feeling of being loved. The attachment process provides the emo-

tional foundation for all future relationships. This secure nurturing attachment encourages the adult to be open, willing to air her views in a clear and positive manner, and to be trusting of other people. By understanding this bond—even if your relationship with your mother was horrendous—you can develop a secure and strong emotional attachment with all the people in your life.

2. *Your mother's rulebook: your mother's and grandmother's spoken and unspoken rules about work, relationships, emotions, separation, and independence.* Your mother's "rulebook," or set of spoken and unspoken rules, is a very powerful force in the family you grew up in and your life. It is the set of rules that covers career choices, money matters, mate selection, children, spirituality, and sexuality, as well as how you emotionally separated and individuated from your mother. You don't think about these rules because they are as natural a part of you as breathing. They are something you have lived by for years. While there are some exceptions to this rule, it generally holds that sons and daughters follow in the footsteps of their mothers and their grandmothers regarding relationships. Even more predictable are the rules for relating and communicating with others, which are all based on your internal rulebook. This comprises powerful spoken and unspoken rules, which guide your behavior, thoughts, and beliefs. Once you are aware of your mother's rulebook, you have to update, rewrite, and make it all your own. Most adults live by their rulebook but seldom consider changing the outdated, nonproductive behaviors and emotional reactions within it. Your mother handed this rulebook to you, but it must be reread, rewritten, and reevaluated for your life to move forward.

3. *Mothering style (daily interactions, behaviors, emotional beliefs, and communication patterns of your mother).* The five basic styles of mothering are the perfectionist mother,

the unpredictable mother, the "me first" mother, the best friend mother, and the complete mother (each style is discussed in chapters 3 through 7). These styles of relating have a tremendous effect on your adult relationships—personally and professionally. They shape how you function mentally and emotionally on a daily basis at home and at work. Whether you are forceful, demanding, and uncompromising or a relatively passive personality depends, to a significant extent, on your mother's parenting style. How your mother interacted with you is a critical piece of your personal information that helped shape your life choices, adult relationships, and overall satisfaction with your life. Understanding your mother's style of parenting provides the foundation for insight into the emotional legacy of your mother factor and thus into your personal and professional life. It is very important to note that the single mother is considered in all the styles above. There is no predetermined mother-child relationship pattern or style because of your mother's marital status. Single mothers make up a very large percentage of all the different combinations of mothers (teenage, married, never married, divorced, remarried, adoptive, etc.) and they fall into the above style categories.

Patty's Story

To give you a sense of how these three areas of daily interactions, behavior, and emotional bonding/communication with your mother influence your adult life, let's take a look at the case of Patty, a fifty-one-year-old, self-employed interior designer in the west Los Angeles area. Patty's mother, Sharon, was a full-time stay-at-home mom. Sharon raised three children, among whom Patty was the oldest. Sharon, for as long as Patty can remember, was always overwhelmed by routine daily activities and was certain she was going to die from a brain tumor. Thankfully, Sharon was never diagnosed with a life-threatening cancer or illness of any type, yet she was convinced that something bad was going to happen all the time and still believes that to this day. Sharon's fear, anxiety, and moodiness defined her style of mothering. At the same time, Patty's father, Frank, traveled three to four days a week during her childhood, selling lumber to construction companies throughout the southwest part of the country. He was always absent from the emotional life of the family and was thus spared Sharon's extreme mood swings.

Patty rebelled against Sharon's chronic mood swings in high school by becoming a heavy drug user. Patty found that the only way to deal with her mother's unpredictable emotional outbursts was to get drunk or stoned on marijuana. Patty's primary emotional connection to her mother was hostility, which was often expressed through constant arguing. Unfortunately, Patty's father spent even more time on the road during her high school years. The level of tension between Patty and her mother exploded on her eighteenth birthday, when Sharon discovered that her daughter was pregnant and addicted to marijuana. Sharon sent Patty to a Bible college in Oklahoma as punishment and to save her from a self-destructive life path. Patty had an abortion and became drug free after moving out of her mother's house. Patty met her husband-to-be, Mark, in college. They married two years later and had three children.

During the course of her eighteen-year marriage, Patty found her husband, Mark, to be as controlling as her mother had been when Patty was growing up. Patty also found Mark to be very moody, anxious, depressed, always worried about something, and argumentative with her and their three children. Patty told me, "The horror of marrying your mother hit me in the face one day, when I spoke to both my mother and Mark on the phone. I couldn't keep their names straight because they felt like the same person to me. I dropped the phone when I realized that I married my mother, I had spent so much time growing up, trying to get away from her. I felt hopeless and stuck."

After that emotional awakening about Mark and Sharon being the same person emotionally for Patty, she immediately entered marriage counseling. Like Patty's mother, Mark didn't believe in the benefit of direct open communication, emotional honesty/clarity, and the need to improve their relationship. Mark divorced Patty because he believed her to be "uncontrollable" and not the same woman he had married many years earlier.

It is clear that Patty's emotional legacy from her mother factor was fully operating in her life years before she even went to college and married Mark. Patty's mother factor was running her life, making decisions before she was consciously aware of its power, influence, and magnitude. Sharon's emotional style of bonding was clearly intermittent, inconsistent, and emotionally avoidant (see chapter 1). Sharon's mothering style was primarily mood dependent. Consequently, Patty grew up without ever establishing a secure emotional attachment with her mother. In turn, Patty became very dependent on others' opinions of her and found herself always being a people pleaser. The problem was that Patty never felt emotionally safe with people and was very concerned that unless they were happy with her, she was in "trouble." This pattern of relating to others affected Patty's business, in addition to her parenting and personal relationships. She was always scared and emotionally distant, so concerned that her close friends wouldn't turn out to be like her mother. This emotional pattern shaped every area of Patty's life and career.

In thinking further about Patty's emotional and personal struggle, she found herself unable to work for anyone in authority. Her psychological experience with any type of authority figure was filtered through her mother-daughter relationship, which was very traumatic and scary. Patty still feels that her relationship with her mother is based on control and guilt. Reporting to a supervisor, therefore, wasn't a model or template in which Patty could function. Her pursuit of self-employment was a result of the need for self-preservation than anything else. Patty's growing awareness of her mother factor allowed her to channel it into a positive influence and simultaneously take more control of her life. Patty is very careful not to blame her mother for their strained relationship or for her personal and professional struggles. She is appreciative of her mother's intervention in her life at age eighteen to keep her from developing a lifelong addiction to drugs.

MOTHERS: REALITIES AND MISPERCEPTIONS

Men and women who experience difficulty overcoming negative emotional legacies tend not to see the connection with their past or believe how events that took place years ago at home could possibly still be affecting their life today. This is a very common blind spot for most adults. Patty, for instance, labored under a number of misconceptions, not only about the negative impact her beliefs had on her relationships but larger mother-daughter issues—emotional abuse, anxiety, fear of rejection, problems with authority figures. Such misconceptions cause us to minimize or dismiss things our mothers said and did when we were growing up. Out of a lack of understanding and a need to emotionally survive, many of us convince ourselves that we exist only in the here and now and that what's past remains in the past. Ironically, this mindset gives those past events more power than they ordinarily would have. When we pretend that a domineering, moody, demeaning, or abusive mother could have no effect on us today, we may unconsciously steer clear of or leave any relationship, job, or situation where the other person is tough or critical, thereby missing some potentially great opportunities and never understanding why.

Men, for example, typically are accused by their girlfriends, wives, or lovers of being scared, distant, or noncommittal to intimacy in romantic relationships. This reluctance on the part of many men to commit to marriage or an exclusive dating relationship can be resolved. In many instances, it isn't that these men don't want to be close to their partners or get married. Rather, they subliminally fear that they might re-experience the same emotional trauma of their mother-son relationship if they get emotionally close to someone (a woman) again. The trauma or negative psychological consequences that resulted from a poor mother-son relationship years before can include feelings of being suffocated, demeaned, shamed, emotionally inadequate, hopeless, or completely responsible for another's well-being. The causes are as varied as the men involved. Men and their relationship concerns and behaviors have their roots and foundations in their mother factor legacy. It is imperative for men (me included) to understand our mother's emotional legacy and how it is practiced, applied, and functional. These same behaviors of staying emotionally distant from a partner and friends are also common in women. It is always important to remember that throughout our lives, both men and women struggle with issues that arose from our mother factor.

When you become aware of the realities versus the misconceptions, however, you are much more likely to recognize how your unconscious beliefs affect your personal and professional relationships and then take constructive action. This deeper awareness will also assist you in taking full advantage of all the ideas and tools that we will be discussing. By understanding your mother factor, you will begin to increase your level of personal and professional satisfaction and then begin to maximize your potential.

The following true/false statements address some of the more common misunderstandings, blind spots, and denials concerning mothers and their impact on daughters and sons. Mark a "T" or "F" next to each statement, then look at the answer key to determine how well you did and your level of understanding about you and your mother. These questions aren't designed to measure your mother factor IQ but rather to start a discussion within yourself about the impact of your mother on your life—past, present, and future. In addition, it is important to recognize themes of the mother-child relationship—these will increase your awareness of

how your mother's words and actions have shaped your life
choices up to now.

Questions

1. Fathers and mothers serve the same role in raising their
   children.
2. Children can only learn their "emotional intelligence"—
   the ability to have empathy, understanding, and insight
   into other's actions—from their adult life experiences.
   Their mothers don't play an important role in this process.
3. Biological mothers have no more influence on their
   daughters/sons than stepmothers or other nonbiological
   mother figures.
4. Women and men can overcome a traumatic mother-child
   past and develop a positive mother factor model.
5. Mothers affect their sons and daughters for their entire
   lives.
6. It is almost impossible for women and men to learn anything of value from mothers they hate or don't respect—
   past or present.
7. It isn't necessary for girls' and boys' emotional development to have a positive relationship with their mother.
8. Once men and women reach a certain age or level of success, they don't want or need their mother's approval.
9. Usually the emotional and mental wounds people suffered
   as kids will prevent them from being productive, highly
   functional adults.
10. Even when they're quite young, children pay close attention
    to their mother's attitudes and behavior in regard to their
    father, family relationships, work, and communication.
11. Verbal abuse by your mother is much less harmful than
    physical abuse.
12. While people who seem to have come to terms with a

negative mother-child relationship may present a calm facade, they in fact are usually pressure cookers beneath the surface.

Answers

1. False. Mothers serve as role models for how we relate to our world emotionally, mentally, and physically. A mother is the female balance to a father's influence. Each parent serves an invaluable but distinct role in a child's development. It is crucial to begin to understand your mother's contribution to your relationship history and future, your emotional functioning, and your personal goals. Your mother plays a major role in who and what you are in your life.

2. False. As odd as that question sounds, approximately 30 to 35 percent of adults firmly believe in the theory that nature is more important than nurture in shaping an individual's mind. Parents are considered secondary influences. The nature versus nurture argument dismisses the invaluable role a mother has in developing and shaping her child's emotional intelligence, relationship potential, and communication styles. Mothers are part of every adult's psychological profile and a timeless influence regardless of the quality of the relationship. A mother has a role in a child's life that is special and transforming throughout his or her life.[4]

3. True. Mothering is not limited to biology. The term *stepmother* is a legal term, but in a relational context, the prefix "step" has little bearing on a woman's true effectiveness as a mother. Given that approximately 67 to 70 percent (US Census 2000 and *Time* magazine, November 26, 2007) of all families today are some type of blended, nontraditional family (children not living with both biological parents), we see that relationship styles and emo-

tional functioning are often influenced by a stepmother or adoptive mother. A mother figure, whether biological or not, will have a tremendous impact and influence on a child's upbringing. It is also possible that more than one person—a biological mother and a stepmother—can have a big impact on a child's life and his direction.

4. True. Not having a mother or having a strained relationship with a mother does not sentence you to repeat the past or continue the negative legacy. You can make the necessary changes to excel in your life and relationships. Your ability to understand rather than blame your mother is one of the keys to personal and professional success and it's the basis of appreciating your mother factor. While anger and hatred are strong short-term motivators, these two emotions can't sustain your relationships and career, nor can they meet all the demands necessary to develop personally and professionally.

5. True. Even after your mother dies, she will still affect your personal relationships and life choices. No matter what sons and daughters say to their mother in a fit of rage—for example, "I'll never be like you"—or how much they try to distance themselves as adults, their mothers still cast a long shadow. Typically, people undervalue their mother's impact on their lives until after her death. Even then, many men and women don't see how a mother's influence extends past personal traits into their adult life and choices. The values you carry concerning your life and how to treat people were formed many years ago in the context and backdrop of your mother-daughter or mother-son relationship.

6. False. All daughters and sons learn an enormous number of things from their mother. It is quite possible to move emotionally beyond your anger, lack of respect, and hatred of your mother. Analyzing the mother-child rela-

tionship can yield valuable insights that will help make you a better parent, partner, supervisor, friend, and person. These insights can help you make the necessary adjustments in personal relationships and allow you to move to the next level in your life.

7. False. At times, some young boys seem as if they do not need their mothers, especially in the wake of a bitter divorce or a sudden remarriage. Some girls also may appear to be so independent or so close to their fathers that they foster the illusion that a relationship with their mother is of no particular consequence. In reality, every son and daughter seeks and needs a relationship with his or her mother. The natural craving for an emotional motherly bond must be acknowledged and understood as a normal mother-child need. Denying this natural impulse creates a void, one that will play itself out in various areas of an adult's life. People who dismiss this natural emotional phenomenon may also be in denial about the need to build strong relationships with family members, partners, friends, and colleagues.

8. False. *Regardless of our age, we all desire our mother's approval.* Approval is part of our psychological wiring and a naturally occurring mother-child dynamic. Unfortunately, you, like many others, may never have received that approval/love while growing up—or received it rarely or randomly. Developing your own self-approval, self-acceptance, and self-love is re-creating your own mother factor legacy. Many people choose instead to seek these qualities from people in the workplace, in friendships, or in another mother figure. Many times, people look to a boss or authority figure for maternal approval and acceptance, which, as we'll see in later chapters, can create all sorts of relationship problems and issues. Issues that result from a missing or absent maternal emotional

bond will never be adequately resolved in the workplace
or in the outside world. Mother factor issues have to be
resolved on a personal level regardless of their nature or
magnitude.

9. False. Growing up with a conflicted, strained mother-
child relationship is not a reason to repeat the sins of the
past or continue to punish yourself through poor life
choices, self-defeating behaviors, or depressed thinking.
You don't have to avoid people who offer constructive
criticism or run to people who are weak and ineffectual as
a way of feeling emotionally safe. Nor do you have to
become abusive to the people in your life as a reaction to
your childhood abuse and neglect. You control your life
choices through new insight about how you were raised
and the style of mothering that shaped your childhood.

10. True. Sons and daughters watch their mothers closely
when it comes to relationships and their behavioral/emo-
tional treatment of other family members. Many children
develop the skill of observing these interpersonal skills by
watching these behaviors from a distance, without being
noticed. Some people contend that they never really paid
much attention to these issues while growing up. But usually they blocked out what may have been unpleasant
experiences: Mom and Dad screaming at each other about
having no money for the bills or Mom complaining that
no one appreciates her hard work around the house. Your
approach to conflict resolution, emotionally charged
issues, communication, and personal ethics all likely
come from observing your mother's attitudes, actions,
and beliefs in these critical areas.

11. False. As horrific as physical abuse is, verbal abuse is
equally destructive and toxic to a son's or daughter's
spirit, mind, and emotions. Children carry those hate-
filled words, scared feelings, and accusations in their

hearts and minds, in many cases, all their life. Cruel words, mean-spirited badgering, and constant criticism erode a child's developing sense of self and will lead to future problems with relationships, partners, and parenting (unless these issues are addressed and resolved). The lack of trust and a sense of danger is what the child learns to feel while growing up. Adults who demean and belittle others often come from homes where their mothers were verbally abusive and emotionally aggressive with them. Their behavior is a reaction to their mother-child relationship. They have to demean people in order to feel good about themselves—it is a constant cycle of abuse. In addition, verbal abuse is invisible. Unlike the physically abused child, the verbally abused girl grows up believing she had a normal mother-daughter relationship. The understandable lack of awareness makes her vulnerable to the effects of this abuse in her adult personal and professional relationships. She often doesn't seek professional help for the psychological and emotional damage done to her self-esteem and never acknowledges or articulates how awful she feels about her mother's abusive behavior—past and present. Given the lack of overt physical evidence (broken arms, black-and-blue bruises, swollen faces), she tends to minimize the long-term damage that verbal abuse has caused. Consequently, she carries the emotional damage and pain into both her personal and professional lives.

12. True. People in high-pressure situations or circumstances often have perfected the art of appearing outwardly calm, while inside the pressure builds. These symptoms can cause sleepless nights, panic attacks, ulcers, and chronic anxiety as well as physical problems that negatively affect their decision-making abilities or even worse, get them to quit their jobs. An emotionally supportive, caring mother

provides a child with the inner resources necessary to cope with all types of stress, including personal challenges. She helps her child gain the self-esteem and coping skills that serve him well in school, work situations, and adult relationships. Some of these children may respond to stress with anger, depression, or frustration, but inside they're capable of managing the stress and continuing to function effectively on emotional and cognitive levels.

THE THREADS LEADING BACK TO MOTHER

The majority of men and women who want to change their lives are very clear about *what* is not working. However, when asked about *why* they think they're having problems in their personal and professional relationships, most don't have a definitive answer. Usually the discussion quickly lapses into an admission of the frustration of nagging ongoing problems, with no clear plan or way to stop the emotional pain.

In fact, posing the questions about a son's or daughter's mother factor often creates more anxiety than it does relief or clarity. It can be overwhelming to learn that there are certain behaviors that might be problems in your life and that the solutions to those issues exist and lie in your mother-child relationship. Todd, for instance, had never really questioned why he had a pattern of repeatedly dating women who were emotionally unavailable to him or whom he had to take care of. The idea that there might be an emotional connection between his poor choices in partners and his relationship with his emotionally distant mother seemed to be a very interesting concept to him. Todd was surprised by the suggestion that there was a direct correlation leading back to his mother in what appeared to be more than a random selection of unsuccessful romantic relationships over a fifteen-year period. He began to realize that his unresolved mother-son emotional issues were keeping him in a repetitive cycle of self-doubt and despair.

The following may help to illuminate some of the underlying connections between your emotional functioning and your mother's legacy. The idea is to show the naturally occurring phenomenon between a mother and her adult daughter or son. The first part describes some of the common behaviors and feelings that daughters and sons have reported. This is followed by issues of the mother factor and their connection to these behaviors, feelings, and beliefs.

Daughters' and Sons' Problematic and Positive Behaviors and Their Connection to the Mother Factor

- Unconsciously choosing unavailable partners—Mother's inability to show daughter/son unconditional love: she avoided an emotional bond.
- Inability to commit to a love relationship—Mother's over-controlling or overprotective behavior.
- Sabotaging career and personal goals—Mother's constant criticism and lack of approval of daughter's/son's choices and behavior.
- Inability to be assertive and to express one's opinion—Mother's low self-image and fear of failure.
- Inability to trust one's own instincts and motivations—Mother's chronic verbal and nonverbal message about how to feel, think, and act. No development of a separate personality from the mother.
- Overwhelmed by volatile emotions, thoughts, or actions—Mother's anxiety about the expression of emotions, her poor communication skills, and her overdependence on others' opinions.
- Difficulty maintaining an intimate adult romantic/sexual relationship—Mother's own unresolved issues about intimacy and her own problems with sexuality.

- Unclear about a life direction or career path—Mother's need to keep her daughter/son emotionally close because of her own abandonment issues.
- Suffering from separation anxiety and guilt for making life choices that don't include one's mother—Mother's own arrested developmental progress of becoming an independent adult.
- Strong sense of purpose and confidence to take risks—Mother's guidance in helping her daughter/son form life goals.
- Compassionate understanding of others and your ability to create your own fulfillment—Mother's emotional mentoring and leadership on becoming a high-functioning adult.
- Ability to have strong emotional connections without losing your identity—Mother's ability to assist her child in differentiating from the parent-child relationship.
- Ability to form one's own life and opinions—Mother's own emotional maturity and a tolerance for differences.

You can see from this short list that the mother factor is a very active force on and component of many levels in your adult life. This is just a sampling of the multiple connections and threads of your mother factor that are part of the fabric of your daily life and relationships. We are going to explore the breadth and depth of your relationships, your self-esteem, as well as your sense of self and the emotional context of your life from the perspective of the mother factor to better understand your legacy and your future. You may be very surprised and relieved to know that some of your lifelong issues can be resolved from a better understanding of your emotional legacy.

Chapter 1

YOUR FIRST LOVE
Mothers and Emotional Bonding

I always wondered if my mother really ever accepted me. And the things I liked. She wanted me to get married and have kids like she did at age twenty-five, I instead went and lived in Europe for seven years. Yet, I knew deep down my mother always loved me. That bond was never broken by my rebellion.

> —Lisa, age forty-two, single

The only connection I have with my mother is guilt. If I don't call her, see her, or listen to her for hours, I am in big trouble. I hate the pressure and sense of panic I feel if I don't do what she wants. I am very scared when women get angry. I can't handle it.

> —Evan, age twenty-seven, single

It is clear from Lisa's and Evan's statements that they have very strong emotional bonds as adults with their mothers even though each statement is in stark contrast to each other. Lisa has a very loving bond with her mother that allowed her to experiment with different life choices and travel the world. She never feared that she would lose her mother's love and support because she chose to follow a different life path than her mother's. Evan's emotional bond was/is based on taking care of his mother's emotional needs. He never learned about or valued his own opinion. He clearly knew what his mother's demands were for him and his life. The fear of disappointing or causing his mother to be angry has been the major driving force in his daily life. He would do almost anything to avoid her anger. These two examples point to the ongoing power of the emotional legacy of mothers and its affect on their adult children regardless of age.

If we are going to really understand the depth and magnitude of our maternal emotional attachment, then we have to look at how we first connected to her as a child. This is our first bond, and it therefore carries such an extraordinary power and lasting influence. Since our life is made up of a series of relationships, and the foundation of any relationship is attachment, then this bond is very important.[1] As the word *attachment* suggests, it involves the way in which you related to and bonded with your mother while you were growing up. The dictionary defines attachment as a "feeling that binds one person to another; devotion; with regard," which isn't a bad way of summarizing this highly significant concept. Without attachment, meaningful relationships would not exist and we'd all feel very isolated from one another.

MOTHERS → CONNECTION → TIMELESS

Regardless of our age, we all need, maintain, and develop attachments (i.e., ranging from no attachment to extremely strong) to the people and events in our life. Our connections with people, objects, places, homes, and experiences are all part of our emotional attachment style. By "style," I mean the manner in which these things give meaning, purpose, and value to our life. Our life is made up of a wide range of attachments and various emotional bonds. There is nothing in your life that you value and cherish (whether family, children, career, health, friends, vacations, holidays, etc.) that isn't a form or reflection of your bonding attachment style. For example, people may argue that they don't have any emotional ties or attachment to their house, but when it is destroyed in a fire, they feel absolutely lost and emotionally devastated. Why are these events such an emotional loss?

These adult reactions to certain events that carry a surprising amount of emotional energy have their origin in our first love relationship, and that is with our *mother*. Our attachment history and emotional intelligence (the ability to understand and respond to different feelings and thoughts) began in our mother-child relationship. It is a foregone conclusion in the psychological community that the mother-child relationship has the power to direct, impact, and shape a person's entire life. It is a very common mistake to dismiss and minimize the power of the mother-son/mother-daughter relationship. Developing a deeper understanding of your legacy isn't about blaming your mother for a less than perfect attachment or love, but rather comprehending what you have learned and experienced and what you know you need to change.

The academic research pioneer of attachment theory is Dr. John Bowlby, a British psychiatrist who firmly believed that no experience has "more far reaching effects on personality development than . . . a child's experience within his family."[2] The initial bonding experience with our mother is the first time we begin to create a sense of who we are, especially in relationships and how we feel about people. This process, which started in pregnancy, birth, holding, cuddling, and feeding, provides the critical factors that make an infant feel safe, secure, and comfortable in the world. The attachment drive and the need for it never diminishes throughout our lifetime. The people and things we feel emotionally connected to may change, but the core emotional, mental, and psychological need for emotionally safe attachments never vanishes. The barometer of our overall mental and emotional health is measured by our ability to form and maintain meaningful attachments and connections.

If you ask a hundred new mothers to describe their experience of "attaching" to their new babies, you will likely get a hundred different answers. One mother, Betty, who is thirty-eight years old, said, "I was completely overwhelmed when I held my son for the first time." Kerri, twenty-seven years old, said, "I felt immediately bonded and connected to Sara when I saw her."

Regardless of all the different responses to bonding with our mother and her with us, the initial bonding experience with our mother is the first time we begin to learn about who we are, how we feel, and how we relate to others in our world. Many people will say, for instance, that they never felt emotionally close with their mother and that it isn't an issue in their life today. No matter how close to or far from you feel, or felt, with your mother emotionally, each experience is a form of attachment and emotional bonding. Attachment has many styles, and each one is significant in its long-range influence as demonstrated in enduring behavioral patterns. This initial mother-child attachment experience may be one of the single greatest indicators of our functioning in future relationships, partner selection, parenting style, emotional satisfaction, and overall level of achievement in our life.

ED AND DENISE—PRESENT-DAY APPLICATION

According to Bowlby, this mother-child relationship creates the template, model, and style that we will relate to in all subsequent relationships.[3] For instance, Ed, thirty-four years old, finds that he experiences his girlfriends as distant, manipulative, cold, "psycho," and unaware of his needs. Closer examination of Ed's initial emotional attachment with his mother reveals that she was preoccupied during Ed's childhood with developing her law practice. This is not to say that mothers should not have professions or careers; many children thrive under these circumstances. Ed spent most of his time as a boy with babysitters or relatives. Ed's mother was unpredictable in her emotional outbursts and believed yelling was a form of showing concern, according to him. What is really operating in Ed's current romantic relationships is a reflection of his early bonding experience with his mother, not his inability to find a great partner. His style of bonding attachment with his mother was distant and distracted. When Ed's mother would scream and yell, she deeply scared him. He never imagined that those early emotional experiences with his mother could have such a lasting impression and impact on his current relationship patterns.

Our early perception, whether it is conscious or unconscious, of our mother-child relationship affects the way we experience our world for the rest of our life. This is a very serious truth and may be one of the major roadblocks to your maximizing your potential in every area of your life. These early perceptions are very evident and operational in how we function, relate, and communicate in our closest relationships. This issue is of paramount importance and unfortunately is dismissed by some people as "psycho babble." Without Ed's connecting his current behavior to his early bonding experience, he would lose the critical information needed to improve his life. Change would become very difficult, if not impossible.

Ed's ongoing experience of continuous frustration with intimate relationships has its roots in his mother factor legacy. When this dynamic was explained to Ed, he began to see how he continually replayed his emotional frustration/deprivation in his love life. He began questioning why he was drawn to women who weren't emotionally available or psychologically unstable. He then began to deal with his sense of repeated emotional deprivation (never believing that his emotional needs would be met). He grew weary of his continual frustration based on a choice that created a sense of emotional emptiness. Once he understood this pattern, Ed took a different approach regarding the type of women he dated and found attractive. He pursued women who had the same desire to be emotionally involved. He found that he really didn't enjoy the emotional drama that he had created with women in the past—drama that mirrored the familiar pattern of his mother-son attachment. Ed made the direct connection between his present emotional behaviors to his emotional legacy, which opened the door for him to change a lifelong, troubling relationship pattern.

Denise, forty-two years old, represents another type of mother-child bonding. Denise continually complained that she couldn't find the right guy to marry and have a child with. Denise had married her boyfriend from graduate school when she was twenty-six years old. They were married for six years. Rather than starting a family, she focused solely on her career in business finance. Denise divorced her then husband, Bruce, because he wanted to have children at the time. Economics wasn't an issue; they were both financially secure in their careers. Denise didn't believe that she would ever have children with Bruce unless she did it on his timetable, which wasn't hers, and she left the relationship/marriage.

Shortly after her divorce, Denise started dating divorced fathers because she believed they would want to have children with her when she was ready. Denise met George, a divorced father who was thirty-five years old and had two children, ages eight and eleven. They lived together for five years. Finally, Denise broke up with George when he refused to get married and have a child with her.

The bonding/attachment process for Denise with her mother was very strained during her childhood. Denise's mother was absent when Denise was between the ages of four to seven because of a mental breakdown. Denise rarely remembers being around her mother or having a strong sense of who and what she was. Denise always longed for her mother's love and time. She believed that her mother loved her, but didn't think that her mother felt emotionally close to her during her childhood. As an adult who was focusing on this problem, Denise began to realize that her chronic insistence on and ambivalence toward having or not having children was really her own conflicted feelings about her mother-daughter relationship. She had suppressed and displaced the loss of her mother and her mother's avoidant/distant attachment style by focusing solely on her career. Her conscious and unconscious avoidance of her painful emotional legacy caused Denise to create the very situation she wanted to avoid: being single and having no children.

Denise thus buried her emotional pain and fears of intimacy (avoidance style of bonding) and focused exclusively on her career. She soon realized that successful business dealings ultimately require a relationship with the client—who is more than an object and may be a person with emotions, and that business is more than just making money or closing a deal. Denise began to realize that her panic about having children was really about her sense of loss and fear that she could never heal her painful mother-daughter relationship. Denise realized that she related to people the same way her mother related to her—from a distance. Denise was repeatedly told by her intimate partners and colleagues that she was cold, aloof, emotionally distant, and very shy. Her range of emotions and her relationships were a direct reflection of her attachment style: distant/avoidant.

Denise eventually admitted that she really hadn't wanted children. She had convinced herself that the only way to reconcile with her traumatic childhood and be a better woman than her mother was to have children. Denise felt that doing what her mother didn't was the only pathway to heal her childhood. When Denise realized this, she stopped dating men with children and decided it was her choice whether or not to create her own family. The intimacy she craved was available to her once she made the conscious connection to her past/legacy. She no longer had to avoid her pain or fears of being alone as if she were still a child. As of now, she has not had children, but she remains open to the possibility.

Ed and Denise both began to realize that their current attachment styles and intimate relationship patterns had their roots in their mother-child relationships. They both found this long-term connection to their past very powerful and eerie, which was enough of a motivation to make an immediate change. Neither of these adults lacks intelligence, common sense, or personal responsibility, and both have tremendous psychological insight and wisdom. Though what took them time to see might be obvious to others, we should be aware that we all have our own blind spots. Knowing that we all have an emotional legacy from our mothers and trying to understand it might be part of the solution to our own ongoing issues with intimate relationships. This insight applies to all of us, regardless of our relationship status (married, divorced, single, widowed, gay, straight, etc.) and traumatic relationship history. *It isn't the issues we're aware of that cause us all personal heartache, but the ones that are just outside our conscious field of vision and reach.* Consider the following ideas about your attachment style, emotional patterns, psychological needs, intimate wants, and unspoken fears. Consider the parts of you that are wounded and have been covered up by years of painful frustration. It takes courage to open up these painful issues—but realize that the alternative isn't working. The old way of handling your legacy by avoidance, denial, fear, or lack of insight isn't an option any longer for dealing with your attachment and intimate issues. Change is in the new way you approach old problems. Let's look at some new perspectives on your relationship history.

ATTACHMENT/BONDING ISSUES REVISITED

It's very possible that you had a very secure attachment to your mother from which your personal life has benefited greatly. If that is true, you are roughly in the select 10 percent of all mother-child attachment styles. This number is based on approximately twenty years of my professional practice, which showed that a large majority of men and women I've counseled want a different type of relationship than they had with their mother. Chances are that your relationship with your mother fell somewhere within the spectrum of attachment styles. The spectrum ranges at one end from securely attached to intermittent to avoidant to depressed attachment at the other end. These varying degrees from close, secure emotional attachment to very distant, depressed attachment are important to understand. Each of these four styles has its own set of characteristics, strengths, weaknesses, side effects, and long-term influences. You have experienced all four types in the context of your wide range of relationships (personal, business, family, mother-child, social) over the course of your life. You, too, have a predominant style that tends to guide and direct the majority of your daily interactions with people. Your style impacts all the different levels on which you engage with others. Without reading any further, what do you think your attachment style is? If you are unclear about your style, ask your partner or a close friend what he or she thinks. You might be very surprised by his or her response and begin to see your life from another perspective.

The powerful and exciting news is that regardless of the type of attachment style you had with your mother, *you can overcome its negative side effects and change the way you relate and bond with other people.* The first step in changing your emotional attachment with others is to understand how you bond with your intimate and close friends. It is in these very close relationships that our personal issues get exposed, resolved, and can be continually repeated. As I've stressed, the majority of your personal issues in relationships (trust, fear, jealousy, abandonment, emotional deprivation, etc.) have their origin in your mother-child relationship. All our emotional strengths and weaknesses started with this all-important bonding process.

The following list of statements are intended to give you some new ideas, perspective, and emotional insight into your inner emotional life. Attachment is a very intimate issue and is at the core of all our relationships and meaningful encounters in our life. The list is divided into two parts—attachment/bonding issues and mother bonding issues. As you read this list, be aware that a given behavior, feeling, or thought is worthy of a check mark if it represents a recurring theme or behavioral pattern that has a strong emotional pull in your present life. You don't need to exhibit the described attachment behavior or mother issues all the time in order for that behavior to deserve a check mark. Whatever is your first response to a question is usually the most honest and accurate answer.

Attachment/Bonding Issues—Your Checklist

___ You have difficulty starting and maintaining close, intimate relationships.

___ You tend to avoid close, emotional relationships with colleagues, neighbors, and friends.

___ You prefer to keep personal issues, matters, or concerns about your life to yourself.

___ You enjoy the opportunity to share your feelings and thoughts with a close friend.

___ You have or had a partner with whom you share your intimate thoughts about your life.

___ You would consider yourself to be a "people person."

___ You experience personal difficulty developing and maintaining positive relationships personally and professionally.

___ You have great difficulty with relationship endings: personally, professionally, and intimately.

___ Changes in your workplace, family, or intimate relationship cause you a great amount of stress/fear.

___ You have a pattern within intimate relationships of feeling an exaggerated sense of abandonment (i.e., always perceiving people as leaving you).

___ You deliberately avoid, whenever possible, emotional encounters and/or emotional exchanges with people.

___ You feel insecure about your place in life (i.e., career, relationships, friends, family, and partner).

__ You tend to be emotionally clingy or aggressive when under stress.

__ When people are emotionally expressive or show strong feelings, you are immediately uncomfortable.

__ You prefer to avoid any display of strong feelings about/toward the people you care for and love in your life.

__ You are most comfortable expressing anger/rage rather than other emotions.

__ You experience periods of feeling lonely and isolated. These sad emotional episodes have occurred for many years.

Mother Bonding Issues—Your Checklist

__ You feel that your mother knows the "real" you.

__ Your mother-adult child relationship is based on mutual respect and understanding.

__ You can express a difference of opinion to your mother.

__ Your mother was emotionally close to you as a child.

__ You didn't feel responsible for your mother's feelings and life while growing up.

__ You have emotionally separated from your mother.

__ Your mother tended to express only anger and frustration when she was upset.

__ Your mother would express both positive emotions and negative emotions in a balanced manner to you.

__ You didn't fear your mother's mood swings (present day and past).

__ You felt safe with your mother growing up.

__ You have a difficult time trusting women.

__ Your mother was actively involved in your life as a child.

__ Your mother expresses very little interest in your life as an adult.

__ You speak with your mother only when you call her or initiate contact.

___ Your mother is mad or disappointed about how your life has turned out.

___ You speak with your mother less than once a month.

___ Your mother was depressed or unhappy when you were a child.

___ You can't remember very many positive things about your mother-child relationship growing up.

___ Your mother was emotionally controlling with you growing up and continues to be now.

___ Your mother is emotionally very dependent on you now.

___ Your mother depends on you for her emotional support and happiness.

___ You and your mother have ongoing emotional tension in your adult relationship.

___ You live with your mother in spite of your need to be independent, because she prefers it.

___ You have great difficultly saying no to your mother.

___ You resent how your mother treats you as an adult.

___ Your mother doesn't like your intimate/marriage partner.

___ Your partner/wife/husband complains that your mother still has too much emotional control of your life and adult decisions.

___ When speaking with your mother, the conversation always ends up being about her.

___ You wish you and your mother were emotionally closer—better friends.

You will find that these two lists begin to give you a new perspective on your mother-daughter/son relationship. If you had no check marks or fewer than three, you need to reread this list and stop editing your responses. This list was deliberately designed to address a very wide spectrum of attachment styles and combinations of mother-child relationships. It is important to mention that many times men more than women will dismiss or ignore the enormous impact that their mother had on their emotional development and relationship patterns. This blind spot, which I've noticed in my professional life, is a very problematic area for most men to realize and address. Women, because of the same-sex identification, tend to be more aware of this timeless impact and bond. And both men and women who have had a conflicted, traumatic, turbulent, and painful relationship with their mothers are very aware of the influence and residual effects of that relationship. For those individuals, many of whom have suppressed their pain, it is a challenge to look at their mother without becoming enraged or depressed.

If you found yourself checking only the negative comments about attachment and negative thoughts about your mother-child/mother-adult relationship, you should seize this moment to begin the process of change. Think about why you checked those statements and what they mean to you now.

Most of us don't think about the way we attach or connect to our partners, children, family, co-workers, clients, or friends, because it is merely something we have been doing all our life. Attachment is like breathing, it is automatic and it enables you to have a life. If you stop breathing, you are dead. If you stop forming attachments, you are isolated from your world and yourself, which is an emotional death. It might seem very challenging to change the way you breathe. But if it were causing you to lose consciousness and pass out, then it would be necessary to think about changing it. The same analogy can be used for attachment: if your style of relating is causing you tremendous emotional pain, repeated relationship failures, rejection, rage, multiple divorces, and professional failure, it is well worth your time to revisit how you respond to this fundamental human need and universal experience. *Attachment is the breath of your emotional life.* Ask yourself, how is your emotional life? Is there anything discussed in this chapter that jumps out at you? Every area of your life is a form of attachment or is related to emotional bonding. Absolutely everything! Your entire life is driven, directed, and influenced by your attachment style. Your life is a composite of various types of relationships. The glue of all relationships is attachment. How does your attachment style hold, bond, and create meaningful relationships for you?

Don't despair if you think your approach to relationships is wrong, dysfunctional, or in need of a serious overhaul. It is crucial to remember that as you begin to change your approach to life regardless of your prior history, *your life is in front of you, not behind you*. Your primary concern is to focus on what you can change, improve, and develop in your future. If you find yourself obsessing about your mother and the drama you experienced with her in the past, then you should read chapter 12 first—to resolve your resentment. Remember that holding onto your resentment is like digging two graves: one for the person you resent and the other one for you.

Fortunately, there is an unlimited number of things you can do to redirect your life and relationships. Don't buy into the hopelessness of past relationship failures or your inner critical voice that will keep you from trying new things and relating to your world in the way you have always desired. Most change is based on your ability to step away from what you know and try something completely different. This isn't a self-help approach, but rather a different life approach. You need to create a different mindset to create new behaviors. To help you do so, let's define your particular style of attachment based on the following four styles: *intermittent*, *avoidant*, *depressed*, and *secure*. Each style has its very own characteristics and approach that derived from your childhood development and pervade your adult functioning.

INTERMITTENT STYLE OF ATTACHING

As the name implies, the intermittent style of relating is a combination of safe emotional connection, secure bonding, little or no emotional bonding, and/or a complete emotional miss. This style of attaching/relating is unpredictable, irregular, and erratic. It is these ongoing inconsistent and unpredictable emotional connections and misses that create problems for the children of this mothering attachment style. Such children later have trouble bonding in adult relationships. The continual emotional connections and misses cause profound psychological damage in children who take their pain into adulthood. As you grew up, your primary emotional needs (love, support, concern, empathy), physical needs (shelter, food, clothing), and mental needs (eye contact, physical contact, communication) were met. Then, for no apparent reason you found your needs—emotional, physical, or mental—not being addressed or taken care of by your mother. It is these early regular misses in a child's life from birth to age ten that shape and form a young person's view of the world—and that become an enduring problem. Your adult view of relationships may still be your childhood view, only with thirty more years of frustration and deprivation added to it. You cognitively knew your mother loved you, but why would she not be aware of your everyday life experiences, disappointments, accomplishments, losses, and masteries? Your emotional experience of your mother wasn't a consistent experience of love or safety but rather one of ongoing disappointment and frustration.

If you came home from your best girlfriend's house with tears in your eyes or a blue ribbon for winning the fourth-grade baseball tournament, your mother joined you in your emotional state of despair or excitement. You loved those special moments when you bonded with your mother and hoped they would never end. Then, over the next three weeks, your mother seemed completely unaware, distracted, and uninterested in your activities. She was like a different person with no sense of you or what was going on in your life. Then on the fourth Tuesday of the month (completely random), your mother responded to your low, sad, or great mood after school with empathy, compassion, or joy—whatever the occasion called for. The problem with such erratic behavior is that the child can never count on his mother being involved or emotionally present in his life or helping make decisions on a regular basis.

This style of attachment of uncertainty and inconsistent mothering creates over time a child's fear that the world isn't a caring, safe, or loving place. The child hopes that the world/mother is safe and caring all the time. The repeated emotional inconsistency develops a relationship pattern of fear, insecurity, and deprivation in the child. The continued lack of a consistent attachment in the first ten years of a daughter's or son's life breeds a deep sense of mistrust that any of his or her needs will be met or acknowledged in any relationship. Adults who find themselves feeling emotionally needy, insecure, unimportant, shy, alone, and unloved often have this attachment style in their mother-child history. These feelings have their roots in early childhood frustration, which are caused by repeated emotional failure between a mother and her child.

Mothers, who are emotionally intermittent with their child for personal reasons such as substance abuse, divorce, mood swings, immaturity, unwanted pregnancy, their own maternal deprivation, and lack of concern for their child, don't comprehend the magnitude of the problem of being inconsistent. They don't bond to their son or daughter with any pattern or logic. These mothers know that they love their child, but they don't have the emotional substance to maintain a consistent emotional attachment or bond. Such a mother wants to attach to her baby but can do so only on an infrequent basis, thus she forms an inconsistent pattern. These mothers exhibit this bonding pattern regardless of age, life experience, education, social status, economic power, and career success. The pattern can be found across all lines of families, religions, races, and cultures. It is very problematic because it eventually creates a deep sense of deprivation in a daughter's or son's life. These children are either in a chronic state of disappointment or one of emotional fulfillment. There is no in-between or middle ground with this mother-daughter/son relationship. This child is either feeling loved or emotionally frustrated. In the teens through early twenties, these children will be very quick to emotionally move away, separate, and develop their own identity—family. These daughters and sons do this to help create a stable, consistent, secure emotional bond in their own life to compensate for their childhood emotional deprivation.

Present Day—Intermittent Bonding Issues

People ask me all the time, what causes a person to be anxious? The intermittent attachment style is the foundation for an anxious personality, an addictive personality, or a person who has a mistrust of the world/people/relationships. Nearly all these surface behaviors likely have their origin in this mother-child relationship. In order to compensate and offset the emotional frustration and fill the mother-child void, people turn to other sources. Many men who have addictive or anxious personalities (i.e., workaholic, gambling, anger issues, excessive drinking, promiscuous sex/womanizing, chronic infidelity, adrenalin rushes, etc.) suffered through their childhoods with an emotionally inconsistent mother. These anxious behaviors are used to cover up the pain and loss of a deprived childhood. Now as adult men, their life looks like a runaway train going downhill, with no break in sight every time an unpleasant feeling occurs. The anxiety is so great that there is no conscious awareness that these feelings or behaviors are remotely related to their mother-son relationship. These men can be very charismatic and simultaneously unable to form a stable, nondramatic, secure emotional attachment with a woman/lover/wife. It isn't for a lack of desire but rather for a lack of insight that men/sons of this attachment style aren't able to create the stable, emotionally safe relationships they crave. It is possible to change this relationship pattern and create a secure, peaceful, and supportive bond with the people in your life. But change is possible only if this mother-son attachment style is fully understood along with its powerful residual effect.

Women who experienced this mother-daughter bonding dynamic will also develop an anxious personality and addictive behaviors as a result of their chronic emotional deprivation. Many times this daughter/woman will become a compulsive shopper who is chronically in debt, a controlling personality in relationships, a chronic complainer about her life, depressed, overweight, sexually irresponsible, emotionally clingy in relationships, unable to express her feelings, extremely body conscious, excessively concerned with exercising, emotionally driven with any interest or project, prey to bouts of depression, loneliness, panic attacks, and a sense of worthlessness. All these behaviors and feelings are in service of off-setting her chronic sense of disappointment and deep-seated emotional frustration.

The need for a close emotional bond is the unresolved issue for this daughter. Any and all behaviors used to cover up and compensate for the lack of a close emotional relationship with her mother will have this type of heightened drive and compulsive nature. Whether you're a man or a woman, the compulsive nature of the above behaviors is the "red flag" warning that your attachment-emotional bond is lacking, and it is having a negative impact on you and your life.

Intermittent Bonding—Your Checklist

Answer the following questions on whether and to what degree your life is being adversely affected by the inconsistent attachment style you experienced as a child. It is necessary to mention that we all have experienced a combination of the four attachment/ bonding styles, but there is a predominant style that characterized your mother-child relationship. Consider the following questions:

__ Do you have a difficult time handling emotionally anxious situations in your personal relationships?

__ Do you find it difficult to express your feelings of disappointment without becoming aggressive or angry?

__ Do you dismiss the importance of being emotionally close and open with your partner?

__ Do you prefer to be a loner, shy, or emotionally distant in your social and professional worlds?

__ Does your closest friend/partner/lover know when you are upset, sad, depressed, or happy?

__ Do you value your feelings?

__ Do you believe that relationships are important and the emotional oxygen of your life?

__ Do you prefer to be alone or with a friend when you are upset?

__ Do you drink or use drugs when you are alone and emotionally upset?

The more yes answers, the more likely that your relationship attachment style is being influenced by the inconsistent attachment mother-child pattern you experienced as a child. The wisdom and beauty of insight is that it creates the opportunity to change your present-day relationships and emotional bonds and to develop a more fulfilling style. At the end of this chapter, we will discuss some of the ways to change and create your own style of positive bonding and relating to others in your adult life.

AVOIDANT STYLE OF CONNECTING

The avoidant style of attaching is very different from the intermittent style. This is the mother who didn't express emotions of any kind (love, fear, anger, hope, etc.), nor did she show feelings, passionate thoughts, excitement, or an enthusiasm for life. This clear pattern of not expressing anything would possibly incite a very strong positive or negative emotional response from anyone. The inability to bond—whether as a result of fear or reluctance—is the driving force in this mother-child relationship. The avoidant attachment style lacks emotional expression, passion, or any type of demonstrative action or behavior. There is little to no physical contact, such as hugging, or empathic communication between the mother and child. No embracing, hand-holding, saying "I love you" or emotionally comforting words as a child leaves for the first day of second grade at a new school, or as a seven-year-old goes to bed at night.

The avoidant attachment style is all about keeping proper emotional distance from events and people, including a daughter or son. For the child of this type of mother, physical expressions of love, concern, and support are absent from the relationship. Hugging, a kiss on the cheek, back rub, a supportive look, or emotional word of encouragement, and other nurturing behaviors aren't part of this style. Adult children, when describing their avoidant mother, will use terms such as "cold," "aloof," "emotionally disconnected," and "unable to express love."

The ongoing relationship issue of the avoidant attachment style is that the child grows up wondering if he or she is loved. These same children as adults then question if they are lovable and worthy of someone showing affection to them. Daughters and sons raised with this attachment style become accustomed to and comfortable with no emotional expression. The natural bonding process of emotional communication is undeveloped and not used by these adults. A sense of isolation and loneliness is common in these adults because they've not experienced the natural emotional, mental, physical, and spiritual connections that occur in most relationships. Many times, when someone else shows a strong emotional response or behaves passionately, an immediate panic is experienced. Close encounters of all types aren't part of these adults' relationships or their style of relating to people. There is an automatic reflexive action to be distant, which causes these sons and daughters to have a difficult time forming close nurturing bonds. The idea of sharing feelings, thoughts, and emotions and having a close rapport is in contradiction to how these children developed in their mother-child relationship and as individuals in relation to the outside world.

True Story—Changing Avoidant Attachment

I have a client who comes to see me only during the holiday season. This year was particularly different for Stan, who was acknowledging how emotionally distant he tended to be with his feelings and thoughts. Stan, a divorced fifty-seven-year-old, had never told his three adult children that he loved them. Stan was a man of few words, and deep emotional expression wasn't a natural or comfortable behavior for him. He spoke to his adult children only when it was time to send them their annual tax-free inheritance gift check. Stan didn't have the need nor did he see any reason to verbally express "soft" emotions to his children, colleagues, or girlfriend. Stan never joined his adult children or his girlfriend's family during the holidays, birthdays, or any type of celebration. In order to avoid these occasions, Stan would work extra shifts at the hospital as an emergency room doctor. On this particular Christmas Eve, Stan was the only doctor on duty at the ER.

A young couple brought in their four-month-old baby boy, who had a cold and labored breathing. Stan examined the boy, and his condition continued to worsen. Stan tells me the following the story:

> The mother is the same age as my daughter, twenty-six years old, and her husband looked like my oldest son. I felt an immediate sense of concern for them, like they were my kids and that was my grandson. I never feel this way when I am working or doing surgery. I am always all about business, diagnosis, and treatment. I put the baby in our Intensive Care Unit immediately

and the boy died of pneumonia complications two hours later. When I walked into the waiting room and I had to tell this young couple the worst news that any parent could hear, I couldn't talk. I was so choked up with emotion that they both stared at me in disbelief. The mother screamed when she saw me: Not my baby. All I could do was shake my head up and down. She got up and shook my shoulders so hard and kept screaming: Not my baby—not my baby. The father buried his head in his hands. I have never cried at work or remember being so overwhelmed with emotion. All three of us stood in the ER. waiting room sobbing. I am a cardiologist and have seen and experienced thousands of deaths. This baby's death broke something down inside of me, I couldn't hide from it. I was flooded with sadness and despair for this couple, the baby boy, and my life. I went to my kid's house the next day on Christmas. My kids all stared at me when I showed up unannounced because I hadn't spent a Christmas with them in fifteen years. I told them the story and we all cried. My daughter Amanda, who looked like the baby's mother, gave me a hug after hearing the story. I can't remember the last time I hugged or got a hug from my kids. I can't hide from my life anymore.

Stan immediately changed his attachment style from being avoidant to being warm and more attached and expressive to his patients, colleagues, children, and girlfriend. Stan had been in couple's therapy with his girlfriend about his emotional distance, lack of passion, and cold, sterile personality. Stan decided that if he remained distant from his feelings and the people in his life, he would die alone and miss out on what's really important: *relationships*. Stan married his girlfriend on New Year's Eve the following year.

Stan's behavior and demeanor are typical of adult children who grew up with a mother who had an avoidant attachment style. As an adult, he was viewed as a loner, recluse, and detached outsider in the emotional atmosphere of his medical practice, family, social life, and romantic relationship. The lack of emotional, mental, and physical connections was a major impairment in all the areas and facets of his life. What is important to remember is that Stan felt a wide range of emotions and feelings that he never considered valuable or necessary to share. Like many people, Stan lived his life only in his head, skipping his emotional/feeling and physical side. Avoidant men and women, regardless of age, want to unzip their emotional straitjacket and begin to express their life and all that is in it.

Unzipping Your Emotions—Checklist

Consider the following questions about your avoidant behaviors and style of bonding with the people in your life. These automatic avoidant behaviors have their beginnings in your mother-child history. Many times, emotional avoidance is a survival mechanism that a son or daughter develops within a chaotic and "crazy" family. These avoidant behaviors don't usually work well thirty-five years later and can be changed to expand the quality and substance of your life. The reasons for them are as varied as the people who have an avoidant lifestyle/attachment style. Ask yourself:

___ Do you prefer to be alone than with your friends?

___ Do you find it difficult to share with your close friends/ partner your emotional issues/feelings?

___ When do you find yourself emotionally, mentally, and physically engaged with others?

___ Would you consider yourself a straightforward, non-avoidant person when it comes to conflict?

___ When you are happy, excited, passionate, and/or enthusiastic, do you allow people to see that side of your personality?

___ Who in your life currently is emotionally attached to you? Who are you emotionally attached to—and do they know it?

___ What is a common, ongoing theme and style of your emotional communication with your partner?

___ While growing up, was your mother distant or avoidant in her attachment style to you?

___ Would you consider yourself to be generally an emotionally avoidant person?

___ What things in your life on a personal, professional, and social level do you avoid?

___ What would you like to stop avoiding in your life?

___ Does the display of strong emotion make you feel uneasy?

Again, it is important to understand the questions that you answered yes or no to. These questions are designed to get you to ask yourself whether you might have an avoidant attachment style. Awareness, insight, and understanding of your attachment issues are the quickest way to revolutionize your life in all the areas you desire. When people acknowledge their pattern of emotional avoidance, they immediately feel a deep sense of relief and begin to feel the unlimited possibilities for their future. Avoidant emotional attachments cause tremendous internal crises in adult men and women because they feel the constant need to keep everyone else happy and content. The need to avoid any uncomfortable emotional feelings (i.e., frustration, anger, rejection, confrontation, panic, anxiety, and sadness) becomes a full-time occupation and very consuming. It is a life-changing moment when you stop avoiding your feelings and embrace them.

DEPRESSED STYLE OF ATTACHMENT

Your mother might not have been diagnosed as depressed, but she may have lacked energy for the role of motherhood. Your mother may have connected and bonded with you at times but seemed generally overwhelmed by the responsibility of having you as her child. There wasn't much happiness or excitement that your mother experienced or shared with you. Your mother (married, single, widowed, or divorced) had very little energy for nurturing activities and for creating an emotional bond with her child. The depressed attachment style has a list of characteristics that make it different from the other three styles of relating: *unpredictable mood swings, emotionally distracted, overly dependent on the child to meet the mother's emotional needs, unaware of other people's actions or feelings, little concern for the child's needs and desires, fearful, chronically complaining, unhappy, unmotivated, careless with the child's well-being, easily overwhelmed, negative, abuses substances, and is at times suicidal.* This isn't a complete list, but it begins to paint the picture of this type of mother-child emotional bond.

The daughter or son of the mother with the depressed attachment style grew up wondering if she or he was the cause of the mother's deep-seated unhappiness. The biggest liability of this attachment style is the overinflated sense of responsibility that these children have for the people in their lives. As a young child, all you knew was that your mother didn't seem happy with you around the house. She wasn't happy about the good things you did or accomplished. Your attachment to your mother was centered on her and the mood she was in at that moment. Children of mothers with a depressed attachment style become very aware of the emotional drain and work it takes to keep a relationship going. In spite of the huge emotional load these children carry for their mother, they consider it their job and responsibility to make her happy. These children/adults grow up rarely considering or knowing their own feelings, thoughts, or emotions. This is especially true when it comes to bonding/attaching with close friends, family members, and intimate partners.

Your mother's depression might have been triggered by your father, job loss, money worries, family death, relationship issues, or chemical imbalance, but the depressive nature of your relationship was always present. Whether your mother's depressed attachment was caused by outside events or was a chronic preexisting condition, it communicated a lack of interest in you. Children of a depressed mother tend not to know how they feel or what they want—they might not even know to consider such questions. Yet these children are excellent in reading and meeting the needs of others and thinking about other people's thoughts. This behavior is commonly referred to as "codependence" and is one of the biggest attachment secrets of this style. The child's emotional, mental, physical, and spiritual developmental needs are rarely, if ever, addressed by the mother. These children grow up believing that the only way to bond is to be the other person's caretaker, regardless of the consequences of those actions.

If your mother had a depressed attachment style, the driving force consciously and unconsciously in your life was and is to make the people around you happy. If you don't do that, the love and emotional support you want from these people will be taken away or the potential for them will be lost. This belief is irrational because it is based on your giving and never receiving what you truly need. The bottom line of the depressed attachment style is that the child (you) learned that everything in a relationship is about the other person (mother). In this relationship, you don't have an opinion or a right to have a choice. This is a very common behavior to a greater or lesser degree in adult children of this attachment style.

The depressed attachment style can beget adult relationships that are verbally, physically, emotionally, or sexually abusive. The victim feels that on some emotional level this abuse is a form of love, concern, and secure attachment. In the entertainment industry, there is a common belief: *there is no such thing as bad attention; all attention is positive, regardless of its nature.* Abuse, regardless of the pain it causes, is an emotional connection. This belief may be true, but it is dangerous. The reality is that the abusive relationship is a hostile attachment with extreme negative side effects—the oppression of the victim. The need to be loved, feel loved, and have that need met is the natural driving force in all humans. We are genetically wired to crave love, attachment, and attention. The adult child of the depressed mother may confuse abuse as a form of love and positive attention. The confusion of love and abuse may have its roots in the mother-child attachment history. Abuse in any relationship is emotionally charged and all-consuming for both parties. The abusive emotional energy is a strong attachment and requires both parties to focus only on the abuser. The distorted emotional relationship allows for the ongoing abuse in all its various degrees to continue. The codependence belief is that the child/partner/friend/colleague is solely responsible for everything in the relationship. This attachment pattern is the only way that these relationships can function, survive, and perpetuate the psychological "craziness." This pattern of connecting is a serious roadblock that bars the codependent adult from having a healthy relationship. It is very difficult for adult children of depressed mothers to see the need to change their relationship patterns, because they have been raised to care for others, regardless of the personal cost or dire consequences to themselves. The need to change these self-defeating attachments is a very serious issue. The first step is connecting with others without having to "fix," "take care of," or "mend" the people in their life.[4]

Stopping Abusive Attachment at Its Roots—Lynn's New Style

Lynn grew up in Malibu, with a house on the beach. Her mother divorced her father when Lynn was five. Unfortunately, one year after the divorce, Lynn was taken away from her mother to live with her father. Lynn never lived or spent much time with her mother again while growing up. Lynn's father, Mike, was a criminal attorney and always had questionable people around the house as clients. Lynn and her father were always trying to help—fix—these people when they had trouble with the law. Mike wasn't able to "fix" his wife—Lynn's mother. Lynn recalls that both her parents were depressed during her childhood and she became the parent to both of them. The only difference between her father and mother was that her father was able to work, and he made a lot of money.

Lynn became extremely responsible as a child. She developed the pattern at age fifteen of always dating men who needed a lot of support, help, and nurturing. She continued this pattern of taking care of men into her adult romantic relationships. She felt that the only way that she could emotionally attach to people, especially men, was to be the expert caretaker. Lynn found herself at age thirty-six, single, broken-hearted, financially ruined, and feeling hopeless of ever getting married. She realized that she had created these unsatisfying relationships because of her style of attachment. Lynn stated the following:

> I always feel responsible for everyone. Brad, my last boyfriend, his mother hated me. I did everything possible to get her to like me. I allowed her to insult me to my face and I never spoke up for myself. She told her son—my boyfriend—in front of me at several family dinners to date a more mature woman. I of course took this awful woman to lunch to explain my good intentions with her son. It was crazy, the woman hated me because she was afraid of sharing her son with me. I never felt like I could ask for what I wanted from Brad—all I wanted was for him to tell his mother to stop criticizing me and leave me alone. Instead, I take her out three more times for lunch trying to convince her that I am a great wife for her son. Each lunch was more painful and humiliating than the last one. This woman called Brad's last girlfriend to see if she was still interested in her son. After that incident, I knew I couldn't keep trying to please everyone in my life, especially an angry boyfriend's mother. Her rejection of me was literally killing me. I was sick every three weeks with some type of serious flu or sinus infection. I ultimately had to break up with Brad because he wanted me to fix things with his mother. Brad didn't want to deal with having to separate from her or setting limits with her. I knew all along that this relation-

ship wasn't right but I just couldn't stop myself once I got emotionally attached to Brad.

Lynn's story represents the experiences of many of us who have struggled with our mother's emotional legacy of codependence. Lynn knew that she couldn't continue to relate to men the way she had in the past because she experienced the same thing every time: *emotional despondency*. Men and women with a depressed attachment style struggle to have their natural human needs met without having to endure the horrors of being codependent in their adult relationships. Lynn knew that if she wanted to have a satisfying romantic relationship it would start with her developing a secure attachment style.

Codependence—Depressed Style Checklist

Consider the following the questions. Codependence might be a very difficult issue to see or address in your life. If you recognize that your mother-child attachment style is of a depressed nature, then look at these questions as a key to finding your emotional blind spots.

___ Have you ever loaned money to your intimate partner against your better judgment and at a time you couldn't afford to do it?

___ Have you ever been repaid money you loaned to your partners, friends, family, or associates?

___ Have you solely supported your dating partner?

___ Have you tried to "fix" your intimate partner's life?

___ Are you always worried about the other person's thoughts, feelings, and emotions?

___ Do you have tremendous abandonment fears in your relationships—regardless of the reality of the situation?

___ Do you always think about the other person's response to your conversation prior to having it?

___ Do you always consider the other person's response to any issue before your own?

___ Is it much easier for you to know the other person's feelings, thoughts, and emotions about an issue rather than your own?

___ Do you become emotionally depressed when you feel that someone is upset or angry at you?

___ Do you avoid expressing your own thoughts and feelings on an issue in order not to upset the other person?

___ Is it more important to you to keep the peace than express your true intentions or feelings?

These are a few of the issues surrounding the depressed attachment style and its underlying codependent behavior. Recognizing your codependent-depressed attachment style might feel as though you're looking into the back of your head. You can't view these issues with the clarity that you would if you were looking at someone else's pattern of bonding. If these questions and the description of the depressed mother-child attachment feel like your relationship style, don't panic. These questions are designed to give you an idea of how your mother's emotional legacy is impacting your adult relationships and shaping your everyday behavior.

SECURE ATTACHMENT STYLE—
WHAT WE REALLY WANT IN A RELATIONSHIP

This is the attachment style that perhaps 10 to 15 percent of us had in our mother-child relationship while growing up. The secure attachment style is the consistent emotional experience of having your physical, mental, and emotional needs met as an infant and throughout your childhood. The repetition of such behavior created an emotional foundation of trust and reinforced the feeling that the world is a safe place. Men and women can develop a similar secure attachment style in their adult life and can have the type of intimate relationships that we all desire. As you read this book, it is important to note that your mother factor is yours to learn about, understand, and change where you desire. No one else will do it for you and no one else has the power to change it. It is your legacy now and yours to use more effectively. This isn't about changing or blaming your mother but changing your own emotional life and how you relate to your world. Many times, sons and daughters get caught up in attempting to fix their mother, which quickly becomes a losing battle and leads to more frustration and anger for all parties involved. Regardless of what your mother did or didn't do, this is your journey and pathway to change.

The feeling of powerlessness about changing old behaviors is an outdated belief. This book is all about your options and the potential to re-create your life regardless of your age, mother-child history, and past disappointments. A sign of mental health and emotional growth is your ability to develop secure emotional attachment with the people and things currently in your life. We have discussed at length the pitfalls of the other three attachment styles; now it is time to focus on the emotional style and attachment pattern that you are beginning to move toward in your adult relationships. The secure attachment style is the only type of emotional bond that we want to form with our intimate circle of partners, family, and friends.

The secure attachment style is shown in the mother's capability to listen, emotionally read, and understand the needs of her baby as he grows up. This style is about the ability to meet the emotional, physical, and mental needs of the child from birth onward. The secure emotionally attached mother is able to pay attention, show concern, and provide loving gestures to her son or daughter. The baby becomes accustomed to having his or her needs on all levels met and satisfied. A child's perspective of the world is shaped and formed by the mother-baby attachment style. Your original worldview was fully developed by roughly the age of six and still influences your perspective today.

Ask yourself:

- Is your world emotionally safe?
- Do you believe that your needs get met/understood in your relationships?
- Do you believe that your emotional needs are valuable enough to discuss with others?
- Do you believe people can be emotionally consistent with you?
- Can you be emotionally consistent with the important people in your life?
- Can you trust your intimate relationships to meet your needs (emotionally, mentally, and physically)?

These questions all have their answers in your early mother-child attachment history (prior to age five). Understanding your personal worldview of relationships is critical if you are going to amend and change your emotional legacy and style of attachments. Remember that a secure attachment gives the child a feeling that his mother is consistent and loving. A regular, predictable, and stable emotional bond allows the child to develop without significant emotional crises or blocks to his potential. The child feels loved early on in life because his mother makes him feel important with her consistent and appropriate behavior. Her repeated actions (eye contact, verbal soothing, hugging, holding, listening) over time build a strong emotional foundation in the child that conveys to him that he is important and valuable to the world. The secure emotional bond breeds and develops in a child the courage to become a leader and take personal and professional risks, the ability to follow his dreams, the desire to become a mentor, and the confidence to change the world. It is never too late or too early to develop an emotional base that is secure and consistent. The baby knows that his mother has his best interest and concern at the heart of her actions and words. These babies grow into adults who are able to be generous and loving and who can show concern for someone else's feelings and thoughts.

As result of this secure attachment, these children continue to grow up to excel in relationships and careers and as individuals. A secure emotional attachment allows a daughter to bond with her peer group, take healthy risks at school, take demanding courses, go on dates, be empathic with others, trust friends, and feel a sense of belonging with other people. We all need to develop trusting, secure attachments in our adult lives. The secret of emotional attachment is that we all share the same basic human needs regardless of our history, nationality, economic background, race, and spiritual beliefs. The basic five needs you've developed from your mother factor are *trust, a sense of belonging, concern/empathy, security,* and *love*. All of your relationships, regardless of their nature and function, are made up of a combination of these five elements. Everything you do in your life starts with a relationship with yourself and is followed by the different relationships with all the people, things, and activities that surround you. The secure emotional bond builds a foundation of trust that allows a daughter to explore and experience her world all through life.

For those who did not have a complete mother, it is never too late to build and develop a strong and deeper sense of trust and emotional security. *Remember, everything in your life centers around relationships.* Your primary relationship—first love with your mother—was the start of your emotional and relationship legacy.

Later in the book, we are going to discuss how to build, expand, and re-create your mother factor legacy—which is in part made up by your attachment style. To help you assess how secure your mother-child attachment style was, see how you respond to the following relationship questions. These questions will give you an idea of how much or how little you attach to the people in your life in a secure and trusting manner. Use a scale attachment from 0 percent (no attachment) to 100 percent (extremely secure).

- Do you consistently offer emotional support/concern in the workplace to your colleagues?
- Do you feel that most people trust you—are they willing to share their feelings, hardships, and successes with you?
- Do you find emotional strength in your personal relationships?
- Did you feel emotionally secure with your mother while growing up? Why did you feel that way?
- Do you form secure attachments in your adult life—in all areas?
- Do you trust the opposite sex?
- How much is trust an issue in your relationships?
- Are you a trustworthy person?
- Who is the most important person in your life? Does this person know his or her value/importance to you?

It is essential to remember that even if your relationship/attachment with your mother was painful and full of disappointment, it is possible to move your life in a positive direction and resolve these early issues that are based on your mother factor. The application of developing a secure attachment style is in the third section of the book. Right now, let us just consider how your life would be different if you felt emotionally secure and loved in your relationships.

Chapter 2

How You Can
MAKE YOUR MOTHER FACTOR WORK
in Your Adult Life and in Relationships

I realized at about age twenty-eight that my mother never listened to me. I have the same pattern of not listening to my friends or boyfriend. I know now that my mother never listened to anyone verbally or emotionally in our family. It didn't interest her to be emotionally connected to us.

—Rachel, age thirty-one, single

My mother was the emotional glue in our family. There was nothing that she didn't know, care about, or didn't feel. My mother felt everything for the family. She was our role model on emotional issues. She held us together.

—Duane, age forty-nine, married

W e have discussed thus far how your first love was your mother. That love relationship started with your emotional bonding and attachment to her in the womb. Those early attachments, emotional connections, and feelings between you and your mother were the start of your emotional education. You have learned many things in your life that go far beyond reading, writing, arithmetic, and reasoning. Your emotional functioning is your higher learning. Typically, the least understood area of your formal training and adult life is the emotional component, which directly involves you and your mother. This education never stopped, and you are still realizing what you learned from your mother about relationships, feelings, communication, and relating to others, for example. Your full comprehension of your mother factor legacy is critical to your future and the direction of your life. We all know this on an unspoken, subconscious level. It is the unresolved issues that are below the surface that make this process difficult for us all. There is nothing in your life that isn't currently touched, influenced, and impacted by the emotional influence of your mother. For those who challenge or argue this point, I ask the following question: *Tell me how you felt at your mother's funeral? If she is alive, tell me how you would feel about going to her grave site and seeing her casket being lowered into the ground?* Women and men of all ages will automatically consider the strengths of the mother factor after visualizing or having experienced their mother's death. A person's psychological resistance to the concept of a mother factor legacy may be telling in itself. The resistance may be emotional evidence of its power and misunderstood nature. Adults tend to resist only the things that are frightening to them. For many of us, dealing with our mother factor falls into the category of overwhelming.

The quotes above show again the residual power of the mother-child connection. It is a timeless bond for women and men. My professional experience has repeatedly shown me that it isn't gender that is the best indicator of the influence of mothers; rather, it is the person's degree of insight into the relationship that matters. Women and men who understand their mother factor legacy are aware of some of the common pitfalls of that relationship. These issues have to be acknowledged and, if needed, worked on in order to remove the classic ball and chain around your leg. The more understanding, clarity, and resolution you have regarding your relationship with your mother, the more opportunity you will have to create the type of life you desire. Your understanding of this very complex relationship gives you the freedom and choices to pick and choose how you will respond to life—professionally, personally, romantically, sexually, and emotionally (there is no limit to your future).

PRESENT-DAY APPLICATION—
THE INFLUENCE OF YOUR MOTHER FACTOR

The unexplored areas of your mother factor legacy are the only issues that will stall out your life. The glass ceiling, emotional blocks, and repeated relationship failures all have their roots in your mother-child history. The more you uncover for the purpose of change and growth, the more your old roadblocks will begin to crumble and disappear. The connection between the following behaviors to these seemingly unrelated themes in your life are worth examining for the purpose of changing your emotional attachment and belief system. Don't dismiss the present-day influence of a troubled mother-child relationship that occurred thirty years ago or more.

- You have automatic anger and rage reactions to minor misunderstandings.
- You have uncontrollable, angry outbursts at work and at home toward loved ones. You scare people with your anger.
- You have chronic feelings of failure, regardless of the outcome.
- You struggle with anxious feelings/have a history of panic attacks/fear not being in control in any circumstance.

- You are very controlling of people, events, partners, and money.
- You have commitment phobia in intimate relationships—can't date past a certain time period (a recurring pattern).
- You are unable to trust people—mistrust and paranoia are common emotional experiences for you.
- You repeatedly have intimate relationship breakups—unable to maintain a long-term, emotionally significant relationship.
- You fight with your children about loving/respecting you—beyond typical parent-child arguments.
- You have emotionally or physically abandoned your children—regardless of your marriage status.
- You have eating issues—body image obsession.
- You are unable to maintain a stable, nondramatic romantic relationship.
- You are unable to commit to a career path or take the necessary steps to develop your career potential.
- You have strong personal feelings of disdain (shame) about yourself and dislike your life circumstances—have feelings of worthlessness.
- You lack personal relationships—professional, social, and romantic.
- You are overly sexualized but avoid emotional contact in personal encounters.

How many of these behaviors ring a bell for you and your relationship with friends and others? These very common adult behaviors, personal beliefs, and feelings about your life are all strong indicators that your mother factor is running your life, and you're not. It is essential to recognize the value of understanding that much of our adult distress is related to our primary relationship model and legacy.

Regardless of your life circumstances, you will begin to see that there are appropriate, legitimate, and positive changes that you can emotionally, mentally, and psychologically implement to move your relationships to the next level. Your life is a composite of relationships in the home, outside the home, and within yourself. As much as the media, talk shows, schools, and cultural institutions describe mother-child interactions, a full appreciation of this dynamic is still rare. The mother factor isn't about blaming your mother for your current struggles but quite the opposite. Our purpose here is to understand the issues, identify them, and consider the real possibility of proactive change. Then you will see the invaluable role that your mother factor has played or plays in seemingly unrelated personal issues and relationship struggles. One of our goals is to use your mother factor as leverage to move your life past your blind spots and particular pitfalls. Remember, it is our emotional and psychological blind spots that we spend our lives running from or avoiding.

In the following five chapters, we are going to discuss the various mothering styles we all experienced growing up. Each style has its strengths and weaknesses that still influence us as adults. It is crucial to start noticing that there are numerous threads from your present-day concerns, struggles, and strengths whose origins date back to your mother. Making the emotional, mental, and psychological connections of the events of your current life with the recurring themes that have shaped your life is the main point of this chapter. We have already examined how your emotional attachments in all the different types of relationships must be looked at in terms of your mother factor legacy. A prime goal is to start seeing the direct connection—cause and effect of many of your emotional blocks, negative self-beliefs, successes, and relationship issues in terms of how your mother's legacy influenced you. Many of your recurring relationship problems, disappointments, and issues have large pieces of your mother-child relationship in them. This may sound simple or obvious to an outsider looking into your life. The key is for *you* to see the powerful connections, threads, and recurring themes.

The five mothering styles are the perfectionist mother, the unpredictable mother, the "me first" mother, the best friend mother, and the complete mother. Each mothering style has/had a tremendous influence in shaping your relationship patterns, attachment style, and emotional functioning (e.g., the ability to tolerate and handle frustration and to experience joy). Each style has a particular issue or negative side effect (except for the compassionate/mentor relationship), which needs to be understood in the context of your adult life today. This concept is further explained in the chapter on the complete style of mothering.

THE PAIN FACTOR—HOW MUCH MORE?

We are going to explore the five most common relationship and emotional problems that adults struggle with on a daily basis. These struggles might seem completely unrelated to your mother factor but, in fact, they are very much related. They have profound emotional, mental, spiritual, conscious, and unconscious connections to your mother. These struggles typically manifest themselves as *personality conflicts, communication issues, anxiety, envy, anger, hostility, emotional immaturity, shame, guilt, depression, loneliness, intimacy issues, addictive behaviors, eating disorders, body image obsession, commitment phobia, masculinity-femininity concerns, and nagging self-doubts.* The straightforward practical approach—there is no other way to emotional clarity and health—to these difficult issues is your pathway to change and resolve. Regardless of your deep sense of feeling overwhelmed, panicked, powerless, and hopeless about your personal issues, none of them is beyond the hand of change (your hand). Past failures are for the purpose of learning what doesn't work in your relationships. Use your perceived failures as a starting point for your personal and emotional transformation.

The above list represents a wide range of powerful problems

that may seem beyond the realistic scope of change. As a psychologist, I have repeatedly found in my professional and personal experience that roughly 80 percent of the successful resolution of our problems with relationships and within ourselves is the mere recognition of those problems, whereas 20 percent is the actual proactive change. There is an old saying that overnight change takes fifteen years. The recognition part can be a very long, painful process, taking many years and involving significant life-changing events. Unfortunately, the recognition usually comes through severe emotional pain, such as that from a divorce notice, pregnancy miscarriage, financial ruin, death, friendship betrayal, criminal arrest, losing a family member to an addiction, family rejection, child custody battles, and so on. The circumstances and the people involved in these traumas are endless. *We only consider change when our pain threshold is exceeded.* Then there is no other option than to make these necessary adjustments to our mother factor legacy. No one is beyond the power of emotional pain as a tremendous motivator for change. We are all psychologically wired for life change after a painful and stunning experience. This is the way humans make changes. Everyone has a mental, emotional, and psychological breaking point, which becomes the opening for significant change. *Emotional pain is one of the strongest motivators for personal change.*

Emotional pain will always blow open all of the doors in your life—guaranteed—particularly the doors of your life that you prefer to keep bolted shut.[1] Your personal pain will expose your defense mechanisms and relationship blind spots in ways that require your immediate attention. It is the emotional resistance from past disappointments that create avoidant behavior in these life-changing moments. Emotional resistance, denial, and avoidance over time become the problem, thus covering up the root of the real problem. These defensive behaviors are very sophisticated and can short-circuit any possibility of change and personal satisfaction. Our aim here is to make the unconscious self-defeating, self-limiting beliefs conscious. Once these behaviors are better understood, exposed, and recognized, then change can be easily implemented. Insight leads to inner personal, psychological change and creates new options that never before seemed possible or attainable. It is the insight into and shift of your internal belief system that opens new doors in your life to exciting, innovative possibilities. Without gaining new insight into your emotional functioning in the problem areas of your life, your personal roadblocks will remain in place, creating future problems. Ultimately, your emotional pain will come flooding back and bring you to the same issues: different day, same issues. Eventually, the metaphor of the closed doors in your life—unresolved issues—will need to be addressed to reduce your emotional pain. Life has a way of pointing out our blind spots, and it is our responsibility to take action on these new insights when we understand them. Part of the 80 percent of recognition is your commitment to stop creating your own emotional pain and personal crises. When adults stop creating relationship "drama," the core issues can then be competently resolved.

The concept of change by understanding your mother factor legacy may be a new idea or perspective. Being open-minded to changing your emotional legacy requires you to be adaptable in your relationships, where your mother factor may be in control. The power of your mother factor likely translates into your attachment style, relationship pattern, and emotional intelligence—these core relationship elements may need to be redesigned for your further personal success. For you to be more proficient in emotional matters and in understanding relationships, you will need to begin seeing below the surface of a particular problem. Blaming your partner, finger-pointing, or accusing all men of being insensitive or all women of being moody isn't an acceptable excuse for your relationship issues. Many times, your critical attitude, cynical belief, or your repetitive complaints are deeply rooted in your past. These feelings have never been clearly identified or recognized as limiting to your life. Gaining insight into these old beliefs, frustrating relationship patterns, and anger—without blaming your mother or condemning your family history—will bring you to a new level of insight, emotional functioning, and personal freedom. These changes will give you the necessary tools to create change in your present-day relationships and take your future in the direction you choose. These changes will reduce your need to create situations, relationships, and arguments in which your emotional pain will be the primary source of motivation for change.

Stacy's and Mark's Emotional Pain—The End!

Stacy was referred to me by one of her longtime childhood girlfriends for "control issues" with men. Stacy, age thirty-one and engaged, grew up with a very unpredictable, moody mother-daughter relationship. Stacy was only five years old the day her father died, and she remembers his death as if it happened yesterday. After that day, Stacy and her mother, Linda, never spoke of her father's death. Stacy told me the following story:

> My mother has been depressed since the day my father died. I have never spoken about my father's death to this day with anyone. I have just powered my way forward and not paid much attention to my feelings. The problem now is I am starting to have very severe panic attacks. I wake up anxious and go to bed anxious. My fiancé is so passive that he slows me down, but he can't handle my stress anymore. My mother is really like my daughter. I am the parent and have been for years. My mother can't function without calling me ten times a day, it is so tiresome. Yet we both do it, we are so connected that it is really wrong. I feel like I have my mother in my back pocket and I can't leave her. I have horrible guilt over getting married because my mother has never remarried. I know it isn't my fault but I feel responsible for everything that has to do with her.

Stacy acknowledged here that her anxiety is about her fear of abandonment and her feelings of shame. For the first time, she discussed her father's death, but the underlying issue was her fear of losing her mother. Stacy began to see that her sense of shame— feeling defective—and anxiety were an active part of her ongoing mother-daughter relationship. Over the next twelve weeks, she began to change her emotional attachment to her mother and to her boyfriend. She worked on resolving and understanding her sense of abandonment and her deep, paralyzing sense of shame. Stacy actively changed her emotional relationship with her inner circle of friends. One of Stacy's new behaviors was not having to be the "hub" of the world for her mother and boyfriend. She now began to allow plans, details, and conversations to develop naturally, not always taking responsibility for the outcome. In addition, she learned that her feelings of inadequacy had nothing to do with her but were the residual effects of the crises of her childhood. Stacy always felt that she was somehow responsible for her mother's well-being and couldn't ever resolve her mother's grief. The long-term effect for Stacy was always feeling the need to be perfect so her mother would "get better" and not be so sad. Stacy felt inadequate because her mother never functioned at her full potential. Once Stacy gained insight into her role and changed approaches, her panic attacks stopped and her anxiety dramatically diminished.

Mark, fifty-two, woke up on Halloween morning with a white business envelope on his pillow. He opened it and read the divorce notice from his wife of twenty-four years. Mark knew that Brenda was unhappy at times, but he had no idea she was considering a divorce. He had been told by Brenda to move out of the house on three prior occasions for being "emotionally" unavailable. Mark always felt that whatever he did for his wife was not good enough, inadequate, or wrong. He found himself being increasingly yelled and screamed at because Brenda wanted him to have several millions of dollars put away for their retirement. She had always been scared that she would die penniless and end up being a "bag lady."

Mark has spent years building a graphic arts company in Los Angeles. His company recently tripled its profits on a monthly basis. The biggest month of his company history ended with Brenda serving him a summons for divorce.

Mark came to my office and told me the following story:

I have been trying to please my wife since we met. I love her, I don't want a divorce. Brenda thinks that whatever I do isn't enough, or good enough for her. She is convinced that I am the cause of all her problems and fears. I have spent twenty plus years pleasing this woman. I have tried everything I know to calm her fears about being poor. We live in a 5,000 square foot house and have no money worries, none. There isn't anything I wouldn't do for her. I feel like a complete loser. I really get what those love songs are all about, I am wiped out. I have given my soul to Brenda every day of our marriage. I have been faithful, never cheated, or wanted to. There is nothing I can do to please her. Her rage at me is so confusing. I feel like crawling back into bed and maybe this nightmare will be over, and this is really a bad dream.

Mark continued talking to me over the next several months and began to realize that his marriage relationship was based on his codependence with his mother. Mark's mother, Mary Anne, was very critical of Mark and his father. Mark remembers growing up feeling that art work wasn't what his mother wanted him to do. He realized that his need for love was based on his ability to be the perfect husband, father, and businessman for Brenda. Mark never set any emotional boundaries with Brenda with regard to money, her verbal abuse, or her chronic complaining. He realized that he had set up his marriage based on his codependence and depressed emotional attachment to women. Mark began to consciously understand that many of his marital issues were really his mother-son problems replayed in the present day. As a young boy, he never felt loved or cared for by his mother unless he did exactly what she wanted and demanded.

Mark began to change his relationship style and set emotional boundaries with his ex-wife over money, child support, and her chronic complaints. He had never said no to Brenda or his mother. He no longer felt panic or anxiety when Brenda was enraged with him. He began to see himself as a valuable person without having to please or take care of the other person. He stopped worrying about what other people would think if he made his own choices. This was a very liberating belief and action for Mark.

Both Stacy and Mark made significant changes in dealing with their relationships by directly addressing their mother factor legacy. Stacy stopped taking responsibility for her mother and new husband. Mark began to realize that his feelings about himself were based on his wife's approval of him. These stories are very powerful because they point out the endless connections we all have to our first love—our mother. This bond shapes our feelings and emotions in our current adult life. Both Stacy and Mark are very insightful and psychologically sophisticated adults who were absolutely in the dark about the fact that their intimate relationship issues and emotional functioning had their origin in their mother-child dynamic.

FIVE MOTHER FACTOR EMOTIONAL ROADBLOCKS

One of the most common complaints about relationships from men and women, mothers and fathers, siblings, marriage partners, blended families, and singles who are dating is that the problem is outside of themselves—"I am not the problem, he/she is!" The concept of the "problem is outside of me, it is not my fault, they screwed up" is one of the biggest deterrents to change. It is difficult for any of us to honestly view ourselves as part of the problem. Many times, we are the biggest contributor to the issue or conflict, though we rarely see our role in the problem. Acknowledging our role and responsibility for the problem immediately removes or begins to move the emotional roadblocks of the mother factor from our life.

The majority of our psychological issues can be traced back to these five fundamental core issues: *shame, emotional deprivation, codependence, fear of abandonment and intimacy,* and *anger.* These very common human feelings, emotions, and behaviors can be found in all areas of a person's life. No one is immune from these struggles from time to time in relationships. The problem is the lack of personal awareness of how these stumbling blocks continually operate in your life. It is the repetitive nature of these issues that causes men and women incredible amounts of pain and suffering. These five widespread adult behaviors can create devastating relationship problems (intimate, professional, and social) in a person's life. The key question again is: can you begin to understand and recognize your own roadblocks in your world of relationships?

Another point is not only the number of times you experience these feelings but the degree of their severity. Do any of the above emotions leave you feeling like a four-year-old in an adult's body? If you answered yes, then you know how problematic these feelings can be in your relationships. For instance, people who struggle with severe codependence issues in their relationships know it is the major driving force in how they emotionally connect—how they attach in relationships. Another example is if your business partner doesn't call, you immediately assume that there is a serious problem, and you are flooded with feelings of shame. These types of extreme automatic emotional responses are indicators that your core mother factor issues are being activated. What is the trigger, attitude, or emotional concern that causes you tremendous pain, anxiety, or panic? When do you feel your emotions the strongest?

Shame is the strongest and most powerful paralyzing human emotion. Shame is often an abnormal emotional reaction to an event, situation, or action. It is important to remember that shame isn't guilt.[2] Don't confuse the two emotions; they are completely different. Guilt is a direct response to an action or behavior. Guilt can be used as a moral compass to correct or amend your behavior. Feelings of guilt can be a source of valuable information and ethical insight. Shame has no ethical value or purpose. Shame isn't activated by action; it can be brought on by a thought, a painful childhood memory, a sexual thought about a friend, a harsh verbal exchange, or a glance at attractive woman. Shame has no moral use or psychological benefits to its victims. Shame, unfortunately, is a common daily experience for millions of people: wives, husbands, single people, adults in every type of relationship. Shame is the most misunderstood psychological roadblock of the five and is extremely troublesome. It is experienced in degrees of severity from mild to moderate to high to extreme. What degree of shame have you experienced in the last six months? What was the situation that triggered it?

Shame is the collection of distorted feelings, irrational thoughts, and critical core beliefs you have about yourself. These feelings are based in your fragmented self-beliefs, which leave you constantly feeling defective. You may feel that you're a phony, not good enough, a failure, stupid, an incompetent adult, a poor lover, a bad parent, a useless employee, an awful supervisor, an incapable person, and a horrible human being. None of these feelings are based in reality. They are a distortion of your true self. You struggle with thoughts of worthlessness, feeling like a fraud in your relationships, as if you were damaged goods and no one would love you if they really knew you. There is a fear that if your partner, spouse, employer, or close friend really knew you, then your true and awful self would really be discovered. People steeped in shame live every day thinking that they are imposters to all the people they love in their world. Shame causes its victims to experience an overwhelming sense of fear for whatever they do, because it is never good enough, regardless of the positive outcome.

No matter how much money you make, no matter how many

people you serve, love, heal, or save, these emotionally debilitating feelings leave the victim (you) an empty shell. Given the right circumstances, these shameful feelings will flood your·mind and heart without a moment's notice. Your face turns red, your stomach drops, your heart rate increases. No matter what, you have a physical response to these feelings of shame. One of the keys to healing your shameful beliefs is to recognize the circumstances that trigger these feelings within you. These feelings were learned as a direct result of your mother-child relationship: It is difficult for any of us to accept that these feelings aren't natural or remotely accurate about us. There is no amount of praise or personal achievement that can offset shame-based feelings and thoughts. Shame has to be healed from the inside out. *Shame is an "inside job," it is not outside of you.*

It is critical to remember that shame has no purpose or use in a relationship. Experiencing shame is like pouring acid on a rosebush and then wondering why the bush immediately dies. Shame can and will have the same effect on any kind of relationship or emotional bond; that is, if it is left unchecked. From every mental health perspective, psychological research, or family theory, shame ruins relationships and all the people involved.[3]

We will discuss in the section on mothering styles how shame is developed, learned, and carried into adulthood and all relationships. Shame can be seen as an "emotional cancer." If the roots of shame in the mother-child relationship aren't understood and resolved, its power and toxicity will continue to increase in a person's life to the point that it will completely control him or her. Put a check next to the following questions if they apply to you in your life, your relationships, or your feelings about yourself.

Shame Checklist

* Do you randomly feel inferior to your partner, friends, and colleagues for no apparent reason or external cause?

__ Do you feel far less competent and capable than you appear to the outside world?

_•_ Do you feel like "damaged goods" and not worthy of a great relationship?

__ Do you feel that you are a phony—faking and hiding your real self from your relationships?

__ Have you ever discussed, revealed, or told anyone about your feelings of inadequacy?

_•_ Do you think your career would be different if you resolved your shameful feelings, beliefs, and wounds?

__ How much of a role does shame have in your personal relationships?

_•_ What would your life look like to you if you weren't chronically held back by your feelings of shame and hopelessness?

__ What is one of your emotional triggers for a bout of shame and fear?

_•_ Do you regularly call yourself a "loser"?

__ Who made you feel shame while growing up?

__ Who and what shames you today?

__ Do you find that you will shame someone when you are feeling vulnerable and scared?

__ What is one thing that you are most ashamed about? (This may be something that you have never revealed, even to yourself.)

__ Does your mother-child relationship have emotional shame?

Seriously consider the checklist and the relevance of these questions and answers to your present-day relationships and your feelings about your mother. If you answered these questions in the affirmative, consider the possibility that part of your relationship frustrations, poor self-esteem, and chronic frustration with the people you are closest to has an untreated shame factor.

Emotional deprivation is a close cousin of the shame family. Emotional deprivation is a direct result of the mother-child relationship. It is the repeated life experience of not having your primary emotional, physical, and mental needs met, understood, and valued. This type of deprivation is a result of an interrupted, inconsistent attachment process between the mother and child and the emotionally absent mothering style. These early life disappointments teach you that your needs and wants will not be met or addressed. Emotional deprivation is a result of many, many emotional misses between the mother and child growing up. These emotional misses are the by-product of the mothering style and attachment style. These chronic misses create in the child a belief, based on her life experience, that her core needs aren't important to the world or the people in it. *Emotional deprivation is the collateral damage of a repeated psychological pattern of neglect between a mother and child.*

The maternal relationship for the child becomes a place where his or her feelings, needs, and emotional development aren't met, understood, and encouraged. Many times, these children who experience emotional neglect look and behave like they are orphans, even though they have a home with a seemingly loving family. These children grow up feeling very lonely and emotionally unable to connect with their loved ones. This all-too-common experience of profound neglect, which creates deprivation and loneliness, isn't limited to any culture, community, or economic group. It is as widespread as head colds are in the winter. It is a complete mistake to think that these events are related to wealth or poverty. Emotional deprivation has no boundaries and is a powerful force in many adult relationships today.

The nagging feeling of neglect in close relationships is one of the best-kept secrets in a person's life. No one wants to feel needy or insecure, either in relationships and or in his place in the world. Emotional deprivation has to be healed and resolved from the inside out. There aren't enough compliments, hugs, or friends to remove the deep sense of feeling unimportant and emotionally neglected. When these feelings converge, the victim may dive into addictive habits in order to numb the pain. One of the psychological components of addiction is the deep sense of emotional deprivation. It is very difficult for a deprived adult to be patient or calm when she is feeling neglected or unimportant. All addictive behaviors (sex, gambling, drinking, illegal drug use, excessive exercise, overeating) have their roots in a person's sense of deprivation and neglect. It is a very powerful emotional habit cycle to break. This wound started with you and your mother. This is such a powerful dynamic, because, if your mother didn't value your emotional life, who ever will?

In an adult relationship, emotional deprivation will often take the form of the man or woman being "needy," "clingy," "attention hungry," "lonely," "desperate for a partner," and "overly attached." All these behaviors have their genesis in emotional deprivation. You believe that what you really want in life, in a relationship, in your career, and for yourself will not happen. There is a constant emotional hole in your life and nothing seems to fill it or remove it—that constitutes emotional deprivation in action. Deprivation is a result of long-term maternal negligence, inattention, and carelessness. It is sometimes difficult not to start blaming our mothers for our emotional pain and struggles. It is very important to not go down the road of anger and blame. It is a dead-end highway with no outlet and will only stall your personal growth and progress.

Emotional Deprivation Checklist

___ You have a recurring theme in your relationships of not having your needs met.

___ You have a personal belief that what you really want will ultimately not happen.

___ You have impulse control problems.

___ You have feelings of insecurity in your friendships?

___ You struggle with feeling lonely or isolated?

__ You hate to be alone or have no plans on Friday and Saturday nights.

_•_ You feel like there is a huge hole in your emotional life and it never seems to go away or get filled up.

_•_ When you feel deprived, you tend to overindulge with alcohol, drugs, shopping, or eating to relieve the pain.

_•_ The concept of "delayed gratification" isn't one of your strengths.

_•_ You have addictive habits when you get anxious or worried. You consider these behaviors as adult fun, even though they negatively impact your life.

_•_ You frequently have emotional waves of insecurity and emptiness.

__ You have a difficult time expressing your emotional needs in your relationships.

_•_ You don't value your needs and dismiss them as unnecessary.

__ You seldom feel loved, cared for, or understood in your adult relationships.

__ You don't express your true feelings or needs in your close relationships.

_•_ You tend to become obsessive about cleaning and household chores.

__ People would describe you as obsessive in your intimate relationships.

Again, consider these questions as thought-provoking and exploratory; they should give you a new perspective on the root of your anxiety, obsessive behavior, and feelings of neglect and loneliness. It may seem like a stretch to connect your sense of "never having enough," loneliness, neglect, and lack of love to a sense of childhood deprivation, but there is a link. Try to trust this process, because your emotional legacy of neglect can be changed to a legacy of fulfillment and emotional satisfaction and self-confidence. It is important to understand the breadth, depth, and width of your own emotional roadblocks. No matter how over-whelmed you may feel, creating a new opportunity to change the course of your life isn't beyond your reach.

Codependence is a natural mother-child bond to a point. If the other two roadblocks mentioned above are toxic, then this road-block is the "silent killer" in adult relationships. Codependence is one of the most underrated issues in all types of relationships, cre-ating enormous problems for all parties involved. You learned as a young child that the only way you can have your emotional needs met is to give away everything you have to the other person. Your mother-child relationship became a situation where you learned to take care of your mother's emotional needs at a very young age. The roles of nurturing got switched in your life before you could read. You became the psychological adult, or your mother needed you to help her emotionally through her life. Your emotional caretaking of your mother was a life-changing experi-ence. Today, your adult relationship pattern clearly reflects your early life despair of being the caretaker, the "parent," instead of the child. It would be interesting to know how many children by the age of five knew that they were the primary emotional care-takers in their family. This powerful family role for a young child is very damaging to her natural emotional and psychological development. The natural stages of childhood are aborted in a codependent mother-child relationship. This daughter doesn't have the chance to "be a kid." Instead, this child grows up wor-rying about the family and her mother. It is very difficult to be a child when you are always feeling responsible for everyone and everything in your family, especially your mother. These children are called "parentified." They become the parent's parent and emotional caretaker. This is a very common occurrence in divorces, when the parent uses the child as her emotional support and they become close friends. This child, regardless of age, car-ries the emotional burden of being the child and mother/parent.

If this rings true for you, you were acting as an adult at a young age, looking out for your mother's emotional welfare and mental health. It was the early lessons of taking care of your mother that trained you to automatically do the same in all your adult relationships. This turns into self-destructive behavior and leads to the poor choices that a codependent adult makes to save a bad relationship. The problem starts when you feel that the only way you can emotionally and mentally function is to have the other person's permission. Feeling loved, accepted, belonging, and joining another person's life becomes a codependent issue when you automatically do all of the nurturing and emotional caretaking. Your relationships are unconsciously set up for you to do all the caretaking, nurturing, and loving. It is this out-of-balance approach to relationships that creates codependent relationships. It is the lack of emotional stability, balance, and your sense of a valuable self that are the major problems in a codependent approach to the world.

Adults who have codependent issues will have tremendous difficulty setting emotional boundaries with people. If this is your issue, you will speak and think for your intimate partner, worry about other people's problems, take responsibility for things that don't involve you, and always worry about the other person's well-being. You don't know yourself outside of the context of being a "rescuer," "healer," and caretaker of others. Both men and women alike will get involved in relationships professionally, socially, and romantically that are based on their being the nurturer and caretaker.

Codependence is having a one hundred-pound steel ball chained to your leg and wondering why you have problems walking forward. Codependence doesn't allow for the natural flow of give-and-take in a high-functioning relationship. One person has to be the giver and the other the receiver. There is no room or chance for the other person meeting the needs of the other. The relationship is based on your doing all the caretaking, worrying, and fixing of issues. When adults become codependent in their intimate relationships, their relationship has a profound lack of emotional equity, balance, and sharing. One person is viewed as more important than the other one. The codependent adult will not consider or even think of her own needs or emotions, and can't make decisions that will empower herself. If this is true for you, your life is based on the other person's happiness and their acceptance of you.

Codependent Checklist

_•_ You worry excessively about other people's problems, issues, and relationships.

__ You tend to get involved in other people's affairs even when they don't involve you.

_•_ When your partner is upset, you have to find the solution for him/her.

__ You don't trust your closest friends in your life to understand or emotionally care for your personal needs.

_•_ You were your mother's emotional caretaker while growing up.

__ Your primary relationship pattern is to find friends, lovers, and co-workers whom you can "fix."

_•_ Your relationships, friends, social life, and career involve people who rely on you to fix or solve their personal problems.

__ You never question the purpose of your relational role of "caretaker."

_•_ Your family life is centered on your being the primary emotional person and problem solver.

_•_ You don't or can't say no to anyone.

__ Your personal struggles are about the enormous burden you carry for the people in your life.

_•_ You feel most comfortable in a relationship as the caretaker or savior.

___ You always take full responsibility for any issue, problem, or concern in your intimate relationship.

___ You have never considered the option of not being the primary caretaker in your personal, professional, and private world.

This is a very focused examination of the powerful pull that the codependent emotional relationship has on smart, loving adults. It is difficult to see that maybe your way of relating to people is the reason and source of your deep frustration, relationship dissatisfaction, and pain. It is hard to perceive that you might be the main contributor to your emotional pain, not the people you date or your friends. There are many other ways of relating to people that will give you the love, sense of belonging, and support you desire.

Fear of abandonment and fear of intimacy are some of the most misunderstood feelings in adults of all ages. The sense of being abandoned in a relationship is the direct result of your early mother-child attachment bond and mothering style. You might have lived with your mother and seen her every day of your life, but something wasn't right. You now find yourself with these nagging fears about relationships. Where did these feelings originate? These two feelings—fear of abandonment and fear of intimacy— are on different sides of the same coin. If you are reluctant to be involved with people romantically, socially, or professionally, it has to do with your sense of emotional terror. This deep-seated terror is the emotional, mental, and physical response that enables you to remain distant from people and their emotional contact. This is an automatic response in you; it is the result of the early childhood trauma between you and your mother. You experienced a sense of emotional loss that had a very substantial impact on your young mind, hindering a sense of psychological comfort in being close to people. You avoid being emotionally vulnerable and open to people at all costs. It isn't a natural act for you. Your unresolved, unexplored, and buried terror creates relationships that will leave you alone and out of harm's way. Isolation, emotional distance, and aloofness feel like the only choices in your adult relationships.

The childhood traumas that result in this problem vary from person to person. But some typical patterns emerge, such as being emotionally distant, dating married or emotionally unavailable partners, never being in an intimate relationship, having no close friends, living in isolation, and an inability to commit to a close personal relationship. Many times there was a death in the family that fractured the mother-child bond or a significant event as well as a distant, unstable, and/or volatile style of mothering. Many men struggle with making a commitment to marriage or an exclusive relationship. Their difficulty making a commitment isn't because they don't love their partner but because they are terrified of reexperiencing the horror of their childhood. Men and women alike will do anything to avoid the possibility of reexperiencing their unpredictable childhood. Many of these adults had an emotionally smothering mother, an abusive mother, an alcoholic mother, a psychologically unstable mother, or a mother who was reckless with her child's emotions.

For instance, a mother who is reckless is unable to understand that her actions and decisions aren't made in the best interest of her son or daughter but for her own benefit. These children grow up without ever feeling the security and sense of being loved and cared for by their mother. These children experience the world as a cold, unloving, and tough place in which to live. These adults survive their childhood but are often very scared, unwilling to ever open up their heart and emotions to that type of pain and abuse again. The core issue that underlies these classic relationship blocks is the fear of reexperiencing the early horror of childhood. These fears are deeply rooted in the terrifying chaos that defined their mother-child relationship. The stories of the terror that young children were able to survive and overcome are endless.

As adults, they now will find ways to develop distant emotional attachments while maintaining a sense of safety. The need for emotional protection is the primary goal against being emotionally terrorized ever again. It is this strong desire against ever feeling the terror of loss, abuse, and helplessness that keeps adults from fulfilling loving relationships. These unresolved events create within a child the need to survive and the resolve to never again put himself in a position of feeling emotional pain. These adults design their relationships on all levels—socially, professionally, and personally—so they will never again be vulnerable to anyone. Their powerful fears of relationships helped create in the child/adult the conscious and unconscious motivation of never reexperiencing their childhood terror.

The problem with these defense mechanisms against intimacy and abandonment is that life doesn't always cooperate with these blocks. In fact, life has a way of forcing you to confront these nagging fears and may help move your emotions out of a traumatic legacy. Adults from all walks of life continually confront these issues until they resolve them, otherwise they will remain emotionally paralyzed in their childhood-mother dynamic. For someone who didn't experience a traumatic childhood, it is impossible to understand these issues or the reason behind these avoidant behaviors. Often, people will marry or develop an intimate relationship with someone from a completely different mother factor background. They select these well-adjusted partners consciously and unconsciously for the purpose of remaining secure and safe with loved ones. These marriage or relationship choices are an excellent place to work out the trauma and terror in a loving atmosphere.

Regardless of your past trauma, it is possible to make significant relationship changes and move closer to people without panic or terror. Everyone craves the love and attention that comes from opening up and being your true self in a relationship. This is the timeless pursuit of the ages and still the top priority of our lifetime.

There is no amount of therapy, counseling, or Internet research that will replace the power of being in a loving, supportive professional, social, or personal relationship. This is a basic human need and drive that everyone has to address and satisfy in life.

Fear of Abandonment and Intimacy Checklist

_•_ You will allow people in your life to see, know, or be within a certain emotional distance.

__ You have difficulty pursuing or maintaining close emotional relationships in any area of your life.

__ You believe that the world is cruel and mean to you.

__ You fear being abandoned more than other people.

__ You will avoid people who share strong emotional experiences or expressions.

_•_ You don't like to hug or be touched.

__ Relationships aren't something that you are good at or comfortable with.

_•_ You break up/leave an intimate relationship before you are left or abandoned.

_•_ The idea of being "emotionally abandoned" is very terrifying to you.

_•_ Your childhood feels too scary or painful to even explain or share with people.

_•_ You are scared of having children of your own.

__ Women scare you.

__ Men scare you.

__ Your best friend is an animal—a pet.

__ You don't see the value or purpose of expressing loving emotions, thoughts, or gestures to the people in your life.

__ You avoid emotional expressions and people who make them.

__ In a relationship, you always have to be in control.

__ You would rather leave a relationship than work out the issues in it.

__ Long-term intimate commitments are very difficult for you to make.

__ You have a relationship history of cheating on your intimate partner or committing adultery.

The fear of abandonment and fear of intimacy are very real roadblocks that people struggle with every day in relationships. Adults make some of their biggest life decisions based on avoiding these two fears. Ultimately, everyone has to resolve and find a safe, secure, and positive place emotionally to connect with others. This process might take several marriages, numerous career changes, and a lifetime of searching, but the result is worth the effort. These two fears alone aren't an excuse for anyone to live a life isolated and removed from their potential. *People don't die from feeling abandoned, but they do die emotionally, mentally, spiritually, and physically from avoiding it.*

Anger is the biggest and quickest deal-breaker in any type of relationship. Unresolved anger is toxic to the giver and the receiver. The unresolved reactionary anger can't be tolerated in any type of adult, parent, intimate, or professional relationship. The explosiveness of an angry, raging outburst is very disorientating for all the people who experience it. The emotional stability and balance of the relationship, regardless of its context—professional, athletic, romantic—is negatively impacted. It is overwhelming for men or women of all ages to experience the full force of a bucket of anger dumped on them. Men and women suffer many personal, professional, and intimate relationship failures because of being unable to handle their powerful, personal anger issues. There isn't an area that isn't adversely impacted by unresolved anger. The problem for the adult with anger issues is finding the source. The pathway to discovery always includes a visit to the mother-child relationship.

Make no mistake, we aren't discussing an appropriate response of frustration and annoyance to a particular situation.

Those responses don't compare to unresolved rage and its inappropriate use. The natural reaction of anger is for the sole purpose of alerting us psychologically that our emotional boundaries are being pushed. Our core feelings, boundaries, and beliefs about our world are guarded by our emotional fence. When that fence is broken down, run over, or violated, the internal alarm sounds—which is our anger response. This natural reaction is our "humanness" in action for the purpose of survival. Our reaction to our emotional fence being violated doesn't require that we use lethal emotional force to protect it. It is the chronic, automatic, and reflexive use of rage, violence, and lethal emotional force for everyday circumstances that is extremely problematic. These types of responses don't work in anyone's world, career, or family.

If you find that you feel completely out of control emotionally when you are engaged in anger, then it is your primary defense against feeling vulnerable. The type of anger I am referring to manifests itself as explosive and emotional, resulting in harmful expressions, character assassination, and verbal and physical abuse. It is the collateral damage that is incurred when adults haven't healed their emotional wounds.

No one argues that road rage, verbal abuse, or domestic violence is tolerable or remotely acceptable. All these manifestations of unresolved anger are usually connected to the mother factor. Many times, men who beat their wives, girlfriends, or other women were beaten as children. These adult men can't understand why their mother never stopped the beatings or why they didn't stop their father from beating them. The degree, severity, and intensity of these raging episodes started in the man's childhood and have gained momentum over the years. There is nothing happening in a woman's or man's life that would explain this level of rage—anger that is triggered by a bad driver, lost Internet connection, late appointment, or your child's being moody. It is the overreaction to normal life events that are the most telling signs of unresolved anger—hidden emotional pain. The key is to understand that your anger is a cover for critical emotional wounds that haven't been understood, resolved, or amended. This insight can begin the healing process. No one wants to be a "rageaholic" or an abusive person. It is the lack of emotional insight, lack of knowledge of your emotional past, and lack of courage that continues the cycle of rage. This type of anger that people carry in their soul isn't resentment, hurt feelings, or misunderstanding; it goes back to the mother-child relationship. Many times the anger is covering up wounds that are so painful the person can't verbalize it or express the depth of it.

Anger Checklist

__ Do you find yourself becoming more of a "hothead" as you get older?

_•_ Is your fuse getting shorter in your personal relationships?

_•_ Do simple things set off your anger?

_•_ When you are angry, do you feel out of control at times?

__ When you feel emotionally vulnerable, what is your first response? •

__ When someone blames you for something, what is your first automatic thought or action? •

__ Have you ever been told by a partner, close friend, or supervisor that you have "anger management" issues?

__ What triggers your anger?

__ Who in your past could push your buttons and set off your anger?

_•_ Were you angry as a child?

_•_ Was your mother an angry woman in your childhood?

__ What role models did you observe for the proper display of anger?

__ Do you experience the difference between healthy and unhealthy anger in your life?

__ Who in your life currently sets off your anger? Do they know it?

___ Have you ever become physically violent when you were angry or enraged?

___ Have you ever hit an intimate partner during a verbal fight?

___ Do you consider yourself an angry person?

___ What is something that always upsets you?

___ Were you physically beaten as a child?

___ Are you attracted to "angry people"? Do you date angry men?

___ How many times is your anger connected to your sexual activity?

___ Do you scare your children with your anger?

This anger checklist is very powerful and is the starting point of your healing. This subject could very easily be termed the "anger factor." We have all lost our composure and acted unlike our usual predictable self. This discussion isn't about those moments but something much bigger and deeper. Men know when they have anger issues and will try to keep them suppressed and/or out of public view. Women struggle with how to use their anger in a productive fashion without being labeled a "bitch" or a "she-devil." If you could add questions to this checklist, then you know your issue. Remember that anger, rage, and aggressive hostility all come from the same source—your emotional pain. Your pain is the fuel that can destroy your life or be the impetus for change. *Finally, anger isn't a gender issue but rather a mother-child issue.*

ROADBLOCK SUMMARY

These five lists are emotionally and psychologically charged and are designed to be used for motivation and personal change. The five roadblocks were designed to point out some of the behavioral blind spots that many of us operate under at stressful times. These mother factor issues are all common at particular moments in our relationships. Do you know your "crisis" moments after reading these five lists? It is important to know and remember the severity, degree of confusion, and long-term relationship impairment that these roadblocks have created. Repeated disappointments and emotional blocks cause all of us daily problems and endless frustration. Think about your most troubling relationship issue. That problem is likely related to or is one of these five roadblocks. It is the recurring theme and cycle of frustration that these lists are designed to expose and change. Reread all of these lists and see which one seems the most familiar to you. If one of these five sections seems very familiar to you, that is your starting point to reexamine your mother-child relationship.

If none of these five lists apply to you, speak to your heart or look more closely at some of your personal and relationship issues and take another look. Don't allow yourself to slide away or make excuses for not making the core emotional and relationship changes that you have desired for yourself. We all have mother factor sticking points at certain times in our life. Having no insight into problematic areas (denial) is a big sign that points to your fear of opening up unexplored areas of your life. It is with compassion, respect, and empathy that I suggest you take another look and open that locked door in your life. It is better you open it than have your partner or a life circumstance do it for you. Emotional pain, unfortunately, has the nuclear ability to blow open any and all issues that we are trying to hide or ignore. In the next section, we will explore the five most common mothering styles that make up the mother factor.

Section II

FIVE MOTHERING STYLES OF THE MOTHER FACTOR

Chapter 3

THE PERFECTIONIST MOTHER

The Unending Drive for Perfection and Love

I always remember my mother was more worried about what the neighbors or cousins thought than what we did or said. My mother lived for perfection and I was always fat and ugly growing up. When my mom died I lost forty-five pounds. I hated the pressure to look perfect.

—Paula, age forty-one, single

My mother preferred me over my sister. I was the first boy and that made my mom look good to my grandparents. I was a complete screw up until I was twenty-eight years old, but I always looked good and acted perfect to the world, my mother always gave me a break because I looked good.

—John, age thirty-three, single

INTRODUCTION TO MOTHERING STYLES

The next five chapters are going to describe in elaborate detail the most common styles of mothering that sons and daughters typically encountered during their childhood. Each mothering style, though appearing separate and individual, in actuality overlaps with the other styles. The two quotes from above are typical of the overlap between mothering styles. Paula and John both are keenly aware of their mothers' perfectionist attitude and superficial approach to life. Don't worry if your mother had parts of all five styles; she clearly had her own distinct style and emotional connection to you. Every mother-child relationship had certain communication patterns, spoken/unspoken rules, expressed and nonverbal expectations, emotional intelligence, behavioral patterns, personality styles, and a particular approach to relationships. All of these characteristics mixed together, every day of your life as you and your mother interacted, and developed into a particular style. The overarching emotional theme to relationships and your life is the sum total of your mother's style, which created the ground floor of your mother factor. Let's consider the ground floor.

All of these elements and countless more of your own personal issues composed the substance and core of your mother factor. Your mother's mothering style was a very integral part to the formation of your emotional legacy and your current relationship status and psychological functioning. A classic example of your mother factor in action is *the intimate partner you picked. How you function in that relationship is a direct reflection and adult application of your mother factor legacy.* Relationships are the driving force of our human experience, existence, and fulfillment. There is nothing you and I will do privately, personally, socially, or professionally that doesn't involve our ability to form and maintain relationships. For instance, I am forming a relationship with you as you read this book. Our personal relationship is growing as you read through the book and experience the power of your mother factor. Relationships matter! Your mother is the original designer and construction crew of your relationship dynamic. Your adult style of relationships and emotional functioning are the power, fuel, and substance of your life.

Regardless of the circumstances surrounding you and your mother (e.g., divorce, death, anger, concern, emotional enmeshment, abuse, anxiety, estrangement, and love), the building blocks of you and your mother's early relationship have created the adult foundation on which you have built your life. This includes every aspect of your emotional functioning, relationships, career, and family interaction. The influences are different for each child with each parent. Your life experience of your mother will be very different than the one with your father. Our focus here is about your mother and you. This isn't for any other purpose than to clarify the power of each parent. Many times, mothers are diminished because their role is so big in a child's life that no one really grasps the magnitude of the mother factor.

This section of the book is going to dive directly into some of your richest treasures, create new insights, and reveal some of your hidden emotional ties. One of the primary purposes of understanding the mothering style you experienced is to show you how the emotional stepping blocks of your life were designed and assembled. Diving into the heart of your mother-child relationship can be very challenging and at times overwhelming. Some of your unconscious or blind spots can be loaded with unexpected "emotional landmines" that have never been defused or disconnected from your life. Now is a great time for you to do this, because you wouldn't have been drawn to reading this book or been interested in this particular subject if you didn't want to improve your quality of life.

All of us have experienced a little of each mothering style in our mother-child relationship. The goal is to focus on the one primary style that characterized your mother's relationship with you and the impact it had on your emotional legacy, adult relationships, and current-day psychological functioning. As a side note, some people might ask why *The Mother Factor* doesn't have a separate chapter for single mothers raising children. I believe, and have professionally experienced, that single mothers embody all five of these mothering styles. In fact, single mothers are often the foundation for other mothers to lean on for emotional and mothering support. Single mothers are everywhere in this book and are just as valuable as married mothers. All the possible combinations of mothers share these five styles regardless of their family, relationship, and marriage circumstances. The bottom line is, if you are a mother, then you have a particular mothering style. Since all daughters and sons have a mother, it is important to know who she is, was, and continues to be in our adult life. The five mothering styles we are going to explore in greater depth are ones we've discussed earlier:

1. The Perfectionist Mother
2. The Unpredictable Mother
3. The "Me First" Mother
4. The Best Friend Mother
5. The Complete Mother

I have found while writing this book that everyone wants to tell me his or her mother story. People will routinely say to me, "Oh, my God, I have got a story for you," or "You need to interview me, I have a ton of material for your book, my mother was a nightmare," or "Can I be a case study? My mother lives with me now." Their vocal inflection implies that their story is "unreal" and that their mother-child relationship was/is very challenging and unique. It also implies that they still have many unresolved emotions and mixed feelings about their mother. My professional and personal experience is that girls and women, regardless of their age (starting at nine and up) are very forthcoming about their mother-daughter relationship, positive or otherwise. Men tend to look at you like the topic of their mother is an untouchable, off-limits, and inappropriate subject. Many of my male clients, guy friends, and male associates don't know how to discuss their mother in a nonjudgmental, neutral, or objective manner. This is always a sign that the mother-son topic is ripe for a new approach, perspective, and healing. Men and women of all ages want to express and tell their mother story. They are excited that someone is finally offering a platform to explore this bottomless topic. All their stories start with their first love and how that relationship unfolded over their lifetime. The problem is how to explain that relationship without becoming overwhelmed or avoidant of the issues and the underlying pain. Consider the following exercise as a start of something new and creative in your life and adult relationships. Remember, if you can discuss your mother in a clear and insightful manner, then you will be able to do that in all of your other relationships.

THE MOTHER SPEECH

This is a great opportunity to begin to experience your mother factor from a different point of view. Visualize yourself giving a speech on the topic of your mother and your relationship with her. If you had to give a five-minute impromptu talk in front of your close friends about your mother factor, what would you say? What information, stories, and feelings would you want everyone to know about her and you? What issues, events, and personal revelations would you comment on in regard to your mother-child relationship? Would you tell only the easy, amusing, and positive stories? Would you describe the struggles that seem very dark and heavy to you? What one point would you want your listeners to know about you and your mother? Would you give a different talk if your mother was in the crowd? If you did or had to speak at her funeral, what would you say about your mother? Consider this exercise before we go any further. You might be very surprised by what things you might say today that maybe you wouldn't have said or thought about six months ago. Verbalizing our feelings is one of the quickest ways to go around our defense mechanisms. Our inner thoughts and emotions tend to come out only when we start to talk about our pain. Thinking and speaking are two very different psychological processes that access different parts of our emotions and repressed feelings. There is only one way to get your story out of your head: *begin to tell the unedited story about you and your mother.*

If you still feel really stuck and angry or can't think of anything positive to say, try this: *Imagine your mother speaking at your funeral!* What would she say about you, your relationship, and her regrets? How would it feel to know that your mother is sobbing about you and your relationship? Don't be fooled by your anger or denial. Every parent (mother, father—we all do) has regrets about not being a better parent and wants their son or daughter to know it. Think about your attitude, feelings, and thoughts trying to visualize this very powerful image of your mother's self-disclosure. Conversely, talking about your mother in a formal setting (to a group) always produces new insights and personal information for you to use.

THE PERFECTIONIST MOTHER

The perfectionist mother has been portrayed in countless movies, literature, plays, and every daytime talk show, usually not in a favorable light. The perfectionist mother is typically an overcontrolling, fearful, and highly anxious woman. For these mothers, it is all about appearance and perfection. The perfectionist mother is a woman who is emotionally driven by the need to look good and have ultimate control of how things appear in her world (you are part of that world). On the surface, this mother looks and acts like she is the hub of the world with no visible worries. One inch below the surface, however, there is a raging river of fear, anxiety, and panic about her life spinning out of control. If things aren't going to plan, which happens daily, this mother tries to manage her anxiety with a hyper-focus on appearance and superficial issues. This obsessive controlling behavior leaves a very strong imprint upon a young daughter or son. This child learns early in life that how she looks is much more important to people than how she feels or thinks. This misplaced value system of appearance versus the power of accepting people for who they are creates an irrational view of how life and relationships work. These relentless attempts at physical and behavioral perfection are really a cover-up for an untreated anxiety issue.

If your mother emphasized physical attractiveness and perfection in your behavior and achievements, your childhood was a series of emotional disappointments. You received the repetitive message that what you looked like on the outside was much more important than what you experienced or knew emotionally, psychologically, or mentally. This hyper-focus on external things, events, grades, sports, popular friends, clothes, money, wealth, possessions, body image, and appearance developed the foundation for shame-based feelings. Your feelings of never feeling "perfect," "good enough," or "not _____ enough" developed into a shame-driven personality and insecure relationship style. This skewed pattern of relating to others was the only legitimate way of gaining your mother's approval and love. All children naturally want to please their mother. Children will do anything to gain the invaluable feeling of maternal love and acceptance. The perfection-driven mothering style became your relationship template for your future. This anxiety-driven model for perfection became how you viewed your self, your abilities, and your importance in the world.

This mother-child bond revolved around the superficial things of life. The only emotional security you felt was constantly reinforced by your mother's expectations that appearance matters more than your inner thoughts, feelings, and risk-taking aspirations (i.e., owning your own business, playing for the Dodgers, studying abroad). Your life was shaped by the chronic need to look good in all your endeavors and actions. The result of the perfectionist mother is your ingrained rejection of your self-acceptance, self-love, and your uniqueness—specialiness. These core relationship and emotional qualities are instead replaced by self-loathing and, in severe cases of perfection, self-hatred. Perfection and the chronic emotional need to be perfect is a form of self-rejection. There is no redeeming mental health value in being hypercritical of yourself and your imperfection. The perfect mother attempts to develop a "perfect daughter/son." This mothering style can be a formula for personal tragedy and the making of a highly self-destructive son or daughter. This child never learns to foster his own inner drive and childhood wishes. The lack of loving acceptance is the dark side of this style of mother, who is ultimately most critical of herself.

The constant emotional thread of the perfectionist mother is that the opinions of others are far more important than your own. As a child, you developed the sense that the entire world was watching you when you failed, screwed up, or did something your mother didn't like. This maternal pressure for perfection caused you to avoid, skip, or become shy of natural childhood challenges. The child's (your) reluctance started in not climbing on the park's jungle gym, not doing the school play, refusing to learn, not participating in team sports, and avoiding peer group relationships. Failure wasn't acceptable, encouraged, or tolerated. You learned emotionally that failure couldn't be endured and that nonperfect risk behavior couldn't be explored. This pressure for perfection was wrapped up with anxiety and fear.

The internal anxiety of always looking good became the barometer of your self-worth rather than your own thoughts, heart, and personal feelings. Several of the missing developmental emotional links in this mother-child relationship include no sense of inner security (feeling OK), safety (absence of anxiety and fear), and self-acceptance (liking yourself). Every child must have these basic emotional ingredients for both childhood and adult relationships. You began to feel at about the age of seven the painful emotional "hole" or a chronic sense of emotional emptiness in your heart. These feelings of inadequacy either grew with intensity or diminished in your heart. The mother factor's message of perfection and "always looking good" created an uneasy sense of insecurity about your place in the world and relationships.

This painful mother-child emotional process was the seedbed for learning to feel shameful about your "humanness"—your ability to accept your natural "imperfections" (i.e., weight, looks, acne, height, skin color, nationality, hair color, sexual orientation, intelligence, etc.). Such "imperfections" were rejected, unacceptable, and intolerable to your mother. There was no psychological room in your mother's worldview for seemingly natural imperfections or common mistakes that all kids need to make. When a mother is chronically feeling anxious, there is no room or ability to tolerate or accept any differences in her child. Every child needs her mother's permission to accept her natural imperfections and childhood errors. The rejection of these natural human conditions and typical childhood behaviors creates a deep sense of inadequacy that becomes part of every relationship that this child will develop. The inner confidence of feeling competent, lovable, and "good enough" is lacking, underdeveloped, or, in a worst-case scenario, nonexistent for this child. This mother wasn't able to teach her child the personal power of self-acceptance and self-respect/love for her natural imperfections. These seemingly obvious nurturing mothering duties of building a high-functioning child aren't part of this style or considered valuable.

Many people believe the definition of perfection is that if you look good on the outside, the rest will take care of itself. In the context of the perfectionist style of mothering, however, the definition is the complete opposite. Daughters who recover from feeling unlovable learn that if they feel great about themselves on the inside, the rest will take care of itself. The outside appearance is a lie that leaves a son or daughter emotionally desperate and vulnerable to many serious life-threatening choices: designer drug addiction, eating disorders, personality disorders, suicide, major physical illnesses, loneliness, and an inability to form and maintain relationships. Learning that your life focus has to start with you and proceed forward to the world is a complete paradigm shift and relationship overhaul.

The intentions of this mother are good. Mothers want to do the best they can for their children. This type of mother knows the value of being responsible and acting appropriately. The problem is where the love and understanding stops for the child. This child becomes severely limited psychologically by this very narrow approach to life, emotions, and being "human." People don't fit into neat and clean categories or a certain look. These children aren't taught or shown by their mother the importance of being "perfectly imperfect"—and this concept is the key to unlocking and creating shame-free children and adults of all ages. We will later discuss how to incorporate this liberating concept into your critical opinion of you and your world. The driving issue behind all eating disorders, destructive drug use (heroin), alcoholism, self-defeating habits, suicidal attempts, and body image issues is your rejection of you and your inherent value. All the different types of self-loathing behaviors are fueled by self-rejection and inability to learn to accept and like yourself. Low self-esteem, feelings of defectiveness, incompetence, and a general sense of feeling worthless are deeply rooted in this mothering style. Regardless of the critical mother-child relationship you had, it is possible to resolve it and stop hating and rejecting your potential. Consider the following list for your "perfect" son or daughter syndrome and the statements that ring true to you.

Self-Loathing—Perfectionist Checklist

- You have daily feelings of hating yourself. These feelings aren't based on any particular event or circumstance.
- You feel everyone is better, prettier, smarter. . . . You don't feel that you are good enough.

__ You have great difficulty accepting criticism or feedback about yourself (you fear not being perfect). *opposite*

_•_ One of your deepest fears is that you will be discovered to be inadequate and unlovable.

_•_ You have difficulty accepting acts of love from your partner, dates, or close friends.

__ You fear that you don't look good enough in your relationships or public situations.

__ You have been told that you have a "narcissistic" personality.

__ You tend to judge people exclusively on their appearance, achievement, and net worth, regardless of their "humanness."

_•_ You don't really care about yourself and tend to be reckless with your life and health.

__ You feel comfortable, and it seems familiar, when someone verbally abuses you.

_•_ When feeling worthless, you consider, or daydream about, suicide.

__ You've been told that you are a "perfectionist" by a lover, close friends, or colleagues.

__ You have had or have an eating disorder.

_•_ You don't believe or can accept that you are "perfectly imperfect."

This hard-hitting perfectionist list may be difficult to take. If you recognize some of these traits in your relationships, then rightly assume that your mother factor is adversely affecting your life and relationships! Your private feelings of well-being in the world are shaped by your mother factor's inner voice in your head. The voice, which we all have, is the collection of years of your mothering style in action that you have incorporated and that has guided your life since early childhood. Unfortunately, the brutal side of this mothering style is the chronic sense that the child (you) were never "good enough" or "perfect." This mother can be exceptionally critical and verbally mean when she

feels that the upkeep of appearances is being dismissed or dis-
obeyed by her children.

The belief system of this mothering style leaves little or no
room to provide for a child to discover his own heartfelt dreams,
personal wishes, or inner desires. The internal conflict that is created in a daughter who doesn't follow her mother's beliefs is
raging anxiety or, in more serious cases, panic attacks. The ability
to create her own legacy is simply impossible until later in her
(your) life, when the burden of being the "perfect daughter"
becomes unbearable. Once you resolve that you aren't perfect, you
can begin to find out what you want to do with your life and relationships. It is never too late to find out what you will do when you
grow up, even if you are fifty-two. Age has nothing to do with creating and designing your own life legacy. What we do in our for-
ties and fifties is as critical as what we did in our teens and twenties. Your legacy can always be updated and properly adjusted to
fit your life and needs.

MOTHER'S PERFECTLY
CONTROLLING BEHAVIOR—WHY?

I have been repeatedly asked by men and women why their mothers
were/are so critical or such perfectionists. The simple answer is that
your mother is passing on to you the relationship she likely had with
her mother—your grandmother. It is important to remember that
your grandmother likely taught your mother how to focus exclusively on the superficial parts of life and ignore one of the most
important parts of a person: *an emotional and compassionate heart.*
Even if you never met your grandmother, if she died before you
were born, she had a profound impact on your mother-child relationship. Don't diminish the impact of your grandmother because of
circumstances that didn't allow for you to know her firsthand. If you
grew up with your grandmother actively involved in your child-

hood, then it should be very clear to you if she had rigid attitudes and beliefs regarding "perfection," "appearance," and "never being good enough." You can't accurately understand or appreciate your mother's struggles without looking back at your generational tree and your mother factor legacy over the last seventy years.

It isn't an academic stretch to realize that your mother likely grew up with a critical mother who gave only love when certain external accomplishments were achieved. The core beliefs, underlying anxiety, and superficial values of this mothering style are immune to change. The anxiety surrounding the appearance of "perfection" is like a brick wall; nothing is going to change it. *You can't change your mother—unless she herself wants to change.* And it isn't your job to change her. You can, however, change what *you* do from this point with your emotions, beliefs, and relationship style.

The perfectionist mother-child relationship tends to be passed down through time, culture, or family history. Your mother-child relationship is a direct product of the last generation and several prior generations of women shaping you. The ingrained behaviors, attitudes, mothering styles, nurturing behaviors, and emotional bonding are all reflections of past generations of mothers in your family. Your grandmother is an untapped source of information and insight to use for your emotional and relationship legacy. You can gather this valuable information from relatives through the family myths surrounding your grandmother. This woman is a force in your life today. You need to decide what type of force she will be in your future. It is well worth your effort to understand your history so the chances of repeating this pattern will be remote.

The emotional pain, frustration, and relationship problems that evolve out of this type of relationship even two generations ago is still alive and well in your life today. Many times your grandmother doesn't get the credit or understanding that she deserves for her contribution to your legacy. Your grandmother, whether dead or alive, played a tremendously powerful role in your mother-child relationship. She gave your mother her mother factor legacy. You can see that this generational emotional pattern is worth understanding because you are a product of several generations of mothers.

Consider why your grandmother would create and raise a perfect daughter. You know firsthand the painful side effects of "perfection": anxiety, self-loathing, low self-esteem, and shame-based feelings. Psychological research has proven time after time that the constant need for "perfection" in an imperfect world is always a formula for creating a chronic anxiety disorder in children. Your mother learned that her value was outside of her, based on her appearance, achievements, wealth, and the way her family looked and acted. These core beliefs were learned to a greater or lesser degree from your grandmother. Never assume that your mother is acting on her own with regard to "perfection" and need for external validation. Your mother or grandmother truly didn't understand the long-term effect the perfectionist mothering style would have on you. Your mother is reacting to your grandmother, based on her own emotional needs, level of self-acceptance, imperfections, and anxiety.

The more you understand your mother's emotional development, the more insight you will have into your own life. The goal is to develop more balance between being perfect and being perfectly imperfect in your relationships, starting with your mother. The following two stories will help illustrate the need to resolve, change, and manage the perfectionist mothering style.

Heather's Story

Heather, a woman in her middle thirties, is an unmarried residential real estate agent with a college degree. She has body image issues and is unhappy about the direction of her life. Heather is extremely thin and tall and seems highly anxious when she is speaking. At first glance, Heather appears to have the world by the tail. She is a top salesperson in her company and is very a popular businesswoman in the community. But she has also had a series of failed romantic relationships, the last three terminating prior to engagement. These last three breakups were especially disappointing, because Heather thought she was going to marry each of the men involved at the time. She also found herself constantly arguing with her mother, Diane, about her (Heather's) life and how she ran it. Heather wanted to seek some professional support and insight into the underlying reasons surrounding her last breakup and the constant tension with her mother. She was currently not speaking to her mother because Diane took the side of the ex-boyfriends in the breakups. Heather also stated to me that she had a "nagging" gut feeling that whatever she did wasn't good enough. It didn't matter what it was, she never felt relaxed or at peace with her work, life, and relationships. She related the following story:

> I have always been my mother's pride and joy. She always treated me like a queen. I just had to look and act the way she wanted me to. I started rebelling in the tenth grade and starting smoking pot. I kept my grades up, stayed thin, and looked the part of a good girl. I was sleeping with my boyfriend the whole time and my mother never knew it. I went to school in San Diego and did very well away from my mother. She and I have always had a push-pull relationship. My mother is a bulldozer and very controlling. My father has never had an independent thought since he got married. My older brother moved across the country after high school and has never come back to visit. I started doing real estate because my mother wanted me to. She has been doing it for years. We are constantly fighting about everything. I find myself acting like a teenager and then really getting mad at myself for arguing with her. I love my mother but we are still too close. I blame her for all the guys leaving me because they have all said that my mother still controls my life and me. They didn't want her to control our marriage. When I stop and think about it, they are right. I have never accepted my role in our relationship.

I have struggled with an eating disorder since high school. The counselors said my eating issues were connected to my mother. I think my whole life is connected to her.

Heather began to see me in therapy to address her mother factor issues and her perfectionist approach to life. When she started to embrace the concept of being "perfectly imperfect," she immediately stopped her food obsession and chronic arguing with her mother. She began to envision and redesign her mother factor legacy in her professional, personal, and intimate relationships. Her first step was to realize that her mother's opinion had become her own. Heather and her mother were one voice in her head. Heather had never really considered or fostered her personal opinions or goals outside of her mother's range of approval. She learned to tolerate her mother's displeasure, disappointment, and anger with her choices. Heather accepted her imperfect body image, her natural appearance, and her career drive as "good enough."

These major shifts allowed Heather to completely recover from her eating disorder, to stop having panic attacks, and to develop a romantic relationship outside of her mother's sphere of control and influence. She also accepted that her mother wasn't going to change. Heather's new outlook changed her entire approach to business and to men. Heather was married thirteen months after our first meeting, changed careers, and moved to the southwest United States. Previously, she had never even considered her own choices, emotions, feelings, dreams, and relationships. Heather had naturally assumed that her mother knew more about her life than she did. Her life had been consumed with always pleasing her mother and looking "perfect." Once she stopped obsessing on her mother's opinion, her energy was focused in the right direction: *her own life*.

Richard's Story

On July 19, 1979, at 2:30 a.m., Richard, seventeen years old, was coming home from a high school beer bash party with his best friend. They were both drunk and had a major auto accident. Richard was the passenger and survived the crash. His friend died immediately. Richard then proceeded to escalate his drinking as a result, trying to cope with this personal tragedy. He drank heavily through college and into his early thirties. Richard had an emotional awakening with his girlfriend at the time. She asked him why he hated his life so much. He stopped drinking a few weeks later because he knew he couldn't control it and he had to stop punishing himself for his friend's death. When Richard came to see me, it was to discuss his most recent romantic relationship struggle and career impasse:

> I have always felt like a failure long before the accident. My own mother wouldn't speak to me still till this day about the accident. My mother was always yelling at me and my sister about our bedrooms, our grades, and our friends, and how we looked. I am in my mid-forties and I still hear her voice in my head "complaining" about me or to me about something. I haven't been married because I just don't want to be controlled by anyone. My mother thinks I still don't work hard enough as a lawyer. I do fine but there is always something I am not doing right. I have a hard time with not drinking because it numbed me out and kept me from my anger. I now use exercise as a release for my anger, anxiety, and depression, I run and workout six days a week. I physically feel great but I can't maintain a romantic relationship. I tend to date women who need help or support. I have been told by other therapists that I am co-dependent and live from a shame-based personal belief system. I think they are right because I don't have any close friends, only a lot of social friends. And all my girlfriends are train wrecks. I feel awful about the things I have done. My drinking

and all the womanizing I have done in my twenties and thirties were out of control. My mother is in her eighties and she still has the power to upset me and get me to do what she wants.

Richard realized for the first time in his adult life that he had the power to change his mother factor legacy of "perfection" and shame to self-acceptance and being "perfectly imperfect." These emotional options, psychological alternatives, and choices were the keys that Richard never knew were available to him. This new emotional awareness and openness began to offset his shameful feelings and triggers. Richard began to apply new positive emotional options and cognitive insights to his relationships. For example, Richard would stop himself from thinking he was a "loser" when a woman would decline his invitation for a date. He would consider that maybe they really weren't a good match— something he probably knew before he even asked her out. The invitation was another opportunity to beat himself up emotionally and mentally. Richard stopped setting himself up for failure, rejection, and shame. Instead, he started taking complete responsibility for his choices and stopped blaming others for the negative outcomes. He then discovered that he was the source and cause of attracting the "wrong" relationships into his life. He came to understand that it was his shameful feelings that he acted on and believed were the problem, not the people in his life.

Richard finally stopped giving his mother's opinion, voice, and anger complete sovereignty over his life. He began to balance his mother's inner voice with his own thoughts, feelings, and desires. Richard stopped apologizing to women, clients, colleagues, and social friends for being such a "late bloomer," and began to embrace and appreciate his life history. He also realized that many of his colleagues found him to be an excellent lawyer, solid legal mind, and brilliant litigator. Though doing well in his career, he realized that he was the one blocking further career development, and he had never seen or understood his role in it before. This was a very powerful paradigm shift for Richard in his relationships and his career. He began to see himself as a valuable, likable, and "good enough" man. This was a completely new behavioral approach, belief system, and positive way of relating to his entire world. The most shocking thing that Richard discovered was that his mother was very proud of his new independence and personal power. He knew that if he didn't take action with his mother-son legacy, the emotional pain in his life would drown him and ultimately lead to his premature emotional and physical death. Life had felt dark, bleak, and desperate for Richard when I met him. He couldn't function under the "perfect son" syndrome any longer and had the courage to take the necessary steps toward a new legacy.

BECOMING SHAMELESS—"YOU LOOK GREAT"

This is a very emotional chapter for sons and daughters of the perfectionist mothering style. I could have added another ten stories that were even more painful and tragic than the last one. This mothering style is a "silent killer" to personal empowerment, self-acceptance, and self-love that every child needs for adulthood. It is near impossible to enter the workplace, marriage, parenthood, and social settings with a sense of confidence and courage if you have the core belief that you are "defective" or "damaged goods." It is a very powerful force to overcome when your worst critic is in your head and is supported by your first love: your mother. You spend the majority of your emotional and mental energy trying to feel good enough for situations, relationships, and careers that you feel don't deserve your love or time. Your life has been about trying to offset the shameful feelings that you experience on a regular basis. The only way out of the valley of despair and panic is your new emotional acceptance of new positive information about yourself.

Your personal growth and new mother factor is about incorporating a balanced emotional, mental, and spiritual view of yourself as "perfectly imperfect." Accepting your genetic and family history as a gift and part of your personality is a new formula for your immediate success and fulfillment. Your understanding and belief that you are "fine" and "acceptable" as you are is critical for all your relationships. This is a very powerful truth that most people rarely, if ever, discover or consider as an option. You wouldn't be reading this book if you weren't on the pathway to your potential in every area of your life.

One of the keys to reducing the power of the perfectionist mothering style over your life is having the imperfect ability to change your life. You are the solution to your self-loathing relationships, lack of self-acceptance, and destructive life choices. You have to get out of the way of your life and allow your positive, self-accepting side and sense of imperfection develop in your heart, head, and relationships. *No one holds more power in your life today than you.* Try that feeling on. Again, no one has more power, influence, or impact on your life than you. People look at me as though I have three heads and carry an axe in my back pocket when I tell them this timeless truth of their own legacy. It is now your turn and personal right to make the relationship selections and emotional attachments that you want but have always feared you couldn't have. You are no longer living under the psychological deception of "perfectionism." You are the mover! You are the only power broker of your "imperfection" and emotional health. No one is immune to the pressure of perfectionism in our culture, but you received massive amounts of it from the day you entered this life. Now it is time to get out of this endless mental cycle of shame, self-doubt, self-loathing, depression, anxiety, and fear of rejection. You own the rights to the rest of your story. No one has the right or permission to write it for you, only you.

In order to gain a more balanced self-accepting approach to your life, you need to start by comprehending your mother's legacy style. Your mother was likely doing what was done to her as she tried to gain her mother's acceptance and love. She likely never questioned this. People tend to dismiss the emotional pain and mental trauma of the "perfect children" syndrome because there aren't any physical marks or broken bones. These children (such as you) grew up believing that unless they appeared perfect or superior, they were unlovable. It is a serious error to diminish or discount the power of "perfectionism," "always looking good," and "never having enough" on emotional beliefs and maternal love. These children grow up with only half the story about their worth in relationships and purpose and life. The other part of the story now is that you have all the power, control, direction, insight, and wisdom to develop and partake of the relationships you crave.

HOW TO BE "PERFECTLY IMPERFECT"

The following steps are designed for all of us and especially children of a perfectionist mothering style. I have never met anyone professionally or personally with a serious psychological issue, emotional wound, or mental trauma who didn't have a background in "perfectionism." There is an untold truth among adults who feel shameful: the fear that their inadequacy will be discovered by everyone in their life at any moment. The following steps, ideas, and suggestions are to provide serious emotional reconstructive surgery on your personal view of yourself, relationships, and role in life. This isn't a neat summary of the chapter, but rather an introduction to your future. You will decide when, where, and with whom you will make these changes to your inner core beliefs and how to apply them to your world. *The bottom line is that your life is in your complete control, not your mother's.*

Step One: Take a second look at your critical inner voice. This may sound painfully simple and obvious, but it isn't. Your critical shameful thoughts, feelings of self-loathing, and subtle self-destructive behaviors are like breathing for you. These automatic feelings that come into your head without any questioning or rebuttal need to be stopped. You need to start recognizing these emotionally debilitating thoughts, beliefs, and choices you make. Think about where these thoughts come from and why. Don't allow yourself the easy way out and assume that they are normal and natural. Shame and self-loathing aren't appropriate at any point in your life. Write down in your new journal (you need one) the feelings you have and where you think they came from. Try to see a pattern and the underlying emotional connections between them and your core picture of yourself. Next, start to distinguish your mother's voice from your own. Many of us have incorporated our mother's voice as ours, without any question or hesitation.

Consider the things you like and dislike about your own beliefs as distinct from those of your mother's. Think of how you might act in a particular situation without fearing your mother's criticism, opinion, anger, or rejection. Finally, think again of your mother's voice and don't minimize it, even if she has passed away or you don't have a close relationship. Your mother, regardless of her present-day circumstances, is alive and well in your head, heart, and emotions. Review the definition of shame and consider how it operates in all of your relationships, behavior, and core feelings.

Step Two: Accept the truth that you are the most powerful person in your life today. This self-acceptance and self-approval is the quickest way to stop behaving in a manner that minimizes *your* potential and dreams. You are, as mentioned above, the most powerful person in your life on every level. No one has control or responsibility over your life other than you. This is the first step into adulthood and to becoming the woman or man you have always wanted to be. This change will impact your emotional life and relationships in ways that will surprise you. Your opinion of yourself is of paramount importance and critical to your relationship path in your adult life. Think about how you give away your opinion, power, and choices to your mother. Your self-loathing is a side effect of not doing, thinking, or believing in your inner dreams, drives, and wishes. Consider three things you have always feared, avoided, and wanted in your life. Write them down in your journal and consider the possibility of achieving them.

Step Three: Embrace being "perfectly imperfect" in all the relationships of your life. Allow yourself to experience the pleasure and freedom of not being under some type of old contract to be "perfect." This may sound silly, but consider the power of forgiving yourself for being "imperfect." When adults forgive themselves for not living up to an invisible standard of perfection or a belief that they are "bad" or "not good enough," life becomes much easier. This shift from self-loathing to self-acceptance will finally allow your emotional life a chance to expand and grow. Very few adults allow themselves the chance to get out from under their internal critical voice. Most children of "perfect" mothers stay trapped in the endless cycle of "perfection."

It takes courage and patience to sit down and put on paper your self-diagnosed problems. Writing is a very powerful way of concretely seeing your inner thoughts exposed. Write in your journal five things about yourself, your history, and your relationships that are less than perfect (i.e., divorce, weight issues, money issues, addictions, sexual problems, etc). Don't be either too polite or too critical; allow yourself to rid your life of these preset beliefs and behaviors that negatively impact every relationship you currently have. Ultimately, you will begin to sincerely enjoy your own company. These types of emotional shifts allow you not to keep up so many emotional walls in your relationships.

Step Four: Create a mantra, motto, or saying that reminds you of your acceptability and new positive core feelings and thoughts. This is much more than taping some cute, catchy sayings on the bathroom mirror and repeating them every morning. It is all about stopping your deep-seated emotional programming of perfection, self-loathing, and shame. Don't underestimate the power of these early emotional beliefs and their connections to your mother. Be creative in your mantra, because it will soon replace the critical voice and feelings in your head and heart. These mantras are a deliberate, conscious reminder of a very powerful, unconscious lifelong self-loathing process you have never questioned. Your life is much more than an artificial standard of appearance or being "perfect." Your life is yours, as are the relationships you form in it.

Step Five: Don't doubt the power of your self-acceptance and self-approval to change your life from the inside out. There isn't a psychological or emotional issue in your life that isn't related to your self-loathing, "perfectionism," and shame. These five steps of internalizing the "perfectly imperfect" self-concept will revolutionize everything in your life. You have the power to change your core feelings, relationships, and emotional connections with yourself and the mother within your head and heart. Think about the personal power you will have when you stop spending your energy on what other people or your mother says or thinks about you. Men and women who do this find that their lives and relationships are much more fulfilling and satisfying.

Write in your journal today how many times you didn't seek someone else's approval or acceptance. Keep track of when you give away your personal power and when you don't. There is a pattern to all these behaviors. Learn why you have these emotional patterns.

SUMMARY

Don't panic or feel more shame if you can't *immediately* comprehend and apply the "perfectly imperfect" concept and the five action steps to your life and intimate relationships. There is no right or wrong path to your continued development and growth. *You are already perfectly imperfect, you just don't know it.* You are going beyond the narrow script of being perfect and becoming the woman or man you have always dreamed of and wanted to become. Consider and accept the fact that you are increasingly becoming more aware of your hidden potential and unlimited sense of being emotionally secure. There is no limit to your life when you feel secure, loved, and accepted by your own standards. You no longer have to live a "perfect life" in order to feel valuable, worthwhile, and lovable. You are "perfectly" ready to do the things that you have held yourself back from until the circumstances were perfect. Achieving perfection is like promising to mail a check and never doing it: the check isn't coming and perfection won't be attained. You can get your life out of its emotionally perfect "straitjacket" and begin to expand it so you can develop your potential in all of your relationships. This pathway out of the valley of shame and fear is sometimes slow but always beneficial and productive. Your continuous effort, new insights, and personal application of feeling, believing, and acting "perfectly imperfect" will return tenfold what you put into it.

Chapter 4

THE UNPREDICTABLE MOTHER
Overcoming Depression and Anxiety

I will never forget coming home from playing outside in the summer and my mother sitting in the dark watching TV. She had no expression on her face and never noticed me coming into the house. My mom always seemed to be someplace else other than with us. I always wondered where my mother went mentally when she stared at the TV for hours. I think it was the only time she seemed happy.

—Debbie, age fifty-two

My mother was very unhappy and depressed when I was a child. My father would always warn us not to upset her and to be really good. My father traveled four nights a week and my sister and I had to handle our mother's mood swings and the continual threats of her killing herself when she got really upset or mad. My mother really scared me and my younger sister when she got angry.

—Linda, age twenty-seven

Depressed, moody, anxious, angry, excessively emotional, and mentally unstable mothers have been the subject of

145

mainstream psychological conversation for many years. This collage of random and chaotic behaviors creates the unpredictable mothering style in a young child's life. These mothers appear "mysterious" in how they make inconsistent emotional connections and parent their children based purely on their mood. There is always a cloud of conflict, impending doom, imminent catastrophe, and judgmental errors surrounding these mothers. They create "crises" in their minds, through their emotions and relationships, and pass them on to their children. Approaching life with constant unpredictability is, ironically, a way for these women to feel in control. Many of these mothers go through several marriages and have children with each new husband. Others remain unhappily married or single as part of their ongoing life drama. These mothers love their children but aren't able to maintain a stable, secure, consistent, reliable mothering style and relationship pattern within themselves or with their children. The public discussion that attempts to explain these women and their random behavioral choices tends to be skewed and insensitive, aimed more toward blaming and finger-pointing. A more complete picture of this mothering style contains the silent, personal emotional struggles that terrify these women and their children. It is very scary and emotionally overwhelming to feel out of control and not know the reason or origin of the problem. When these mothers are able to verbalize their inner thoughts, they don't enjoy being, nor do they want to be, the problem mother or the emotional train wreck in the neighborhood. These mothers genuinely want to develop secure and stable relationships, but they don't have the emotional ability to do so.

The unpredictable mothering style is very problematic for all family members. A young son or daughter will shape their relationship skills around avoiding the terror that is created by the unstable mother-child connection. These children will find a way to minimize the fear that is created by their mother's daily verbal explosions and constant excessive emotional crises. For example,

Linda, as the above quote demonstrates, spent the majority of her childhood trying to please her mother and manage her random mood swings and irregular behavior. Linda explained that one time her mother got so mad with her father that she took all of his work clothes out of the house and burned them in the front yard. The next morning, Linda's mother had no memory of her screaming and burning clothes or the reason for it. She wasn't drunk but in a rage about something that Linda could neither understand nor control. Linda remembered staying home from school at the age of seven (second grade) when her mother was having a "bad day" and needed her support.

These types of nurturing behaviors by daughters and sons are very typical, normal, routine, and necessary for the emotional survival of their mothers. Linda and Debbie (see the first opening quote) were always worried about their mothers' well-being. Their concern turned into an education in psychology early in life. They learned to be the "parent" that they wanted and didn't have. The children of this mothering style learn tremendous people skills and emotional intelligence (ability to understand people and their feelings) by the first grade. These children know that they are responsible for things, situations, and issues that are clearly beyond the scope of a "normal" mother-child relationship.

UNPREDICTABLE AND EMOTIONALLY EXCESSIVE—IT NEVER STOPS

This mothering style not only adversely impacts women but men as well. This would seem obvious, but men are given very little credence when and if they discuss their unpredictable mothers. The daughters, on the other hand, are generally more aware of their mothers' behaviors and more likely to discuss them. Men tend to be more dismissive and avoidant of the chaotic and unstable childhood in which they grew up. The men I have met professionally, personally, and socially are generally ambivalent about the long-term impact of their mother-son relationship. These same men complain that all women are "unpredictable" and that they only meet "crazy" women. They also believe that a calm, stable, equitable, intimate relationship is a myth.

The mother legacy that connects between the present drama and past emotional terror eludes most of these men. Unfortunately, both adult men and women of all ages struggle with their unpredictable emotional legacy and with reliving the terrifying memories. Although women tend to be more candid about their mother-daughter issues than men, it is to the advantage of all adults who experienced this mothering style to be candid and open to the possibilities of changing their legacy and relationship patterns. Yet, all adult children of this mothering style understand—men later than women—the enormous emotional burden and painful issues they have borne.

I met a young man who typified the struggle that both sons and daughters have with this type of mother and her "crazy" approach to life. Josh, a computer systems engineer, age twenty-six, came to see me about his emotionally paralyzing fear of intimacy. Josh described that "awful gut feeling" he had whenever he began any type of emotional connection in a relationship (professional, business, social, and family) with a woman. He admitted to me that when he began to feel emotionally close to or understood by a woman, he immediately started to feel a terrible sense of impending doom and fear. These feelings became so overpowering that he had to stop seeing the woman or resign himself to being emotionally paralyzed. When this happened in business, he would bring his male colleague to deal with the female client(s). Josh dated only women who were in need of being "rescued" or who needed to be "fixed." Initially, he wasn't consciously aware of their emotional needs, but the same issues always appeared in his love relationships. Josh said, "Same girl every time, just a different name and the same story." These types of one-dimensional rela-

tionships of giving but never receiving have been his only relationship model and style. He avoided as much as possible any emotional interaction with women in the workplace or socially. Josh is
in a chronic cycle of internal conflict because he longed for a safe,
intimate relationship with a woman, but it seemed impossible to
him. This pattern also hindered him from making more decisive
business decisions because of his fear of women and their anger.

When we began to explore his mother-son relationship, Josh
told me the following:

> Steve, you have no idea of how I rescue women. It is an auto-
> matic action and feels like my duty. I have no problem finding
> a date but it is difficult not to get involved in an ongoing drama.
> I always seem to take on the woman's problem and make it
> mine. Then I feel responsible to fix the problem and make sure
> she doesn't get mad at me in the meantime. I am always in fear
> of upsetting or letting down my date or partner. I automatically
> assume it is my duty to be rescuer guy and be loving and sup-
> portive. I feel like I get run over by a truck every time I start to
> get to know a woman. I feel this pressure that clouds my judg-
> ment and relationships with women.

I asked Josh about the type of mother-son relationship he had
growing up. Josh replied,

> I was always in fear of my mother. She is still calling me daily
> to let me know her opinion. She never stops, everything is a
> crisis and I need to act accordingly. If I followed her advice I
> would be unemployed and living back at home with her. I have
> always felt that no matter what I do, it is never enough for her
> or any woman. I am very scared of a woman's anger and dis-
> appointment. My mother was always in a bad mood and would
> become verbally abusive and mean. I was always walking on
> eggshells as a kid so I wouldn't upset her or set her off into an
> emotional rage. My mother would throw things, hit me, and

scream for hours. There was nothing I could do to stop her or calm her down. She was absolutely out of control.

Josh's story isn't unusual when considering the childhood drama of an unpredictable style of mothering. This type of mother has the most chaotic of the five classic mothering styles. She creates problems, issues, and emotional relationship blocks that can surface in the child's life twenty years after the incident. The circumstances, events, and outbursts are almost beyond belief for adults who have no background with this type of volatility and rage. Adults who aren't familiar with this type of maternal emotional impairment find it hard to comprehend the degree of fear that is created. Yet a large majority of conflicted mother-child relationships have likely had their beginnings in this mothering style. It is the numerous unresolved emotional issues, likely from the prior generation—your grandmother's—that helped create a very unstable emotional foundation in your mother's life. The result is a chaotic legacy passed on from generation to generation. Many daughters who become mothers themselves aren't consciously aware of the depth of their own emotional pain—their own legacy of difficulties or relationship apprehensions. When confronted with these issues, many daughters and sons choose to ignore their inner turmoil until their pain exceeds their comfort level.

INSTABILITY → UNPREDICTABILITY → CRISIS → IMPACTS YOUR LIFE

Children like Josh and Linda will automatically create ways to comfort, care for, and protect their mother when they sense her emotional neediness. This mother is unable to manage, understand, or cope with her own emotional and psychological issues. There is a lack of emotional, mental, or psychological insight into the legacy that this mother carries, so her issues remain unresolved. Life for many of these mothers on a daily basis is simply too overwhelming and difficult. She needs to be psychologically self-contained to take care of her own emotional needs and be aware of the impact of her unstable "mothering" behavior. Moreover, this mother isn't able to maintain a clear emotional boundary between herself and her children. The children become the "parent," emotionally and psychologically. These children become the emotional container of the mother's psychological problems. Young children take on this extremely mature behavior because they know their life is in danger if their mother falls apart. Children will figuratively stand in front of a train or do almost anything to protect their mother, because she is their life source. Children desire for their mother to be stable and predictable. It is a natural genetic trait to pursue a stable and consistent emotional bond and relationship with your primary first love—your mother.

Children of the unpredictable mothering style learn and develop sophisticated ways of keeping their mother from self-destructing. Josh and Linda both learned how to keep their mothers from attempting suicide on a regular basis. They would find ways to distract their mothers emotionally. The goal was to refocus the mother's attention on something other than killing herself. These children grow up with a tremendous ingrained burden of needing to take care of people: friends, relations, and everyone's emotional issues. Children like Josh and Linda become adults who will struggle with trying not to fix or repair all of their relationships. The term *codependence* accurately describes their relationship style, emotional legacy, and emotional attachment. These same children have tremendous guilt when they aren't in the caretaker role with their mother or the loved ones in their life. The level of guilt, uneasiness, or anxiety about not nurturing can be paralyzing and emotionally debilitating. The codependent behavior can often be like an addictive drug: the withdrawal is more painful than the ongoing self-sacrifice and dismissal of their life. Codependent behavior impedes a person's ability to see clearly and to set the necessary boundaries that all relationships require.

Unfortunately, unexplained emotional and psychological explosions are the cornerstone of this mothering style. Adults have tremendous difficulty recalling the horrors of their childhood and the fear they felt when their mother would lose her temper. These adults will avoid any type of emotional or personal relationship that has a familiar behavior pattern. If they don't avoid the drama, they will continually choose the same unpredictable relationships and traumatic outcomes. The emotional drama becomes the mainstay of these adult children's life and their sense of self.

Depression, anxiety, anger, screaming, hitting, excessive panic, and unpredictable emotional reactions are the daily, or at least weekly, life experiences of these sons and daughters. All of the emotional reactions are fueled by unresolved anger, which is covered up with anxiety or depression. The mother randomly and unconsciously misuses these emotions for the purpose of offsetting her unmet emotional needs. This is a mother who is usually emotionally and mentally immature and not capable of raising or guiding her children in a positive, productive manner. The mother's emotional issues are so extreme and severe that they control her life, thinking, and mothering. The children fast become the emotional adult, parent, and hyperresponsible person in the family.

The impending fear of the mother's becoming upset or out of control is a very horrifying thing for any child to experience. It is a powerful relationship pattern and emotional connection to change in adult relationships. Once a child learns and experiences the emotional benefit of being a "caretaker," "nurturer," and "healer," it is very difficult to ignore the power and control that is gained from that power position. These early emotional experiences help create a codependent personality—an adult who is consumed with other people's issues, concerns, and relationships. These adults aren't able to focus on or understand the power and choices that they have in a relationship other than being the "mother" to all people involved. This behavior is universal for men and women. No one is immune to the pitfalls of being the mother's "parent," "hero," or "savior." A codependent element can be found to a certain degree in many mother-child relationships. Those same "mothering" skills aren't productive when they are the only relationship skills used, however. It is the sole use of care-taking patterns in adult relationships professionally, socially, or intimately that cause a daughter or son to become codependent in nearly every relationship.

DRAMA QUEENS AND KINGS

Checklists for the Unpredictable Mother Factor

The following lists have two different purposes. The first list is designed to accurately pinpoint some of the problematic behaviors of your mother and their long-term effect on you. The second list describes what you do or don't do in your relationships. Consider these two lists as informal self-diagnoses of your unconscious, codependent behavior and emotional excess, as well as a means to gain psychological insight and resolution for unpredictability. Many times we believe and act as if life really is as dramatic as our mothers believed and acted. Even though we cognitively know the sky isn't falling or that the sun will rise tomorrow morning, we are still a product of our mother's parenting and bond.

Mother

- Your mother typically acted in an unpredictable manner.
- Your mother would express her anger and frustration in a very aggressive and unpredictable manner.
- Your mother usually was in some type of "crisis" with her relationships and partner.

_•_ Your mother would become very abusive (verbally, physically, psychologically) on a regular basis.

_•_ Your mother took her anger and frustration out on you.

_•_ Your mother had extremely unpredictable mood swings.

_•_ Your mother complained that no one loved or cared about her.

_•_ Your mother depended on you emotionally.

_•_ Guilt, fear, and panic are natural reactions when you don't help or assist your mother.

_•_ Your father didn't know how to emotionally contain your mother's rage.

_•_ Substance abuse (alcohol, marijuana, illegal drugs, painkillers) was common practice in your house.

_•_ Your mother's life was constantly consumed with her issues, emotions, and crises during your childhood.

You

_•_ You have been called a "drama queen" or "king" because of your excessive overreactions to regular life issues.

__ You have difficulty being direct or honest with people because you fear their reaction.

__ You have been called a "people pleaser."

__ You feel overly responsible for your friends' happiness when you plan something or have a conversation with them.

_•_ You have difficulty focusing on your own needs and concerns without feeling guilty.

_•_ You feel overly dependent on other people's opinion of you.

_•_ You don't value your own opinion as being the most or as equally important as those of the people in your life, including your mother.

_•_ You would describe yourself as a "rescuer" in your relationships.

_*_ You have a high degree of anxiety concerning people's anger or any sign of frustration directed toward you.

_*_ You don't like how you act codependent in relationships.

_*_ You take responsibility for other people's actions, emotions, and feelings. This is an ongoing theme in your relationships.

_*_ You feel most comfortable with a crisis or emotional drama.

__ You have been accused of "creating drama" or unnecessary crisis in all of your relationships.

__ You have difficulty maintaining long-term stable relationships.

_*_ As an adult, you still feel overly responsible for your mother's feelings and traumas.

__ You have a personal history of extreme emotional reactions and behaviors to "everyday" life events.

_*_ You are psychologically resistant to being compared to your mother (you fear you have similar behaviors to hers).

__ Currently you and your mother don't get along or speak.

This is a very exhaustive list of your and your mother's behaviors, beliefs, and emotional reactions. It is important to gain new psychological insight into the impact of being raised with an unpredictable mothering style. Don't minimize the fact or be discouraged that you might be attracted to a little excitement in your relationships. The key is to remember that your life isn't based on a series of manufactured dramatic, emotional upheavals or chronic chaos. *Your life is your conscious ability to make clear choices that empower your dreams, relationships, and sense of self.* Having the ability to understand how your present-day reactions, relationships, and emotional health can be completely different from your childhood legacy is your primary goal. A clear mental health marker is your ability to make your own choices without the fear, guilt, and prewritten script of your childhood. Adults who haven't come to terms with or reconciled themselves with their chaotic and traumatic childhood will automatically repeat the same self-defeating emotional patterns. Guaranteed!

We are all destined to repeat our past mother-child pitfalls unless we get new information, more knowledge, and greater insight about ourselves. The lack of insight and in-depth understanding, as well as denial and little self-exploration into your mother-child relationship, is a formula for disaster. You remember from the last chapters the intense emotional pain that this legacy can cause. If you have experienced one-tenth of the feelings and behaviors on the previous list, you are more than ready to resolve your history and take full control and responsibility of your present-day emotional life and relationships.

Many of my professional colleagues are psychologists who work with the Los Angeles County Department of Children and Family Services (DCFS), and they see this mother-child pattern repeated several hundred times a day. The kids, regardless of age, are attempting to survive their childhood and are hoping their mothers will change. The mothers in the "system," who experience tremendous personal struggles, aren't limited to any particular social or economic bracket or life circumstance. This type of behavior is widespread, with no regard to social barriers, race, or education. In the more severe cases, the children are often taken away from the mother by DCFS. Whenever drug use is introduced into this mothering style as a coping mechanism (usually the underlying reason for drug use), however, the mother will often lose her children or, worse, her life. In the other roughly 80 percent of these mother-child relationships, the situation is still highly problematic but not beyond the control of the mother and her support system.

The dark and unresolved side of the emotional legacy of the unpredictable mothering style is that it can promote codependence, passive-aggressive personality, borderline hysterical personality, and/or emotional insecurity and mental instability in the child. Despite these labels, these polarized emotional reactions aren't insurmountable. Many of the children who went through the "system," and others who have lived with their unstable mothers, have overcome their mother-childhood legacy. The pathway out of the valley of despair starts with recognizing the depth and origin of your self-defeating behaviors. Your ability to honestly and openly examine your relationships, emotional behavior, belief system, and own style is the pathway to a much calmer, more fulfilling, stable life and high-functioning relationships. Taking a step back from your emotional triggers, reaction patterns, and recurring relationship problems is a necessary step in rewriting your emotional legacy.

EVERYONE HAS A STORY— CHRISTINE'S JOURNEY

One of the most painful mother daughter stories I have heard came from a couple who met with me about twelve years ago. Christine wanted to improve the communication between her husband and herself. This seemed like a very sound and appropriate approach for couple's therapy. It took only a few therapy sessions, however, for Christine's anger, constant irritability, and emotional outbursts to appear during our discussions. Christine first presented a very calm demeanor and a soft tone of voice. She would suddenly "switch gears" for no obvious reason and start yelling at her husband, Howard. These verbally explosive encounters would cause Howard to sit still, with no expression on his face. No matter what Christine yelled about, Howard wouldn't react at all to her unpredictable behavior. Christine seemed to almost lose her mind when she became so angry. I found myself to be absolutely stunned by the degree of anger and rage that she would express in our therapy sessions over seemingly minor issues (e.g., taking out the trash, Howard phoning her).

It was overwhelming to witness these painful outbursts and the despair in Christine's voice and actions. She was inconsolable and seemed to be yelling at someone in her head. Her rage was clearly directed at someone else who wasn't in the room. Christine wouldn't look at Howard when she launched into an explosive verbal episode. Howard would look at Christine with a blank stare, as if he couldn't believe she was screaming at him that the family computer was not working. Their two children would run and hide when Christine got angry with Howard. I also felt like hiding in my office when her energy and emotional tension became so extreme.

Christine would begin to explain a situation and, regardless of the circumstances, her voice would become increasingly louder. The level of intensity and the rage that was in her voice just didn't seem to fit the situation she was describing. Howard would stop talking when she became so angry and aggressive toward him. He would "zone out" and emotionally leave the room. She became so angry that she once threw a book at him in my office. She then stood up and told him to go to hell and die. I asked Christine to meet me for an individual session so I could better understand the origin of her seemingly endless frustration and hatred of her husband.

I asked Christine about her mother-daughter relationship and if there was much yelling and screaming in her childhood. Christine told me the following:

> My mother was one of the bitterest and angriest women I have ever met. No one could ever do anything to help her or understand her frustration. My mother had my brother when I was seven and I raised him. We got in a horrible screaming and yelling fight when I was twelve years old about her laziness. My mother beat me with a pair of pliers and called the police on me. I couldn't defend myself or hit my mother back. I always wondered why I couldn't fight my mother in that moment. I ended up spending the next three years in a foster home until I was fifteen years old. I then got emancipated by the courts and solely supported myself. My mother and I never got along again after

that horrible night when I was twelve. I dropped out of school when I was in the ninth grade. I couldn't study or concentrate on school. My whole life was consumed with my mother's resentments. My whole life was a series of disappointments for my mother. She would say the meanest things to me and accuse me of being an awful sister to my younger brother. I couldn't do anything right until the day she died. My mother always expected me to take care of her and shoulder her emotional pain. My rage with her is always just below the surface and comes out toward Howard, when it is really not appropriate. I just get so mad and resent his aloof behavior with me. My mother never got over my unwillingness to taking care of her after getting put in foster care. My mother, while dying from bone cancer, told me it was my fault she had cancer. I ruined her life and caused her to die. My mother never accepted the fact that she smoked cigarettes for forty years.

After several individual therapy sessions, I asked Christine how she had overcome her painful mother-daughter relationship.

I have worked and earned money since I was nine years old. As long as I was working, I felt and still feel valuable and productive. I struggle with not taking on everyone's issues and concerns. My circle of friends have reflected my co-dependence, they all seemed to need my help. Now, I try not to fix everyone as if I am fixing my mother. I am working on not doing that or feeling responsible for everyone's life. I am also not beating myself up about not being a better wife, mother, and friend. Howard really is a good guy and doesn't deserve my mother's frustration and rage that I still hold. My goal is to reduce the drama and emotional upheaval in my life. This has been something I have worked on since I was twelve [she's now fifty-six years old].

RESOLUTION STARTS WITH YOU

It is very clear from Christine's candor that her emotional legacy of "drama," "excessive yelling," and "blaming" has been negatively impacting her marriage, her sense of self, and her parenting, among many things. It was the threat of divorce from Howard that caused Christine to stop blaming him for her emotional pain and terror. Christine made the conscious connection between her present-day anger (marriage) and her unresolved mother-daughter relationship (disappointment). She began accepting the idea that the majority of her emotional overreactions weren't about the issues at hand but were the unconscious reminders of her childhood. Christine began to put her mother's chronic emotional abuse, emotional neediness, and verbal beatings into perspective and leave them in the past. Christine knew it was irrational, but she had in fact felt responsible for her mother's life and death. She hadn't ever been able to constructively express the pain and disappointment with her mother in a nonhostile manner. She and her mother were always a volatile combination. Their relationship dynamic had been hostile for as long as Christine could remember. When Christine stopped blaming herself for her unpredictable mother-daughter relationship, her angry explosions toward Howard and the kids immediately ended. This behavioral and emotional shift in Christine greatly improved the quality of and bond within her marriage, parenting, and professional relationships. The need to displace her emotional pain had finally been resolved and laid to rest in her past, where it belonged. Until that point, Christine had never been able to resolve her mother factor with any degree of satisfaction or emotional relief.

TELLING YOUR STORY—IT'S YOUR TURN

It is your turn to tell your unedited story about your experience with an unpredictable mothering style. The purpose of this exercise is for you to continue to stir up your "emotional pot" of unresolved, unseen, untouched, and untapped issues that are linked to your mother-child history. These old issues that crop up currently with your partner, children, friends, and career can be connected to you and your mother. I want you to seriously consider all the issues, concerns, problems, and crises mentioned in this chapter and the role they play in your life today. Take a piece of paper and write down your answers or answer these questions aloud. Whatever answer comes to mind first is the answer or thought you should consider.

1. What is your primary memory of your mother when you were a child?
2. How would you like your children, partner, and loved ones to remember you?
3. What is the scariest moment of your childhood?
4. Who really knows the scope, depth, and seriousness of your childhood trauma, terror, and fear? Do you really believe what happened or do you dismiss it as unimportant?
5. What is the one issue, problem, resentment that you hold against your mother?
6. How different could your life be without constantly reliving your unpredictable emotional life?
7. What is the one thing you have always longed for from your mother? Can you accept your mother's limitations?
8. Can you accept your limitations in relationships?

Now that you have answered these questions, put them together in a brief story. Go someplace where you can be alone—in your house, neighborhood, or outside, and say your answers out loud. You don't need an audience, but you might try imagining that you are explaining your life to a judge and jury. This is a very powerful emotional experience; it gets you outside of your story and into a third-person perspective. Imagine that you are explaining your life to the judge (a god, universe, any source outside of you) and describing how you and your mother interacted. Tell the whole story to this impartial, benevolent third party of how scary and lonely your childhood was at times. Tell him or her how you have always wanted things to be better or different, but they never or rarely were, and today you are changing that. Don't stop expressing your greatest hope, fears, and issues to yourself and your judge. *This is your emotional legacy being rewritten in oral form.* Your life will change when you begin to sincerely tell your story.

You may find yourself talking to yourself a lot in the next few weeks. Please don't panic, you aren't losing your mind. This self-talk isn't a sign that you have finally gone over the edge of reality or lost your mind. You have opened up an emotional dialogue with yourself that isn't limited to any particular time, place, or situation. Don't be surprised if, while you are driving, walking, or doing something routine, you start to have a flood of new thoughts, feelings, and insights. This is natural, normal, and part of your healing process. The depth of feeling and the need to talk it out are critical. Trust the process and go with it. Don't be surprised by what you have to say and the level of new insight that is developing. Your goal is to get out of the way and allow your inner voice to discuss and reflect on your story. Write down the key thoughts, ideas, and statements that you make. It will be helpful to fully understand your transformation. Later on, go back and read what you said and thought—you will be most surprised.

GOING BEYOND THE DRAMA CRISIS

Being Direct and Emotionally Secure

This mothering style of unpredictability has been very difficult to describe. It has likely stirred up the thousand of hours, events, and emotional pictures that you have witnessed, lived, heard, and wondered about for years. It is hard to describe the terror and un-resolved pain that are created for everyone in these families. But the answer is not blaming, insulting, or metaphorically killing off the mother. These women/mothers would have done things differently if they had the capability, but they didn't. It is now your turn (your responsibility) to put your painful memories, codependence, chaotic relationships, screaming, anger, resentment, emotional trauma, and drama king/queen behavior into the past. The more you genuinely feel resolved and nonreactive to these old wounds, the more personal power you will have in your relationships. The amount of new emotional energy that will be available to you for anything that you put your attention into will be astounding.

It is important to fully comprehend the classic negative and problematic side effects listed above. You can't let go what you don't know you are holding. What are you holding? Consider the following brief definitions and descriptions of unpredictable behaviors. These are the core behaviors that you should start considering letting go of and changing. The following list is a condensed version of the wide spectrum of "crazy" events, beliefs, and behaviors that develop in the context of the unpredictable mother-child relationship.

Emotional Drama King/Queen Behavior: You have an exaggerated fear of being abandoned, unloved, and ignored. You are emotionally unsure of yourself and create situations to draw excessive attention to yourself and your problems. Your first experience of feeling loved and cared for has left you avoiding potential disappointment in all your actions. You don't know how to ask for what you want or need without being "excessive" or extreme. Your life is always in a state of chaos and emotional instability. You have chosen partners, friends, and relationships that become very volatile and chaotic. You don't understand or believe that your emotional wants or needs can be met, properly understood, or accepted. You fear that people don't like you or love you. Your only way of feeling loved or cared for is to have a crisis, chaos, or unstable circumstances. You tend to be addictive with drugs (all types), relationships, sex, gambling, any kind of distracting behavior. You feel emotionally alive when things or circumstances are volatile, crazy, and exciting. You like living on the edge of danger and beyond common sense. You prefer to be near a crisis than to play it more conservatively.

Passive-Aggressive Behavior: You are emotionally avoidant of confronting, communicating, or being direct about your feelings, thoughts, and beliefs. You have tremendous anxiety saying no and fear the outcome of doing so. Instead, you give the response that is desired or expected—not your own. You are scared of being yourself and expressing your true opinion. You feel powerless and hopeless about this type of behavior. In order to feel powerful, you will deliberately do or say things that will sabotage a situation, your partner, or yourself. You don't take any responsibility for your actions when questioned about these behaviors. You appear to be unaware of your destructive behavior, but you know on a deeper conscious level the desired outcome. You know exactly what will cause problems or create a difficult situation for the other person. You gain a sense of power and pleasure when you do things to disrupt, incapacitate, or damage your partner, mother, or personal relationships. You feel empowered and important when you accomplish these tasks. The need to feel powerful and understood is the driving force behind your semi-apparent passive behavior and naive, aggressive actions. It is the inability to be direct and clear with your feelings, thoughts, and actions in relationships that is problematic.

Codependent/Dependent Personality: You are extremely helpful, giving, nurturing, and supportive in the hope of being loved and accepted. You will go beyond yourself to rescue, serve, and take care of your mother, partner, or other people in your life. You tend to do this in every relationship. You feel valued only as a person who is a "giver." The only way you feel lovable or worthwhile is to do these never-ending selfless tasks. These behaviors over time cause you to engage in self-destructive behaviors to keep an unequal relationship going. Your entire self-worth is dependent on the other person's approval and need of you. You have great difficulty thinking about your own thoughts, needs, and self. You spend your life thinking and worrying about what the other person is thinking or feeling. You don't feel secure or emotionally strong enough to express your own opinions and beliefs with other people. *You don't exist if you can't fix, rescue, or save someone.* Your relationships tend to be emotionally exhausting for you. You feel manipulated and many times abused (all forms) by the people in your life. Your constant need for self-acceptance from others causes you to feel desperate and sometimes panic. You are too emotionally paralyzed to pursue the goals, relationships, and material things you desire. Your life is a series of crises and your ability to fix and repair the people in your life.

Avoidant, Anxious, Moody, Insecure: You have extreme mood swings and feelings of despair on a regular basis (daily, weekly, monthly). These feelings occur without any particular prompting or as a result of any external circumstance. When you feel overwhelmed and hopeless, your entire life suddenly feels directionless and lost. These feelings aren't based in reality, because your external life circumstances haven't changed. When you are in this unstable emotional place, you have trouble focusing on your daily tasks. Everything you do or need to do takes a tremendous emotional effort and mental focus. The exaggerated sense of feeling abandoned, unloved, and ignored is exhausting and a chronic relationship fear. In short, it is an issue. You are constantly in an emotional state of upheaval and agitation with friends, partners, and family. Your relationships are very powerful and dramatic regardless of who is involved. The beginning and ending of your relationships, whether professional, social, intimate, or familial, are emotionally charged and mentally consuming.

You don't understand why other people don't experience the same degree of emotional discomfort, unrest, fear, and anxiety that you do. You fully believe that experiencing these emotional extremes is natural and normal. When you are depressed—moody, lacking energy, hopeless, feeling worthless, panicking, anxious, and insecure—you either become completely withdrawn or emotionally aggressive toward your partner. The biggest challenge when you feel these emotions so strongly is not to dump them on your partner, children, close friends, or the world. *You blame the people currently in your life for being responsible for your deep emotional unrest.* All these behaviors reveal your fear of being unlovable or unworthy of positive emotional support. You have felt unlovable and thus have been seeking people's approval since your childhood. Your emotional life and erratic behavior completely dominate your mental and psychological ability to function at your full capacity and potential. Your life is an ongoing series of problems that have a recurring theme and concern: *emotional instability/insecurity.* None of your behaviors or actions ever adequately addresses these internal beliefs and emotional legacies from childhood. These adult behaviors of constant emotional unrest are merely the symptoms of much deeper mother-child unresolved issues and concerns.

WALKING AWAY FROM EMOTIONAL DRAMA AND PERSONAL CRISES

The practical definitions of codependence, passive-aggressiveness, moodiness, anxiety, emotional instability, extreme dramatic emotional behavior, and avoidant behaviors have their roots in the unpredictable style of mothering. The following four steps are very challenging concepts to accept but are easy to follow. The hardest part of change is accepting that change is necessary. At this point in your life, you have had enough pain to want to move forward without any more anguish and drama. It is imperative to move beyond the emotional need for constant attention and people taking care of you.

Step One—Create Personal Boundaries: The psychological concept of setting emotional and behavioral boundaries is for you, not the people in your life. If you can't say no or stop a particular reaction, you will feel out of control and at the mercy of someone else's actions. You can begin to consider the areas of your life that you need to have control over and clarity for in order to progress. Think about one or two behaviors, feelings, or circumstances that cause you to act in a nonproductive manner or self-destructive way. Your ability to set up a program or an emotional game plan is your key to success. Alcoholics Anonymous is a classic example of setting emotional boundaries and managing your emotional impulses.

Everyone needs emotional, physical, and mental boundaries. Boundaries help us define ourselves in the world along with finding our place and purpose. Without emotional boundaries, your ability to create productive and high-functioning relationships will not happen. This is possible only with new insight, support, and knowledge to create personal boundaries in any area of your life. The recognition that you have to monitor your mood swings, feelings, and verbal expressions is the first step in stopping unnecessary dramatic behaviors. All addictions (drinking, sex, drug use), eating disorders, and compulsive behaviors (shopping) are healed by setting emotional boundaries and limits with yourself.

The psychology of creating emotional boundaries and behavioral limits is an effective way to manage and gain control of your emotional mood swings. Boundaries will give you the cognitive insight into your emotional pain and overreactions. Over time, your boundaries will increase, as will your tolerance for frustration. Your increased tolerance for simple problems and relationship frustrations will allow your emotional expressions to be less dramatic. If you are not fully aware of or need more information about your mood swings and personal drama, ask your partner or close friends. They have experienced your "meltdowns," dramatic behavior, and hostile communication. They are the people who know you firsthand and can give you the valuable support and clear insight that is necessary for your personal growth. Think of two areas or triggers that set you off.

Step Two—No Catastrophization: This is your cognitive ability to stop, look, and listen to the problem, issue, or feeling. If you don't give yourself the chance to run away with an idea or old fear, then you can stop panicking. It is your new emotional ability to step back from a problem and consider other options or opinions. Pausing and rethinking your emotional "hot spots" will give you the control and clarity that you crave.

You must accept the fact that you were trained to exaggerate the importance of a particular action, issue, circumstance, or personal conflict. You would then immediately imagine the most horrible outcome that could possibly take place. This was/is your internal thinking and emotional process. When you think this way, with this type of emotional and cognitive approach to your life and relationships, everyday events become crises. Immediately assuming the worst about another person or business decision impairs your ability to think and understand the actual person or event. Your energy is spent on replaying your mother-child drama and conflict in every area of your life. When adults understand this pattern, it is very stunning. Becoming fully aware of it is the way to amend any dramatic behavior or hysterical emotional reaction. Your emotional, mental, and physical overreaction to noncrisis situations is your comfort zone of familiar behavior. The hardest thing about not overreacting is letting go of this old, familiar comfort zone. You know how to be upset and anxious and how to create your own end-of-the-world scenarios. Can you be calm, clear, and confident of your own empowered approach to your relationships? Watch the outcome, it will be very different from what you are used to. You will notice that you have trained the people in your life to expect your "crisis" reaction and to treat you a certain way. Your mother did it with you as a child, and now you are going to change that pattern.

Step Three—Your Opinion Matters Most: If you are going to

resolve any of your unpredictable mothering concerns, you must first start with considering your own opinion as the most valuable. This concept ends the agony of people pleasing and worrying about other people's opinions of you. You will find yourself breathing easier and having much better days if you end this cycle of dependency and desperation. Constantly seeking others' positive opinion will leave you in a very desperate emotional condition. *No one can approve, love, or accept you, unless you do it first.* You can begin to choose whom you want to help, support, love, and spend time with. You are no longer driven by the emotional need to be needed by people. You can stop seeking, consciously and unconsciously, people's love as a substitution for your own self-love. Codependent personalities and dependent relationships have a very strong addictive quality, irrational belief system, and a lack of acceptance. The desire for being loved and supported is normal and healthy, but the desperate neediness found in codependency is not.

The codependent adult focuses only on loving the other person in the relationship. The unspoken hope is that your intimate partner, colleague, children, or friend will take the responsibility and control of loving you. You have never been able to find the courage to truly be yourself and accept, love, and nurture yourself. You learned that to care about yourself or consider your own feelings, thoughts, and emotions was selfish and unnecessary. Your relationships have been centered on the hope that someone will finally love you. Since this basic mother-child nurturing issue was never resolved, it is still a driving force in your adult life. This belief and old behavior doesn't work and leaves you always in a state of panic.

Step Four—Emotional Clarity/Maturity: Your ability to be clear-headed is directly correlated with your ability to reduce the internal tension and fears in your life. It is impossible to be at your emotional or relational best when you are worried or fearful of some unspoken impending doom. Lowering your emotional tension, panic, anxiety, and fear is opening the door to new thoughts, feelings, and emotions. Recognizing that your old familiar feelings are a source of your personal powerlessness and drama is the first step toward emotional freedom. When you realize that your old emotional behavior, overreactions, and anxious thinking are nonproductive forces in your current life, you will achieve a new level of clarity. Your ability to consider other options besides your own feelings in your relationships will take you to a new level of emotional maturity. The cognitive ability and desire to stop your automatic responses to your friends, colleagues, family, and partner is taking control of your emotional legacy. Regardless of the traumatic and excruciatingly painful mother-child relationship you experienced, it is possible to step away from it and be different. Women and men over thirty wonder if they will ever overcome their mother and her legacy. These adults have come to believe that there is more than one way to think, act, and feel. Your life can become a combination of many different perspectives, giving you the hope and courage to change.

If you find yourself getting upset about a missed phone call, for example, and this kind of reaction has been your pattern, then don't allow yourself to follow that old cycle. Emotional maturity is simply your ability to recognize your mental process of coping with stress and tension. Giving yourself the opportunity to look at your life from a different point of view is very valuable. If a building has four corners, it is important to know which corner you are standing on. Try thinking about your new perspective in terms of walking to another corner in the same building to get a different view of your life. Your unpredictable childhood can be viewed from a different corner, with a fresh perspective and new insight. Your new approach to your life is that you don't have to be in a constant series of never-ending disappointments, heartbreaks, and crises. Your pathway out of your valley of despair is considering your new emotional options and choices.

Enjoy the walk away from the old drama to a clear and stable life and fulfilling relationships. The things that you truly crave in your relationships can be accomplished by not creating a crisis or becoming a wallflower. It is possible for you to create the types of relationships that make you feel loved, cared for, and emotionally empowered. This can be done in your career, family, social circle, mother/father relationship, and with your intimate partner.

Chapter 5

THE "ME FIRST" MOTHER
Creating Your Own Life

No matter what the discussion is about, my mother always finds a way to bring it back to her. I could be dying and she would find a way to focus my death on her. It is so frustrating, it is all about her.

—Julie, age thirty-nine

My mother wants to be the center of attention. I am always aware of mothers who need to seen and heard. My whole life has been about my mother's life. Her struggles, disappointments, lost lovers, and her suffering as a mother.

—Doug, age fifty-six

My mother hasn't called me since I moved in with my father. My mom thinks I have betrayed her because I wanted to get to know my father. I haven't lived with him since I was four. My mom considers any affection for my father as something being stolen from her. Everything I have or feel is my mom's. It's my life not hers!

—Kelly Anne, age sixteen

THE "ME FIRST" MOTHER

These three quotes from three completely different people share a common theme and childhood experience. These three people are representative of different age groups, life experiences, different degrees of understanding, and they include both genders. Yet all three of these adult children have one very important thing in common: they experienced the "me first" style of mothering. They were raised by a woman who wasn't able to see her children as separate individuals from her and her life. There are many terms that could be used to describe this very prevalent and common mothering style. This mothering style is in fact considered by many sociologists, psychologists, and family therapists as an untreated epidemic in our culture.[1] According to current research, people are either becoming more "me first" in their relationships, life, family, and careers or they are dealing with people who are self-absorbed. This trend isn't surprising to the children of a "me first" mother, who know too well her approach to the world, life, relationships, and family. This is a very emotionally complex woman, who continuously frustrates her children. These daughters and sons will spend their entire adulthood seeking a positive way to be loved and supported without feeling deprived in their relationships.

For those of you who grew up with this style of mothering, your mother is a series of contradictions that make you feel frustrated and confused. The following question-and-answer section about your mother might help clarify some of her mothering style behaviors and beliefs.

Questions and Answers about My Mother

Who is my mother? No one would question that the self-absorbed, self-centered, and "me first" mother isn't a very complex woman to know, understand, and live with. Her style is very different from the two previous types of mothering styles. This is a woman who can be the most charming, hospitable, funny, smart, friendly, kind, and charismatic person in the room. Then, instantly, she can become cold-hearted, emotionally insensitive, and negligent. These emotional shifts are dependent on many issues, concerns, perceptions, degrees of attention, and her constant need to be "special." She is a bundle of contradictions and emotionally unresolved needs and desires. If this sounds like your mother, you learned by the age of five to please her and keep her from looking "bad." The need for a perfect appearance was always an issue for your mother, regardless of her actual physical beauty.

Why is my mother so harsh toward others? This mother can be very harsh, controlling, lacking in emotional insight, fragile, and very loving all in the same hour. All these behaviors are contingent on the degree of emotional neediness this woman experiences in any given moment. The constant up-and-down emotional behavior is based in her childhood. If your mother experienced a severe lack of maternal approval, love, and acceptance, this will translate into emotional deprivation in her adult relationships. This painful void will begin to show itself in early adulthood as "self-absorption," "self-centeredness," "lacking empathy," and "being the greatest" at whatever. These behaviors are driven only by an underlying need for gaining people's approval and undivided attention. It is a constant unconscious emotional behavior that is always working and looking for an audience or a chance to be heard. Your mother attempted to offset her emotional deprivation (feeling unloved, undesirable) by always telling the world of her overestimation of her abilities and mothering talents.

Why does my mother always make herself better than everyone else? The constant bragging by your mother is likely fulfilling an emotional need of not believing or feeling that she was loved by her mother (your grandmother). Your mother has to keep everyone, including you, at least one step down from her self-perceived importance. This very common compensating behavior is a great yardstick by which to measure anyone who is constantly telling everyone of her greatness, special gifts, and exceptional abilities. Your mother felt and continues to feel inferior, and that is the driving force in her life since childhood. The long-term insecurity about her place in the world has carried over to mothering. The sense of insecurity about mothering caused her to brag to the other mothers about her wonderful children (you). Of course, nearly all parents brag to some degree, but this type of mother goes way beyond the norm. She behaved like this to make herself feel better and to show her peer group, friends, and family that she is the best. You learned at an early age that your life revolved around making your mother feel happy and special. This mothering system works well until the child is about age six. At this age, you first considered your own opinions, independent actions, school friends, and life away from your mother. If your new independent behavior or thinking was not in line with your mother's agenda, you were immediately punished.

Why does my mother only approve of or love me when I agree her? You learned that being loved by your mother meant making her happy at all costs. This was the start of your emotional neediness, deprivation, and feelings of insecurity. Regardless of your age, you still find yourself automatically placating your mother in conversation, personal disclosures, about career choices and friends. You struggle with the need to seek her approval and tell her the truth about your life regardless of the outcome. You have the innate ability to know and understand what your mother needs and wants from you. The problem is that you always feel empty and unloved after doing these "mother pleasing" behaviors. You have learned that all of your conversations will ultimately end up being about her and her life. This is particularly upsetting to you as an adult, because you truly desire your mother's love and support without having to be in her shadow. You always feel frustrated and unimportant because of the absence of focus and lack of genuine interest in your life. This has been a lifelong emotional issue in your relationships: *feeling unimportant and dismissed.* You know that your life is about obtaining and maintaining your mother's sense of well-being.

Why does my mother get so mad at people and then cut off the relationship afterward? The need to be seen as and to feel perfect is one of the primary underlying emotional drives of a "me first" mother. When a circumstance or situation doesn't reflect well on your mother or shows her to be unkind, mean, or self-absorbed, there is an immediate rejection of that situation or person. In order to maintain the emotional defense against such events, the other person is viewed as bad. This type of rejection can be applied to anyone: a family member, friend, partner, colleague, relative, anyone who has emotionally hurt your mother. It is your mother's underlying, vulnerable self-esteem that makes her so sensitive to these "injuries" of criticism or perceived defeat. Although your mother may not show it outwardly, these events may haunt her for years and cause her to feel humiliated, degraded, and emotionally empty. This internal process of rejection is the motivation for such a strong reaction by your mother. Your mother's disdain and rage and never-ending need for a defiant counterattack is her attempt to feel empowered. This emotional process is very typical of your mother and isn't limited to anyone or anything. Everyone in your mother's circle of friends, family, and colleagues is subject to these rejections.

Why is my mother so confident and I am not? When sons or daughters learn to put aside or ignore their own dreams and passions in hopes of attaining their mother's unconditional approval and love, parts of their emotional life are left undeveloped. Children raised with this mothering style are always struggling with low self-esteem. You weren't given the approval for your first-grade finger-painting or your current career challenge, it's all about your mother and her needs. You might also devalue your own thoughts and feelings about what's right for you. Whether choosing a dress, a college, a baseball glove, or a life partner, there are always free-floating elements of self-doubt in your decision making. You have been raised to gain your mother's approval, regardless of her actual knowledge base in all your choices. Your life has been directed to always include her, and that has caused you to doubt your own decision-making abilities. You have learned to consult your mother prior to understanding your own thoughts and feelings on any given matter. *Her opinion is more important and powerful than your own.*

True Mother-Daughter Story

Julie, age thirty-six, is married to Max, age thirty-eight. They finally found a house they wanted to buy. This was their first big purchase after seven years of marriage and three years of house hunting. Julie was told by her mother, Barbara, age sixty-eight, not to buy a house until they had 40 percent of the purchase price in the bank. Max couldn't talk Julie out of following her mother's unreasonable advice on home loans. Julie wouldn't consider making an offer on a house until her mother saw it and approved of it. Julie has been unable to separate and form her own opinions, experiences, and relationships without caving into her mother's wishes. Julie told me the following:

> My mother doesn't mean to control my life, she is single and needs my support. I feel uncomfortable about making a big decision without talking to my mother first. She needs to know. I have always done this and it seems normal to me. Max has threatened to divorce me if I don't stop allowing my mother to run our marriage. I see her only once a week and talk to her on the phone only once a day. I don't see the problem. She knows everything about my life. Max and my girlfriends think I give my mother too much power. I have a lot of anxiety if I think about doing something without considering my mother. Isn't that what a loving daughter does? I am very close to her.

We will discuss later how Julie was able to develop her own opinions and thoughts. She ultimately learned to have an adult relationship with her mother. But before she did, Julie feared that if she didn't include her mother, Barbara would cut her off emotionally. Barbara's pattern of resolving conflict was to emotionally remove, avoid, and ignore family, friends, and business partners from her life. There are times when it's wise to avoid "toxic," destructive relationships, but casting out people for any minor reason is not the same thing. Barbara's automatic self-defense mechanism against feeling inferior—casting out nearly everyone—had been her long-standing relationship model. The chronic fear of abandonment and rejection has therefore been a constant anxiety of Julie's all of her life.

Why does my mother always have to be the center of attention? When someone is fully engaged in telling you about his or her wealth, endless achievements, prominent people he knows, and super-special abilities, it is an indicator of his "me first" mother-child history. Many men and women who are considered highly self-centered and "full of themselves" are in actuality compensating for a deep emotional deficit in their mother-child relationship. This emotional deficit can be passed down from one generation to another of mothers/fathers and their children. Sons and daughters of this mother can grow up to be extremely self-centered and narcissistic, but each gender tends to react differently to the "me first" emotional legacy.

Why does my mother need me to be perfect and better than everyone else? This mother will announce to her son or daughter that she is the best and that you are part of her formula for success. Her need for maternal attention, admiration, positive feedback, and a sense of feeling special in the world was never addressed in her childhood. These issues become apparent in early adulthood as a pervasive, constant pattern of grandiosity and a chronic need for attention (from anyone). There is an inability to tolerate anyone or anything that doesn't reflect well on your mother. Teenagers are very difficult for a "me first" mother to parent, because they will do anything and everything to make her look bad, feel worthless, purposeless, and useless. Many teens of this type of mother have reached their limit of making their mother look good, feel good, and appear as a perfect mother to the world. Often these teens (boys and girls alike) will never resolve their anger, becoming resentful and blaming the world for their struggles. The relationship with their mother is no longer a safe place for feeling good about themselves. Many times, teenagers will become more like their mother in attitude and feelings of personal importance. Sons and daughters will then re-create their childhood experiences with a new partner (a mother substitute) in their intimate adult relationships. This process of becoming like our mother is often underrated and ignored in our society. The unresolved issues with your mother have to be addressed, or you will unconsciously use them as the foundation for your relationships in adult life.

True Mother-Son Story

Larry was fifteen years old and lived with his mother. Larry's mother, Cindy, age forty-four, had been divorced from Larry's father for nine years. After the divorce, Cindy moved out of the San Diego area to Los Angeles. She sold residential real estate in West Los Angeles. Larry had regular visitations with his father, Robert, age forty-seven, every weekend and for half the summer. Larry was suspended from an exclusive private school in West Los Angeles for having sex with his girlfriend in his car in the student parking lot—during school. His mother brought him to me to discuss his current crisis. Larry told me the following:

> Hey, Dr. Poulter, my mother is full of sh——. I caught her having sex in our driveway at home with her new boyfriend two weeks ago. She is such a phony. My mother says one thing to you and does something different at home. She is more concerned about

her image around town then me. She goes home at night, drinks a bottle of wine, and gets drunk. Then she starts yelling at me for being a loser and a screw up. Then my mother threatens to throw me out of the house and tells me to go live with my father. This happens at least once a week. I hate my mother and her phony image of being a great mother, are you kidding me? She is the loser.

After much discussion, it was decided by Cindy, Larry, and Robert that Larry should live with his father during the school year. Larry moved in with his father and immediately stopped acting out at school and fighting with his mother. Cindy admitted that she was very hurt and couldn't understand why her son didn't love her and didn't want to live with her. Cindy had no psychological insight into why her son was angry with her or why he was being self-destructive. She didn't believe that she had done anything to provoke Larry and felt the mother-son issues were all his problems. She didn't believe that her mothering style was a contributing factor to the family crisis. Cindy was enraged with my suggestion that her mothering was a major problem in her mother-son relationship. Cindy "fired" me for not completely taking her side and for suggesting that her mothering style might be part of the problem. In addition, Cindy was furious with me for not recommending that Larry be put in military school.

This mother-son conflict didn't require Larry's removal from his father's home or a boarding school. Prior to this incident, Cindy wouldn't allow Larry to live with his father, even though it had been recommended by numerous school officials, family members, and other psychologists. She didn't speak to Larry and his father for three months after this incident, even though Larry repeatedly called her. She told Larry that she didn't want to speak to him because he hurt her so badly. Cindy did finally call Larry when she was on vacation in Europe with her new husband. Cindy told Larry she couldn't see him during the summer. I continued to see Larry in therapy to help him resolve his anger and abandonment issues concerning his entire family situation.

HOW NARCISSISM—"ME FIRST" MOTHERING— IMPACTS YOU

Before going any further, it is important to clarify that our discussion is about the untreated, unhealed, and unaware mother who is struggling with her own issues of narcissism. Our working definition of the narcissistic/"me first" mothering style is: *a behavioral, emotional, and psychological pattern of grandiosity, a chronic need for attention and admiration, a profound lack of empathy, and an inability to tolerate any critical information about the mother's behavior.*

Isn't everything in life in shades of gray? Everyone agrees that life would be easier if everything involved a simple choice or action. The gray area is appropriate and necessary for all of us to function in daily life. We all have some "me first" impulses from time to time. However, it is the constant superior approach to others, relentless elitism, and incessant self-absorption that characterize the "me first" mother as she lives and operates outside of the gray zone of life and with her children.

It is in these difficult areas of basic emotional intelligence and relationship functioning that the "me first" mother has chronic problems. These problems aren't limited to but include the following basic emotional legacy issues: *lack of emotional connection, constant need for approval, attention-seeking behavior, lack of empathy and compassion, critical of others, sense of superiority, lack of loyalty, self-serving relationships, morals based on opportunity, and the importance of maintaining a picture-perfect perception that she is superior at all costs.* Your mother expects, consciously or unconsciously, for everyone to recognize her special talents, gifts, and exceptional abilities. When you or others don't recognize these talents, your mother will often immediately become enraged, emotionally and verbally abusive, or withdrawn from the situation or family. Such episodes during your childhood forced you to become very sensitive to people's mood swings or perceived mood shifts. You assumed that these emotions or sad feelings were somehow your responsibility. Your own emotional needs, concerns, and nurturing were never addressed or adequately understood by your mother.

Your mother was much more interested in maintaining and developing her own personal status than in your emotional health and growth. You learned that your feelings were centered on her and her needs. She tended to associate only with those she deemed as special or having high status. These friends, superficial associates, "big names," or celebrities were considered by your mother to be "unique," "perfect," or "exceptional." She aggrandized them because of her need to be associated with others more powerful, influential, and prestigious than herself.

The question regarding many adult children of the "me first" mother is whether they will develop the same narcissistic personality traits or become emotionally deprived—longing for nurturing love and unconditional approval. Either scenario is based on the lack of emotional love, support, and little to no focus on the child as a son or daughter. Your life was like the moon (you), always reflecting back the light from the sun (your mother). You were always reflecting back to your mother that she was exceptional. Your birthright created a false illusion that you were somehow more special than the rest of your friends or school buddies. It is this artificial approach to life and the inability to see people as people that was your mother's driving emotional force.

The following two lists are designed to address some of the emotional fallout from the constant programming as well as from the lack of empathy for others. We will see that sons and daughters both react similarly and also very differently to this particular mothering style.

SONS—HOW ARE YOU?

Consider the following list and how you relate to the women in your life, socially, professionally, and intimately. Sons of the "me first" narcissistic mother will treat women how they were treated or they will create a mother replacement. Think about the questions below in order to uncover the blind spots in your emotions and relationships. Next, consider how you view your professional life, social circle, and family. These areas are excellent sources for explaining, revealing, and exposing your unconscious self-centered behavior and emotionally deprived feelings. Your emotional connections, relationships, and sense of self will be greatly shaped by either your sense of superiority or your feelings of inferiority and deprivation. The polarity of superiority to deprivation must be understood in terms of how it operates in all of your relationships. Your emotional attachment and psychological approach to people is your mother factor in action.

There is absolutely nothing you do within a given day that doesn't require your relationship skills and interpersonal competence.[2] You don't want to stay on the fringe of your life by making self-defeating interpersonal choices that alienate others. You have experienced people's displeasure with you and always find it very surprising and deeply hurtful. Your new approach to people and conflict resolution is the opportunity to maximize your potential. This isn't an age issue but a legacy issue. Your emotional insight into your behavior, emotional bonding/attachments, and feelings about yourself is your way out of this rut. It is never too late to make these all-important changes in your life.

Our goal in understanding all of our mother factor styles is to find the balance between these extremes and develop emotional empathy for ourselves and the people in our life. All of these five mothering styles have a polarity dynamic and also share a common middle ground. The key here is to begin to realize how every area of your of life is influenced by your mother-son "me first" legacy. For instance, you may have great difficulty finding the middle ground between your sense of superiority and your sense of desperation. These two extremes make finding your emotional balance in your relationships almost impossible.

The Son's Checklist

___ You are highly sensitive to criticism.

___ You have been repeatedly told that you act like a "know-it-all."

___ You are emotionally defensive when proven wrong in a discussion or relationship, or shown to have any type of misunderstanding of a situation.

___ You have been told by your intimate partner/lover that you are "self-absorbed."

___ You have emotional difficulty in not being close to your mother, regardless of your adult relationship status.

___ You publicly and/or privately view yourself as superior, unique, and very special.

___ You don't understand why more people don't see your special gifts and abilities.

___ You consider only position, power, and money as a true reflection of your exceptional talents.

___ You are easily angered or become emotionally upset when people don't do what you want.

___ Your close friends and intimate partner don't consider you a flexible or open-minded person.

___ You have a difficult time understanding other people's problems, pain, and struggles.

___ You don't fully understand why people are angry about your lack of empathy.

___ You always "get even" with people who have wronged you or hurt your feelings.

___ You have great difficulty compromising with people and

understanding someone else's opinion or disagreement with you.

__ You demand that people follow your ideas, suggestions, or plans.

__ You feel violated, ripped-off, and/or cheated by people, life circumstances, and failed business dealings.

__ Your intimate partner perceives you as a "complainer" and "whiner."

__ You emotionally withdraw—cut off people—when they disappoint you or fail you.

__ You always voice your opinion and consider it the most important.

__ You have a sense of entitlement—you believe that rules, laws, or normal circumstances don't apply to you. The rules are for average people, not you.

DAUGHTERS—LIFE BEYOND YOUR MOTHER

As a woman, you have struggled to find your own opinion and your own voice—not your mother's. Living your life in the shadow of your mother has been one of your greatest struggles. Only women with this particular type of mother will understand, empathize with, and support your struggle. Your mother has been a driving force in your life both positively and negatively. Much of your life has been spent developing your own self-esteem and personal goals separate from your mother's. You have performed the necessary developmental tasks with one eye on maintaining your mother's love and not losing her support. Your other eye has been on your own path and your attempt to make the choices and decisions that fit your life regardless of your mother's opinion. *Your emotional growth of maintaining your own identity with your mother and finding your own individual path, purpose, and intimate relationships has been at times exhausting, frustrating, and very scary.* Daughters of "me first" mothers have the added pressure of making their mothers look good. *No daughter wants to look better than her mother and lose her approval and support.* It is a simultaneous process to become an independent woman and maintain an emotional bond with your mother.

Many women stop their own emotional development and stall their aspirations, careers, and relationships in order not to lose their mother's love. This becomes readily apparent when a daughter enters adolescence. A "me first" mother can become very resentful of her daughter's beauty, youth, and new opportunities. The resentfulness and jealousy can be transfused by the mother to the daughter. The relationship may become very tense and emotionally hostile. Daughters of all ages have the constant pressure of not "outshining" their mother yet still not losing their own sense of self. Many times a daughter will follow her mother's self-absorbed approach to life in order to earn her approval and love. Daughters of the "me first" mothers tend to be either self-absorbed and narcissistic or emotionally deprived and dependent on others.

The challenge for daughters of all ages is not to get stuck in either polarity of emotional deprivation and chronic insecurity. Either end of this emotional continuum is nonproductive and a source of endless frustration. Vacillating between these two extremes is also very problematic. I have never met a woman who wants her partner, colleagues, friends, and social circle to view her as a self-absorbed narcissist or an emotional sponge for approval and love. It is possible to find the middle ground of compassion, empathy, and emotional security by uncovering your fear of being emotionally abandoned. Consider the following list of statements as a source of valuable information for creating new emotional insight. Emotional security and the courage to have your own life, opinions, and choices are very possible and well within your reach.

The Daughter's Checklist

__ You fear your mother's anger, disapproval, and disappointment with your choices (i.e., school, clothes, job, partner, and friends).

__ When you get upset with people, you will emotionally reject them.

__ You spend a tremendous amount of emotional energy worrying about your mother's life and well-being.

__ You view people, friends, and/or relationships as disposable when you are emotionally hurt.

__ You feel that your partner doesn't know or fully understand your special gifts and abilities.

__ You often feel that you are either the best or at least one of the best people in the world.

__ Your partner(s), past or present, consider you "self-absorbed."

__ You are impatient with other people's weaknesses, personal flaws, and shortcomings.

__ You can't forgive or forget an emotional wound, mistake, or misunderstanding.

__ You crave others' approval and acceptance of you.

__ You have a revengeful attitude and a mean streak as part of your relationship style/pattern.

__ You hold grudges for years against people who have personally wronged you.

__ You associate only with people you deem as more powerful, wealthier, or of a higher social status than most.

__ You often feel empty and emotionally lonely in your relationships.

__ Most of your relationships tend to be superficial in nature.

"ME FIRST" INSIGHT 101

The two lists above overlap for sons and daughters. If either list of "me first" descriptions struck a familiar chord with you, take note and mark it down. One item not listed above is this: *You have been described as defensive and aggressive when confronted with your own behavior.* This description is more of a definition of your emotional defensive mechanism than informational. When young children are both chronically dismissed and used as an emotional support for a parent, in this case mothers (fathers also do this), children develop hypersensitive reactions to feedback. The underlying cause for these exaggerated reactions to perceived criticism is that the child's entire life depends on always making his mother happy. The idea, whether conscious or unconscious, of losing her love, approval, and support is overwhelming and traumatic for the young child. Therefore, this child develops a defensive emotional wall against any feedback, accusations, or suggestions of behavior that are less than perfect. The child gains valuable emotional support and praise from the mother for always making her look good. This continuous cycle of approval-seeking behavior by the child/adult can become a nonstop endeavor. No amount of effort or determination seems excessive for this daughter or son in the attempt to win the mother's approval. Often, as daughters and sons focus all of their emotional energy on satisfying and pleasing their mother, they minimize their own feelings in the relationship.

The template of people pleasing via emotional deprivation becomes a sacrifice worth making, in order to be loved. In this repeated process over the ensuing years, this type of behavior begins to lay the foundation for a lifelong pattern of endless and painful efforts to please others at the expense of one's self. Does this sound remotely familiar to you?

It is essential that you begin to understand the emotional interactions that occur within you and in your daily interpersonal encounters. First, you don't have to act superior or desperate for people's love and approval. You can have deep and meaningful relationships without these counterproductive behaviors. The approval and emotional support that you crave can be attained without having to follow your "me first" model. It is in the resolution of your counterproductive, emotional deprivation that you can begin the path toward re-creating your own emotional legacy. Either end of the "me first" spectrum of narcissism or emotional neediness is really two sides of the same coin: *emotional deprivation*. None of the above behaviors are based in a secure emotional foundation from the mother-child relationship. This mothering style breeds insecure adults who attempt to find anchors in life to offset their underlying sense of deprivation and emptiness. The ongoing behavior of superiority, greediness, jealousy, envy, resentment, emptiness, alienation, and revengeful acts are all rooted in the "me first" approach to relationships, family, career, intimate partners, and yourself.

GOING BEYOND EMOTIONAL DEPRIVATION

I have found that no one, regardless of his terrible emotional state or overwhelming circumstances in childhood, wants to be viewed as "desperate" or "needy." The quickest way to ruin a new dating relationship is for your potential partner to see you as emotionally desperate or, on the other hand, extremely arrogant. Another sure way to blow up a relationship, regardless of its context (business, sports, family, social), is for you to feel, act, or become emotionally dependent. Adults of all ages struggle with their unmet emotional needs and the conflict of how to have them understood, met, and resolved. The truth is, we are all desperate and emotionally needy at certain times. The difference is that children who grew up with the other mothering styles haven't had to deal with years of being their mother's emotional support system.

As futile as it sometimes appears, you might try many ways to

win your mother's, partner's, or colleague's approval. You have
learned to put aside or ignore your own passions in hopes of
attaining your friend's unconditional approval. The emotional
process of not accepting or rejecting parts of yourself is undeveloped and undervalued. Adults in this relationship legacy cycle
always suffer from low self-esteem. You automatically discount and
devalue your own inner thoughts and feelings. This isn't about decisions such as what to have for lunch, but much bigger life issues
such as marriage, career, children, family, finances, and your health.
The way out of emotional despair and emptiness is to embrace the
concept of viewing yourself as "good enough" and capable of fulfilling your inner desires. Until you accept your limitations and view
yourself as a capable and competent person, the two extremes of the
"me first" mothering style will be a very powerful influence in your
daily life, relationships, and view of yourself.

You Are Enough—is a concept that addresses the narcissisti-
cally wounded personality. The famous *Saturday Night Live* come-
dian Al Franken, playing the role of Stuart Smalley, made the daily
affirmation "I'm good enough, I'm smart enough, and, doggonit,
people like me!" a very popular household joke. The truth of the
matter is that the comedy routine was not only very funny but
painfully accurate. Don't allow the idea of being "good enough" to
be minimized or dismissed as a pointless saying in your life. The
power of personal acceptance is never a joking matter.

Your unmet emotional needs, wants, and desires can be
resolved by the concept that you are enough. When you shift from
the emotional position of "me first" belief to the emotional belief
that you are "enough," your entire world of relationships changes.
Many things automatically happen, and your life becomes immediately transformed. These changes might take time to be revealed
and experienced, but your inner emotional sense will become
secure and stable. Prior to this point, your entire life has been a
series of emotional disappointments, letdowns, and poor emotional connections. You have spent the majority of your life since

age five trying to receive and maintain your mother's emotional support.

Being emotionally deprived explains how rational, highly educated adults will say and do very insensitive, mean-spirited things to co-workers, family members, their children, and intimate partners. All these immature, nonproductive behaviors have their origin in not feeling emotionally secure and safe. When people feel safe and secure, they can be very generous, forgiving, and compassionate toward others. You have that power and opportunity to do that right now, today in your life. Consider the following steps in developing emotional room in your thinking and relating for being "enough." This concept resolves the emotional deprivation and/or the arrogant, superior approach to people that you used as a means of feeling good enough or emotionally secure—which, for the record, didn't work and left you, the user, in a chronic state of emotional neediness or emotional defensiveness.

Emotional insecurity, emptiness, and arrogant behaviors are all attempts at compensating for a deep emotional lack and sense of adequacy. The driving behavioral force behind all "me first" adults is a deep sense of inadequacy and emotional insecurity. Children and adults of the "me first" mother struggle with many different types of inadequate feelings, beliefs, and nonproductive behaviors. The idea of feeling, being, and acting "good enough" stops the need for attention-getting behavior, celebrity-type friends, and all the behaviors aimed at covering up deep-seated emotional insecurity and neediness. Adult children of the "me first" mother are emotionally drained and tired of always either seeking approval or telling the world to approve of them.

GOOD ENOUGH RULES TO LIVE BY

Good Enough Rule #1—You can change your beliefs, actions, and feelings. You are solely in control of your life, not your mother.

Your issues, problems, and emotional pain are no longer about your mother. They are about you. If you don't make some significant changes in your life, no one is going to do it for you, and things will feel worse. Eighty percent of change is admitting that it is possible, necessary, and too painful to avoid. Twenty percent is actually implementing the change and new beliefs. Your mother isn't in charge of your life or the judge of it. *You are solely responsible for your life.* Do you sincerely believe that it is time to change your legacy? The first step is recognizing what end of the spectrum of the "me first" polarity you identity with. The second is uncovering and accepting how much of your behavior is centered around seeking your mother's approval. Your mother may have passed away, but she still has a big influence in how you approach your life. Self-acceptance takes all the pressure off getting your world to notice and love you.

Good Enough Rule #2—Reconsider your automatic responses, behaviors, and feelings. Acting self-centered only furthers your isolation, emptiness, and emotional deprivation. Your relationships—personal, social, and intimate—are reaching only a fraction of their potential with a "me first" approach. You can choose to be compassionate, empathic, and giving with others. The next step in moving from a self-absorbed perspective or a feeling of deprivation is to acknowledge how these beliefs keep you from achieving what you truly desire. Taking an inventory of how your behavior has affected your key relationships is critical for change. Consider your intimate partner: he or she will be an endless source of information about your "me first" actions, beliefs, and priorities. It takes humility to ask the people closest to you about how you have hurt, ignored, or been nonempathic to them. Allow your closest friends to express their pain, then embrace their insight. Their insight will allow you to focus on the areas that you truly need to explore.

Good Enough Rule #3—You need a feedback loop in all of your relationships and actions. You have a huge blind spot on how you affect people. All theories of communication, social psychology, and sociology consider the ability to have a feedback loop necessary for the survival of an organization or relationship.[3] Without your ability to listen to new information, your relationships will remain stagnant. A system, company, relationship, or person will become stagnant without new information and a flow of new energy. The best analogy of this concept is to try living in a room with a closed window with no fresh air circulating. After a period of time, you will suffocate from a lack of new oxygen. Why should our relationships or personal life be any different? It is a scientific fact that all living systems must have the ability to take in new information or matter for their survival. Similarly, all of us must have a constant flow of new input from the people in our life. Adults who feel emotionally secure have developed the ability to take in new information, new insights, and vital feedback. You can learn to consider feedback and criticism as your opportunity to change and become a different person. Without new information and feedback in your life, your emotional growth will get stuck at either end of the "me first" behavioral polarity. Defensiveness keeps positive changes from happening in your life. Every system in the universe has a feedback loop. You need to develop one.

Good Enough Rule #4—Develop emotional insight into your problem behaviors. Understand why you scream at stupid drivers in front of your children and partner. Figure out why certain events, people, or situations set you off like an unguided missile. Go below the surface of your behavior and find the root cause of it. Don't settle for the "I don't know" answer to your own problems and questions. Too often we spend our time resolving the surface causes, not the underlying pain. Create emotional insight into your own life. We all sincerely know the truth about behaviors, actions, attitudes, and choices. Take full responsibility for the problem areas in your life and relationships. This commitment to being clear about and responsible for your actions and emotional responses is the pathway to secure and powerful relationships.

People are automatically drawn to men and women who possess this type of emotional and mental clarity. The emotional issues, relationship problems, and personality conflicts become much easier to see and appropriately address. Your new insight will guarantee your ability to be emotionally clear and present to resolve your old relationships and to create new ones.

Good Enough Rule #5—Being right isn't always right. Feeling right doesn't make it right. There is a saying in couple's therapy, that *you can be right or you can be in a relationship.* Your conscious need to always be right isn't about the issue at hand but your unconscious need to have your mother's approval. The core issue of being a "know-it-all" is connected to the unmet emotional need for attention and adoration. *Do you believe that if you are right then people will adore, love, and accept you?* Wrong! Instead, what happens is that you aren't aware of how you alienate and push people away from your life. Being argumentative, verbally aggressive, and stubborn isn't going to get you the love and approval you are seeking. None of these behaviors for maintaining your "right" position are worth the emotional cost and loss of friendships. People who insist on being right to the detriment of their partner, business, friends, and life are really arguing about their need for attention, love, and approval. If you don't have to be right, then you can be secure in your views, opinions, relationships, and sense of self. You can learn what the people in your life think and feel because they aren't defending themselves from your verbal aggressiveness.

Good Enough Rule #6—It is an inside job. All of the changes that you want aren't outside of you, they are within your reach. You can meet, understand, and learn to satisfy your own emotional needs. This statement doesn't imply that you should isolate yourself in a cave. Rather, figure out what you need and want emotionally from your relationships and partner. Your personal knowledge of your own life will allow you to pursue those things that are important to you. Your mother or other people to whom you have given your personal power can't do this for you, nor should they. The more you understand your emotional deprivation, the more you can properly address it. This may sound far too simple, but it isn't.

Good Enough Rule #7— Learn to say NO to your mother and develop tolerance for the fear of rejection. Love your mother and know your own opinions, thoughts, and feelings. *Your mother can't define you, or be responsible for you, or do your personal growth for you.* It is all your own choices and decisions now. This step of adulthood requires that we all develop, learn, and employ the ability to say NO to our mothers and the people closest in our life. No one can sincerely say YES until they learn to say NO. Most adults who struggle with others' opinions of them and their mother's perceived power over them have never learned to say NO. Learning to handle the feelings of rejection or the anticipation of them is the key to your personal power and voice. You can't make your own choices if you are terrified of your mother's rage and disappointment.

Good Enough Rule #8—Stop telling the world you are great. You aren't great, but you are "good enough" to be a great human being. Everyone in your world is sick and tired of your ongoing commentary about your special gifts, remarkable accomplishments, wealth, and fame. It is time to move past the little boy or girl who needs constant reinforcement and praise for every achievement. You can spend your energy focusing on what you can do and allow naturally occurring events to reveal your expertise and accomplishments. The process of allowing people to discover your gifts, beauty, talents, and compassion is the mark of emotional maturity and psychological balance. People really don't want you to continually self-promote or brag about your wealth or successes. The adults in your life can and will form their own opinion about what you do or say. You can contain and heal the young child in you by accepting that you are noticed and appreciated. This step of being humble is a very powerful move toward becoming a more complete, well-rounded, high-functioning adult.

Good Enough Rule #9—Humility is your greatest strength. Don't ever forget that humility can open doors, create opportunities, and change your world and the people in it. Can you trust the process of life and that the people you know will recognize you? When you resolve your deep sense of emotional deprivation, all the obnoxious, self-absorbed behaviors will no longer be necessary. Men and women who are humble have harnessed the power of life, so their potential is unlimited. The people surrounding your life will go to the ends of the earth for you, because your humility has given them power and courage in their own lives. The quickest cure for a "me first" style of relating is to focus on the people in your life and give them the support and sincere compliments that they crave. All your relationships will benefit beyond measure from your sense of humility and selflessness. Going beyond your own concerns, ideas, and emotions and perceiving people to be as important as you are will change everything in your life. Learning to be humble is the only way out of this vicious cycle of emptiness.

SUMMARY

There isn't one thing mentioned in this chapter that you didn't already know or hadn't considered before. Now is the time to put all these "good enough" rules together. It is time for you to embrace the fact that you are enough—that you are good enough. It is your life, and this simple concept is as empowering as anything in your life will be. Being "good enough" gives you the courage, self-confidence, personal insight, and understanding of the risks that you want to take in your life. You have the courage to step out from your mother's shadow and go to the next level in your life. Until now, you didn't know that you had control of your life. Adult children of the "me first" style of mothering don't know and weren't taught that they have all the solutions to their own life. This is a very liberating fact when your life has been focused only on pleasing and maintaining your mother's emotional well-being instead of your own.

Chapter 6

THE BEST FRIEND MOTHER

Finding Your Emotional Power

My mother and I both got breast implants together. It was weird to see my mother compare her body with mine. It was at that moment that I really got sad. My mother was living her life through me. My mother had been dressing like a twenty-year-old for thirty years. My mother was competing with me for attention.

—Sarah, age thirty-two

My mother would hang out with me and my buddies when we were in high school. I realized after college and at my wedding that my mother thought she was one of the "boys" with breasts. Everyone loves my mom but she isn't really a mother. She is more of a sister. I realized that my mother needed my friends more than I did. My mother dated one of my friends after my wedding.

—Lance, age thirty-six

FRIENDSHIP AND MOTHERHOOD

The concept of a mother being her daughter's or son's best friend is one of the hottest flash points in motherhood. It is an impossible task. How does a mother achieve a balance between being a best friend and being a parent? The short answer is that she does not. The two roles are completely incompatible and opposite to each other. The mother's role is the setter of behavioral limits, the one who says no, the teacher, the nurturer, the model of unconditional love, the disciplinarian, the secure emotional connection, the positive supporter, and the emotional guide for her children. The "friendship/best friend" style of mothering is the abdication of all of these roles. Either a mother is a best friend or she is a mother. This isn't a black or white approach to mothering but rather a fork in the road of the mother-child relationship. The active mothering approach isn't concerned with being the child's best friend. A mother's role is to set limits and help develop her child's emotional life and desires.

The best friend approach tends to avoid conflict, difficult parent-child dialogues, setting limits, tough love behavior, accountability, and developing appropriate behavior and emotional boundaries for both mother and child. All these good mothering fundamentals aren't part of this mother-child relationship. As a child, you were either raised by your mother or you lived with an older friend. The difference is very clear and apparent to children, friends, and other mothers. The best friend style of mothering is very popular currently because it doesn't require the mother to make the hard parental choices—to be the "bad guy" or the tough limit setter in her child's life. This approach to mothering can be compared to the divorced dad who takes out the kids on weekends and deals only with the fun and easy part of parenting, ignoring discipline and consequences. Any adult child of this mothering style knows that relationships aren't all fun and games but rather a combination of many challenging tasks and responsibilities in addition to the fun.

THE FORK IN THE MOTHERING ROAD

Being a mother and being a best friend are distinctively different and promote within the child completely different emotional outcomes. The best friend mother-child relationship causes feelings of being neglected and can lead to anger. The development of an angry personality starts with the consistent experience of emotional neglect and emotional/physical abandonment—the parent's abdicating her role. The cumulative effect of maternal neglect and abandonment is anger, which can turn into an angry emotional approach to the world. Best friend mothering creates an angry daughter/son by virtue of the mother's being the friend instead of the parent. The emotional needs, developmental milestones, and healthy adolescent experimentation (not drugs) to develop a secure emotional bond are avoided or ignored. Individuation or separation from your mother is either postponed or skipped completely. The problem here is that adolescent daughters and sons need to emotionally separate and individuate from their mother. This is one of the most important milestones within the mother-child relationship.

Separation/individuation is on the same par as emotional bonding in childhood. Unless a young daughter or son is able to successfully separate and form an identity apart from the mother, the child's adult life will be consumed with anger, resentment, and feelings of abandonment. These critical issues are dismissed or avoided in light of other needs and the priorities of a mother-child friendship.

Daughters and sons with a mother/best friend are burdened with being the emotional support system and emotional "glue" for their mother. These children grow up feeling abandoned and lacking emotional support and maternal guidance. They feel as if no one has been watching out for them. They have the profound experience of being "motherless," while still living with their mother. This is a very strong statement that we will consider with real-life examples and a body of supporting evidence. Children truly want a mother in the maternal role, not a friend. As one thirteen-year-old daughter, Stacy, said to me during a mother-daughter therapy session, "I have plenty of friends, my mother isn't a girlfriend. I want her to be like the other moms." I couldn't help asking Stacy, a very bright teenager, the obvious question: What are your girlfriends' mothers like? Stacy answered me with a very strong tone, "That's easy, they pick their daughters up from school, know their friends, act like a mother, dress like a mother, and have a lot of control of their daughters. They leave them alone and don't try to be their friend."

When I say that parents should not be their children's friend, I am not talking about parents being abusive or dictatorial to their children, no matter what their ages. In the best friend mothering style, the child, at approximately seven to ten years old, becomes the special confidante of the mother. The mother-child relationship no longer exists. There is a dramatic shift from mother to girl-friend. It is a woman-daughter or woman-son friendship that is fun, easy, and lacking in any adult guidance in the child's life. The child becomes a friend to the mother. Both assume the role of an emotional partner, even though the majority of these mothers are married or have a significant romantic relationship. These children don't fathom the full residual loss of their mother figure until many years later.

The best friend mother can be found in all types of circum-stances, marriage styles, and relational situations. This style of mothering is very prevalent and currently very popular. It isn't lim-ited to any particular group of mothers (married, divorced, wid-owed, adoptive, single, etc.), education level, career path, or eco-nomic class. Many adult children of the best friend mothering style experience great difficulty finding their place in life, maintaining functional relationships, and creating secure emotional bonds.

When a mother makes the shift from mother to friend, the departure halts the normal development of a child's emotional self, his psychological understanding, and his sense of self-esteem. The natural needs of the child are no longer considered. The avoidance, dismissal, and neglect of treating the child as "the child" becomes a source of profound loss and grief. It is almost as if the child experiences the death of the mother while she is still living. These children, regardless of age, emotional stability, or personal neediness, instantly become a miniature adult. The friendship process hasn't worked for fathers and it clearly doesn't work for mothers either. Children—regardless of age, and particularly from birth to twenty-five—need the leadership and emotional wisdom of their mother. Children always crave their mother's approval and emotional support. Without the nurturing qualities that only a woman/mother can bring to her children, a serious emotional fracture develops in the child's psyche and self-esteem core. This fracture starts the internal emotional wound that in time becomes the source of the child's rage, anger, and resentment. The development of an angry personality happens as a direct result of the maternal nurturing process being aborted.

The best friend mothering style tends to have an earlier crisis point than the other styles because of the requirement of the child to provide emotional compensation early in the relationship. When the daughters or sons reach preadolescence—eleven years old—they are recruited to become the emotional colleague, friend, and confidante of their mother. Adolescents have the challenge of trying to act in an age-appropriate manner without carrying the extra pressure of worrying about their mother. *The common behavioral and emotional denominator of the best friend mothering style is a lack of understanding of motherhood.*

These women (regardless of marital status) have little or no insight or not enough emotional maturity to fully function in the role of mother rather than a best friend. The emotional needs of this mother are so overwhelming and consuming that she has to use her daughter or son to meet them. The child becomes a pillar for the mother's emotional and psychological functioning. Women, for as many reasons as there are mothers, tend to lean toward this mothering style when other areas of their life aren't complete or functioning properly. In order to be evenhanded, men with the same type of emotional neediness or unmet needs will either completely abandon their children or also employ them in a similar fashion. But here we will continue to focus primarily on the mother-child relationship and the mother's emotional legacy.

The best friend mothering style is no different than the "fatherless" fathering style in terms of its negative side effects on a parent-child relationship. By "fatherless fathering style," I am referring to the abdication of the emotional and psychological role of being a support, teacher, guiding force, and emotional backboard for the child. People are quick to point out that most men aren't actively involved in their children's development much after age eleven. These parents aren't consciously aware of nor do they fully comprehend the powerful lifelong influence they have on their children's life. Fathers have been called to account by federal laws and state legislation about physical and financial abandonment and for being irresponsible with their children and their paternal obligations. Men have traditionally minimized their role and the profound impact they have on their children's life.

A common complaint of many women is the challenge of maintaining their maternal role and still having a "life" outside of being a mother. Women have been handed a double-edged sword in the last thirty-five years: be a successful professional and be a successful full-time mother. The best friend mother often doesn't address either of these challenging roles. This is a woman who isn't taking either path of womanhood with any degree of commitment or full understanding.

The best friend mother believes that her life would be over if she embraced motherhood. This devaluing of the motherhood role is similar to how some men respond to fatherhood and choose not to get involved. These types of beliefs and prejudices are the fuel for the best friend mothering style. Regardless of why or how women become their daughter's or son's best friend, it is a very problematic parenting choice and a nonproductive situation for the entire family.

It is important to compare the best friend mothering style with the "absent" or "fatherless" fathering style. People are much more aware of struggles, anger, relationship problems, emotional pain, and trust issues of fatherless children. Unfortunately, the emotional loss and struggle of the children of "motherless" or the best friend mothering style is discounted or not viewed as serious. It is hard for people to accept this theory, because they saw the sons and daughters growing up and living with their mother. The children spoke and spent time with their mother every day, yet the mother-child relationship wasn't what it appeared to be. The appearance of the "ideal" mother is part of the problem, since she may look "perfect" despite her lack of nurturing, emotional support, and unconditional love. People grossly underestimate the power and residual impact of a mother who doesn't follow through on her motherhood responsibility, role, and commitment to her daughter or son.

Consider this idea to expand your perspective: if the first woman you loved in your life decided it was better to be emotionally absent from your life than be engaged in it, how would that affect you psychologically over the long-term?

People are very quick, and rightly so, to point out how the absent father has a negative impact on the father-child relationship (personally, socially, professionally, and intimately). This point is valid and applies equally to the best friend mother. It is a very unsettling idea to consider that seemingly great mothers are doing as much emotional and psychological damage to their children as absent fathers do. The emotional damage, however, is from a different angle and perspective.

BEST FRIEND TRAITS

The following list will help explain and expand the theme on this very complex best friend style of mothering. Adults who grew up with this mother-child relationship struggle with many issues throughout their adult life. Among them are rage, lack of trust, resentment toward women, fear of authority figures, and improper emotional expression of frustration. One of the critical problems with this mothering style is that the child spends a lot of time with his or her mother. The best friend mother is involved in her children's life on a peer level, not on a parental level. The loss of a parent, even though she is physically in your life, is a serious developmental crisis, though it tends to be dismissed as a minor problem in a child's life and future. Children know instinctively when they aren't in a safe emotional relationship and when they aren't protected by their mother. These children will make behavioral, mental, and emotional adjustments in order to serve their mother and gain her approval and love. But the outcome of the loss of a mother will be anger, frustration, and a deep sense of abandonment.

The mother-child friendship will eventually end in a dramatic manner with a painful outcome. There is no natural place for the relationship to grow other than the child continuing to put his or her life, dreams, and passions on hold. Daughters and sons who are their mother's best friend have problems moving out and beyond this role into adult intimate relationships. For instance, the twenty-four-year-old child must separate from his peer support role with his mother, or he will be unable to move forward in his life, relationships, career, and emotional growth.

How do you know if you and your mother were or are best friends? Consider the following questions and how you feel and have experienced your mother-daughter/son relationship. Don't dismiss any thoughts or what appear to be random ideas about you and your mother. This uncovering, exploratory process is designed to reveal your blind spots and legacy of emotional issues. Many adults find this mothering style difficult to understand because it combines peer friendship with being a loving daughter or son. The conflict is in a child's separating his core feelings from how he should be a good friend to his mother. Good friends don't question their friends? Wrong! A good friend does question and is honest about the relationship.

The Best Friend List

__ Did you or do you consider your mother your best friend?

__ How did it feel being your mother's closest friend when your friends didn't have the same type of relationship with their mothers?

__ Do you resent that you were your mother's best friend and she wasn't yours in return?

__ Do you, as a daughter, feel that your mother competes with you?

__ Does your mother dislike all of your girlfriends or partners?

__ Do you have a fear of rejection?

__ How much emotional time do you spend concerned about people or friends leaving your life?

__ Have you been or are you uncomfortable with the personal things that your mother shares with you about her life, relationships, and feelings?

__ Does your relationship with your mother feel dependent and/or an emotional burden and/or a huge problem for you?

__ How do you manage your mother's emotional need for you to be her playmate, friend, and confidante?

__ Do you have frequent emotional outbursts with your mother?

__ How much of your life do you put on hold in order to remain your mother's best friend?

__ Do you tend to feel lonely, unloved, and underappreciated in your relationships?

__ Does your mother demand your attention and time? If you aren't able to give her your time and energy, does she resent you or does she understand?

__ Do you have difficulty expressing your emotional needs, desires, and hopes to your partner or intimate friend?

__ Do you feel anxiety, panic, or fear if you don't speak with your mother during the day or night?

__ What is something you have always wanted emotionally or psychologically from your mother?

This list of questions is designed to widen your perspective and create a deeper and more comprehensive understanding of your mother-child relationship. Many mothers, when confronted angrily by their daughters and sons for being a "friend" instead of a "mother," are in complete shock and disbelief. One daughter, Marissa, age forty-one, explained to me that she felt like a victim when the issue of friendship was addressed. Marissa said, "It is like my mother committed a felony or emotional betrayal and wondered why the victim is upset with her. Mother is clueless about why I am furious with her." Adult children constantly tell me that they don't understand why they are so angry and upset with their mother. Their feelings seem to be unrelated to their childhood and the long-term connection to it. All these daughters and sons know is that they are angry with their mother and feel that she is an emotional drain on their life. Simultaneously, they deeply care about their mother and are unable to have a calm and appropriate relationship with her. Of course, there are adult children who are selfish, who were treated properly while growing up and now don't want the burden of an elderly parent. But that is not what we're discussing here.

Consider that maybe your friendship with your mother wasn't in your best interest or that the emotional responsibility wasn't what you needed growing up. The guilt, fear, and emotional strain of being your mother's best friend wasn't necessary for your personal growth and development. What questions or statements in this chapter have struck an emotional chord in you? Consider why and how that question or questions accurately describe your life both past and present. This new way of thinking is quite different and scary for many adult children. It may feel wrong, bad, or phony to examine your mother-child dynamic. But to re-create your emotional legacy and relationship model, it is necessary to fully understand the "fallout" from your mother.

FRIENDSHIP STORY

Kerri and Nicole: I met an anxious woman named Kerri. Her story started eight years prior to our first meeting. At that time she was forty-three years old and a mother of two teenage daughters (thirteen and eighteen). She was married, self-employed (movie script writer), and a very capable woman. Kerri and her oldest daughter, Nicole, a senior in high school, were like sisters. They would talk all night about boys, Nicole's friends, and the constant drama that teenagers create and encounter prior to leaving for college. Nicole was planning on going to college at New York University in the fall. Kerri became very depressed about three months before Nicole was to leave for college. Three weeks before Nicole left, Kerri admitted to her that she didn't know how she was going to live without her daughter around as her closest friend. Nicole immediately withdrew from school and enrolled in the local community college. Nicole never moved away and transferred to a local university two years later. She commuted to college all four years and then got a job ten minutes away from her mother's house. Nicole, at age twenty-six, hadn't moved out of her mother's house and acted as if she was the parent and her mother the younger daughter. Nicole never referred to her home as her parents' house; it was always her and mother's house. Nicole's younger sister and father weren't part of the close friendship bond that enveloped her and her mother.

Kerri came to therapy when her husband, Stan, threatened to divorce her. The reason for the ultimatum was that Kerri was living her life through her daughter, and Stan felt powerless to do anything about it. Stan told me the preceding story with great concern for his daughter and wife. Kerri admitted the following, "I have always feared that Nicole and I wouldn't be close friends when she left for college or moved away. I have had this need to be close to her since she was born. We have always been close. She is my best friend. I know that Stan feels left out but I need this girl-to-girl relationship. It's a woman thing."

Stan got up while Kerri was speaking and put his hand up to stop her. "I have had it with this girl talk, friendship excuse. Nicole hates having to be her mother's best friend. She doesn't feel she can move away or get married. Kerri doesn't believe it and insists on still speaking with Nicole three to four times a day. Kerri isn't a mother to Nicole, she is a sorority sister and needs to stop it. In fact, Nicole wanted us to do this meeting because she doesn't think Kerri will listen to her."

Kerri and Stan agreed that it would be better for Nicole to come to therapy, to voice her concerns in a neutral setting. I asked Nicole, who was her best friend?

Nicole said the following:

I am my mother's friend, confidante, and sole emotional support system. She tells me everything. I know about my parents' marriage, sex life, finances. I know that my dad is threatening to divorce my mother because of our relationship. I can't have my own life. We have been this way since middle school and it has become more intense as I get older. I feel guilty if I don't call my mother and I hate to call my mother. I am always angry with her or we are having a fight of some sort. My dad and sister aren't even part of our relationship. It's me and my mother. My dad has promised me he will pay for me to move to New York and get a master's degree. My dad wants me to go back to N.Y.U. and get a master's degree, since I didn't go because of my mother. I think my mother would divorce my dad if he did that but I really like the idea.

David and Dana: I met David when his two younger sisters brought him to my office for an emergency family therapy session—during the Thanksgiving holiday. David, a young man in his middle thirties, told me the following without my having to ask any questions:

> Dr. P, my mother (Dana) drives me crazy. She is always complaining that I abandoned her and moved to Wyoming without her permission. I wanted a fresh start and I had to move someplace. I wasn't doing anything productive in Orange County other than surfing and smoking marijuana all day. We now talk only three times a week. Before, she wanted me to call every day and I almost went broke doing it. I haven't had any girlfriends that my mother has liked, never. I am engaged and I will not tell her, because she will find fault with Linda. My mom will not take control of her life and do what she should do. Instead she will bug me and want to know all about my life. I feel very responsible for her and guilty if I don't call her daily. I am now sober and working full time for the first time in my life. I know that without having to be my mother's husband, brother, partner, and emotional support, my life is much easier. I still struggle every day with feeling like I abandoned her and moved away. I was dying, living near my mother. She was constantly in my life, I had no peace. She does this same emotional thing with my two sisters too. They haven't moved away yet. My father is out of the loop, he thinks my mother is crazy. I think that is why she is so dependent on me and my sisters. We all feel it. My mother isn't a mother, she is like a dependent child.

David related further that ever since he could remember, his mother had been especially close to him and his two sisters, more so than his friends' mothers. David believes that since he is the only son, his mother is much more emotionally dependent on and possessive of him than his sisters. Yet his sisters also feel that they are responsible for their mother's life. All three children feel that their mother is an emotional burden on them. They all resent that Dana is always emotionally needy and demanding of their time and attention. David knows that if he doesn't give his mother enough attention, she will become very punitive and vengeful toward him. He moved away three years ago unannounced to make an emotional and physical break from her. Since that time, he founded and developed a thriving construction business and has a steady girlfriend (marriage pending) for the first time since high school. David and his sisters all struggle with being supportive of their mother without being consumed by her.

MOM'S COMMON FRIEND

These two short stories may seem unrealistic, but they are true and actually quite universal. It is a very common phenomenon that daughters, sons, and mothers struggle with and strive for a balanced, appropriate, and healthy parent-child relationship. Mothers of the best friend style, regardless of their child's gender, have the constant psychological struggle of satisfying their own unmet emotional desires through their child. Daughters and sons may react differently to their mother, but the underlying issues, pressures, panic, anger, frustration, dependence, and guilt are all from the same source: *Mother*.

No child is spared the ongoing conflict of an emotionally dependent mother when she is a friend and confidante. Nicole, David, and his two sisters have the same mother factor issue of how to love their mother when they feel enormous amounts of resentment and rage toward her for her dependence on them. The key for all four of these adult children and anyone with a best friend mother is the ability to move past the feelings of guilt, anger, and abandonment. These powerful emotions, left unresolved, begin to fester and can completely derail a young man's or woman's entire life. I've seen men and women in their sixties and seventies still struggling with the same mother legacy issues that Nicole and David are faced with in their twenties and thirties.

Both of these mothers are married, however, it is important to note that *relationship status (married, divorced, single, adoptive, widowed) does not predetermine a mother's style of mothering.* It would be far too easy and convenient to point to a marriage status as the most accurate predictor of a mothering style and emotional capacity. Rather, it is the mother-daughter relationship from the prior generation that is the most accurate indicator of future emotional functioning. It is the unmet emotional needs, unresolved feelings, emotional development, maturity, attachment history/style, self-esteem issues, and understanding of motherhood by the daughters—now mothers—that shape today's mothers. These factors are the most precise pieces that will combine together to create a woman's mothering style, her emotional bonds, and how she lives out her legacy.

The best friend mother is a combination of many unmet emotional issues that demand attention and nurturing by her children. David and Nicole are excellent examples of children who learned how to nurture, show empathy, and be compassionate people as a result of their mother. The problem is that they can't live or fully function without having to shoulder the endless task of taking care of their mother's emotional life. These two adults represent a large segment of the population who are terribly conflicted with feelings of rage, resentment, guilt, and sorrow for their mother's life and emotional state. It is critical for all sons and daughters of this mothering style to emotionally develop beyond the limited circle of caretaking, which creates a sense of neglect and abandonment in them. These children grow up to become adults who feel emotionally neglected. It is the naturally occurring roadblocks of anger, a sense of abandonment, and a sense of emotional neglect that cause smart, creative, and fun-loving young adults to get stuck in a bitter, negative approach to life and relationships.

MOTHERLESS DAUGHTERS AND SONS

If there are three emotional issues that can stop the promise and potential of any son or daughter, it is these three: anger, abandonment, and neglect. It is tough to describe your childhood as "motherlessness" when you saw and lived with your mother every day of your life. *Feeling and being motherless has nothing to do with the physical presence of your mother.* This is more of an abstract description than a literal one. Sons and daughters who have experienced "motherlessness" know it and don't want to argue about their mother's physical presence. Clearly from the stories in this chapter, we can see that physical absence isn't the problem between these mothers and their children.

We have discussed the weaknesses, the many side effects, and core problems of the best friend style of mothering, which can also be described as "absent" mothering. Adult children of this style of mothering need to stop a potential lifelong sense of bitterness and failed adult relationships from occurring. They need to take a big step toward healing and creating a new emotional legacy and relationship style in their adult life. One of the biggest roadblocks to healing is the "guilt factor." Adult children will take a bullet in the head rather than say a critical word about their mother or allow anyone else to describe her in a negative light. Moreover, the classic psychological resistance/reason to deny your childhood pain and struggle is that it will metaphorically drown you. Strong emotions come and go, but your emotional wounds will only worsen with time. You recall from earlier in the book that our emotional pain is the impetus for change. Your pain and anger will spread throughout your life if it isn't addressed by you. Consider the following "motherless" list and rate yourself. This exercise isn't about finger-pointing, accusing, or blaming your mother. If you don't do this, it will never get done. No one can do it for you.

The Motherless List

___ Have you ever considered yourself a motherless daughter or son? If so, why?

___ Do you find yourself craving and seeking out emotionally "safe" and nurturing mother figures in your life?

___ Do you desire a loving and understanding maternal adult/ mentor in your life?

___ Do you have older female role models, aunts, and maternal friends who fill in the emotional gaps in your "motherlessness"?

___ Do you have feelings of guilt if you don't give your mother all your emotional attention?

___ Do you have feelings of abandonment and unexplained anger in your intimate relationships?

___ Do you get angry at your mother for her constant emotional demands on your life?

___ Does your mother expect, assume, and demand that you take emotional care of her?

___ Does your mother resent your intimate partners, lovers, or husband/wife?

These best friend/"motherless" questions are very powerful. How many of these questions did you answer with a "yes"? If you answered any of them affirmatively, you are coping with a best friend mother issue. Many of your emotional choices are motivated by your natural and appropriate need for a loving, supportive mother. We are all wired to need an empathic, supportive mother and an approval-giving father. How these connections evolve over our life cycle determine to a large degree our adult relationships, careers, parenting, and sense of self. If this wasn't true or necessary, adults wouldn't spend their entire lives seeking out these core mother/father emotional ingredients. Many of your unconscious and conscious choices, social/intimate partners, and selection of friends are driven by your need to have positive, nondemanding female energy in your life. We all have a natural need to have positive, supportive, approval-giving, unconditionally loving women in our life.

MOVING ANGER, ABANDONMENT, AND NEGLECT → OUT

Taking anger and resentment out of your relationships is crucial for your present and future. Nothing in your life will flow, develop, or come peacefully into your mind if you're dragging around anger chained to your emotions. Anger is incompatible with high-functioning productivity and loving relationships. *Unresolved anger has the ability to stop and destroy your heart's deepest wishes, hopes, and potential.* The ability to function at your potential in any area of your life is enhanced by your ability to resolve these relationship-killing, self-sabotaging emotions. Although it may not seem true on the surface of your life, your selection of partners and friends, your social circle, and your emotional functioning have all been shaped by your mother's absence in your life. The same holds true if your mother was actively participating in your life. At this point in your life, you know the difference!

This premise seems more palpable if your relationship with your mother was strained, hateful, bitter, and conflicted. As much as you may consciously reject your mother's absence from your life, you are still under its sway and pull. Most adult children of best friend mothers have a tremendous amount of anger, which, unfortunately, is usually directed toward other people—their children, friends, family—and, of course, themselves. It is only wise and prudent to deal with your anger in order to stop the ongoing emotional, mental, and personal roadblocks that it inherently creates and maintains. Your entire emotional functioning is influenced by your anger and resentment. It is essential to remember that your anger is only a smoke screen for the core emotional injuries that the best friend style of mothering creates.

The following list is designed to help you quickly identify some of your deeply buried emotions, feelings, thoughts, and memories that still actively influence your present-day relationships and life.

EMOTIONALLY ABSENT— THE BEST FRIEND MOTHER CHECKLIST

Abandonment Issues

__ Your mother physically left the family because of divorce or some other type of marital/personal problem.

__ Your mother spent large amounts of time away from you.

__ Your mother pursued her own personal interests, hobbies, and goals away from you.

__ You were unable to emotionally connect or bond with your mother.

__ You became your mother's best friend in order to spend time with her and gain her interest and affection.

__ Your mother always chose to do things that were for her benefit or interest.

__ You were scared of losing your mother's attention, love, and approval so you focused solely on her life.

Neglect Issues

__ Your mother paid little or no attention when you had something important to do, say, or experience.

__ Your mother ignored or did not notice your requests regarding emotional support, feedback, and attention.

__ Your mother wasn't aware of your personal concerns, fears, and emotional issues.

___ Your mother wasn't aware of your disappointments, celebrations, or regular activities.

___ Your mother wasn't aware of your personal struggles, issues, or problems as a child, teenager, and adult.

___ Your mother was very consumed with her own emotional issues and wasn't aware of your "cries" for help, support, and love.

___ You engaged in drug use, poor school performance, pregnancies, sexual promiscuity, criminal behavior, and/or reckless choices as attempts to engage your mother's interest and concern for your life.

___ Your mother was more interested in being your friend than being a mother, limit setter, role model, and mentor.

Anger Issues

___ You scare people when you get mad or express your disappointment.

___ You feel "out of control" when you get upset.

___ You have been told by friends, partners, and family that you have anger management issues.

___ You feel constantly angry and easily agitated for minor infractions or trivial matters.

___ You don't like the amount of negative emotion that you express toward people.

___ You resent that your mother didn't participate in your life as a mother but as a friend.

___ Your mother was more interested in her life than yours.

___ The only attention you received from your mother was giving her support, love, and approval.

These lists contain only a few of the factors, issues, experiences, and painful situations that go into the mix of creating an angry son or daughter. The combination of feeling abandoned, neglected, and angry creates the huge ball of fire in a son's or daughter's life. Years of accumulation of these chronic painful and disappointing events produce an angry personality and an angry emotional legacy. All of your relationships are tainted with this underlying rage and frustration. There is nothing in your life that isn't touched, influenced, or negatively impacted by your sense of "motherlessness."

YOUR BEST STEP #1—
ANGER → UNDERSTANDING → EMPATHY

Acknowledging your anger is one of the most powerful steps of defusing it and reducing your emotional pain. This may sound elementary, but people with anger issues, problems, and outbursts aren't open to acknowledging it. If you wonder about your expression of anger, ask your close friends, children, and partner. They will immediately give you the answer you don't want: Yes, you are angry! Admitting you have anger issues allows the defensive angry wall around your life to come down.

Your cognitive and emotional understanding is the key to resolving and putting into perspective all of your emotional pain. Accepting that your mother wasn't or isn't able to give you the love, support, and guidance that you crave allows you to move forward. Your mother, because of her own emotional shortcomings and unresolved issues, wasn't able to give you the maternal nurturing that you needed. Her actions weren't malicious or intended to wound you. Your mother just didn't have the ability or insight to be the mother you wanted or needed. Forgive the crude analogy, but you can't resent a cat for not being a dog. The analogy applies to your mother. The definition of empathy is accepting who and what your mother was and is today (living or not). Empathy also means developing your ability to view your mother's life from her perspective and emotional state. Empathy also allows you to understand your pain and helps you not to be critical or dismissive of it. I sincerely mean this: *If your mother could have done a better job mothering you, she would have. It's that simple.* Mothers love their sons and daughters. They may not have had the ability or insight to show it, but they sincerely did and do. Finally, I have never met a mother who didn't love her children and want the best for them, even though her behavior indicated otherwise. Your development of empathy will directly reduce your anger to the same degree.

YOUR BEST STEP #2— CREATE YOUR OWN MOTHERHOOD

It is important to develop your own network of loving, supportive, understanding, and nurturing women in your life. Accepting your mother's limitations and emotional needs allows you to discover your needs and wants. You have unconsciously created a network of women who support and love you already. This is true of sons and daughters. Begin to understand why you have and need these women in your life. All addictions, self-destructive behaviors, and choices are driven by the need for love, acceptance, and emotional support. It is the loss of these emotional supports that causes sons and daughters to fill the void with compulsive/addictive behaviors. These behaviors are a distraction from the pain and loss of nurturing. The lack or abundance of these natural mothering qualities is the substance and foundation of your emotional life and legacy. Learn what the substance and issues of your emotional life are. What is the one thing you want in your life (that is not material)?

Knowing what you want, have, and need allows you to create relationships that foster your growth and emotional health. Daughters and sons need to have a nurturing support system to function at their fullest capacity in friendships, business, marriage, parenting, and family life, and with themselves. Lastly, it is appropriate and necessary for you to know and comprehend what you lacked with your mother. Then you can understand how to resolve and create a life that meets those fundamental human needs.

YOUR BEST STEP #3—UNDERSTAND YOUR OWN EMOTIONAL NEEDS

There is an old adage that if you know what you want, then you can get it. That truism applies here. Take an inventory of the emotional and psychological issues that are most important to you. Knowing what you crave, need, and desire is critical to resolving your emotional wounds and anger. Anger is only a cover-up for your own unmet emotional needs and unfulfilled desires. Don't fool yourself that your intense fear of abandonment or panic about failure isn't connected to your unmet emotional needs and self-esteem. All of your psychological fears and concerns have their basis in your emotional life. Educate yourself on the issues that are of interest to you. Those interests are the tip of the iceberg to further understanding your emotional process and legacy. It is never a sign of immaturity or weaknesses to know and develop ways to meet your needs.

Make a list of what you emotionally desire and want in a romantic relationship even if you are married with four kids. The needs, wishes, and longings we have in our intimate relationships or potential ones generally mirror those we had with our mother. Intimate relationships have long been considered the adult place to repair and reparent ourselves and to heal emotionally. This is absolutely true about intimate partners, romantic encounters, marriage relationships, and close friendships. It is important to remember that any close relationship, regardless of its context, is a place to allow your emotional legacy to grow and heal. These emotionally safe connections are the lifeblood of our existence and human expression. Without close, loving, supportive, nurturing relationships, people are isolated and psychologically damaged by the absence of such connections.

YOUR BEST STEP #4—
KNOW YOUR OWN EMOTIONAL TRIGGERS

Begin the path to fully understanding the core issues that set you off emotionally and that ignite your anger. You need to be consciously alert and aware to fully comprehend your cycle of anger. You no longer have the luxury to blow up and then claim that you didn't mean to. Those disclaimers are excuses to continue being a "time bomb," to be emotionally out of control, and to be emotionally dangerous. Anger is the quickest way to lose control and do and say things that are permanently damaging and self-destructive. When you become enraged with your partner, children, friends, and colleagues, there is usually something much deeper in you that is being touched rather than the current circumstances. It might feel and seem like the current event or issue at hand, but it isn't. Your unresolved, residual anger will always come out in your present-day relationships.

To get out of this cycle, you must make a list of three or four things that clearly are your "hottest" buttons and personal issues. This list needs to be written down and thoroughly considered. The list automatically creates responsibility on your part for your emotional behavior. For that reason, it will serve as a deterrent. You will soon discover that nearly all of those present-day issues will have their roots in one of the three triggers—abandonment, neglect, and being unloved/rejected. These three core emotions can show up in a thousand different gestures and circumstances. You need to be the expert about your own issues and take full control of your triggers.

Chapter 7

THE COMPLETE MOTHER

Your Mother Factor with a Compassionate Flavor

I don't know what I would do without my mother. She has been my role model and mentor. She is an amazing woman. I have learned the value of communication, mentoring, compassion, and how to handle life's adversities. I would be a lost soul without her.

—Ed, age fifty-two

My mother has been the bedrock of my life. I feel very lucky to have such a great mother and mentor. My mother has always encouraged me to follow my dreams and not allow anyone to put me down because I am a woman. I always know that my mother can give me the advice or wisdom necessary to handle any problem in my life.

—Maria, age thirty-three

THE NEW MILLENNIUM MOTHER

The complete style of mothering encompasses the best parts of the first four mothering styles plus many added features, insights, and abilities. This is a mother who clearly knows what she is doing with her son or daughter. There is no lack of insight or empathy; she is emotionally balanced. The complete mother fully understands the incredible role she plays and influence she will have on her children now and for the rest of their lives. This mother has the ability to figure out what her daughters or sons need, want, and desire, and she helps them to get it or creates the opportunity for it. This isn't a super mom or a "saint," who makes no mistakes or tries to be perfect. She is a woman who could be twice divorced, widowed, unmarried, single, gay, artificially inseminated, or married with seven children. Her life circumstances don't dictate or determine how she is going to be a mother to her children. Education level, age, economics, ethnicity, or personal relationships don't create emotional or social barriers to being the mother of the twenty-first century. Those self-imposed limitations aren't part of her psychological understanding and experience of motherhood. This is a woman who is committed to motherhood, regardless of her career or outside responsibilities. She is a "mother's mother." The other mothers in the neighborhood, at work, and in her social circle will seek out her advice, support, and guidance. The other mothers know that this woman psychologically "gets" the mothering job. Her understanding is based on her own complete mothering style and secure emotional legacy. This mother may or may not have had a horrible, conflicted, self-absorbed mother, but she has used her childhood as a springboard to being the complete mother.

Regardless of her own mother-daughter relationship, this woman, mother, and partner has the keen insight and acute awareness to not miss the opportunity of a lifetime and actively be part of her children's lives. All the kids in the neighborhood want her as their own mother. She is a patient, loving, and nurturing soul. Everyone craves her time and understanding. In the workplace she is the ideal co-worker, supervisor, or company executive. People are comfortable in her presence and respect her opinion.

The complete mothering style probably represents about 10 percent of all mother-daughter/son relationships. It is very important to understand how this mother is able to manage, securely connect with, consistently bond with, and emotionally empower her children so they can excel. These children of the complete mother know they are fortunate to have a mother who can see them as individuals and help them discover their individual paths and dreams. The complete mother is capable of nurturing her daughters and sons so they can successfully separate and form their own identities. Many mothers aren't aware of this all-important step toward maturity and don't prepare themselves or their children to move forward into adult life.

The natural process of separation/individuation between the mother and child starts when the child is about age fifteen and is fully completed when the child is about twenty-five. Unfortunately, for most mother-daughters/sons relationships, this process becomes severely problematic. All the unresolved emotional issues, unmet needs, lack of developmental insight, and fear of abandonment come into play for all involved. The reason the teen years are typically viewed as a "living hell" by mothers is that this separation/individuation process is in full gear. All the unresolved emotional issues and psychological concerns are on the table.

This dual separation process is for both mothers and their children. Neither sons nor daughters have an easy time with this very important life-changing event. Typically, the dual process will be uneventful and conflict-free if the mother was able to undergo the same process with her mother fairly seamlessly when she was a teenager to twenty-something. More often, however, the process was incomplete, and the mother is still separating from her mother while her daughter and son are attempting to do the same with her. The mother will then feel abandoned by her children because she never fully established her own identity and mothering style. The complete mothering style is embodied in a woman who was able to successfully complete her separation and individuation process from the previous mother-daughter generation. Her emotional clarity concerning this process allows for her daughter and son to navigate the challenges of becoming simultaneously independent and interdependent. These children don't have the added burden of attempting to help their mother emotionally separate while they are also attempting to separate from her.

The complete mothering style prepares her daughters and sons from an early age to embrace their life and to take the necessary developmental steps. One reason that this mothering style is called "complete" is that the mother has the ability to assist her children achieve their own sense of autonomy while still remaining emotionally connected to her. One of the hallmarks of being a successful mother is allowing your children to separate and form their own identity in late adolescence. It is crucial for all daughters and sons to take this step in order to function in adulthood with a secure identity and stable emotional attachment style. Each mothering style will either hinder or facilitate this all-important life transition. No one can live at home forever, even though many young adults choose to live with their parents until their early thirties. The reason for some emotionally late bloomers isn't because rents are so high or they can't find a roommate, it is the emotional enmeshment and underdeveloped identity in the mother-daughter/mother-son relationship.

ELEMENTS OF THE COMPLETE MOTHERING STYLE—WHO IS SHE?

The following list highlights some of the critical qualities and nurturing traits that this mother possesses. These qualities, behaviors, and nurturing actions can be learned and become an active part of your emotional life. It is possible to develop these traits and incorporate them into your relationships and sense of self. There is an ongoing academic debate that you can't learn or develop maternal instinct skills, empathy, and compassionate behavior. You either have these abilities or you do not. The argument is completely irrational. If you learned to neglect, ignore, and reject your own feelings, there is no reason why you can't then relearn how to nurture and be empathic to yourself and the people in your life. These skills are necessary for any us to further our own emotional legacy and improve our quality of life.

Your Mother in Action List

- The complete mothering style creates sons and daughters who have the psychological ability, insight, clarity, and wisdom to understand, respect, and appreciate that other people, colleagues, and family members all have their own perspectives. This understanding is empathy in action.
- The complete mother teaches her children by example to have tolerance for human differences. The ability to accept and tolerate personal, intimate, and professional differences is critical to this mother-child relationship. The tolerance for differences is the ability to express compassion for others. There is no personal investment in being "right." People are viewed from a larger perspective and with the understanding that actual differences are natural in all types of relationship settings. Differences aren't viewed by the complete mother as threatening or something to fight over.
- The complete mother of the new millennium is emotionally capable of appreciating other people's feelings, actions, decisions, and choices that are different from her own. The lack of negative judgment and insecurity allows for strong and secure emotional bonds/attachments to be formed and maintained. This emotionally intelligent position is taught to her children through mentoring.
- The complete, compassionate mother demonstrates leadership qualities, including her ability to say no to peer pressure, to her children, and to other family members. Her

resolve is real and is exhibited in the face of potential consequences: personal, social, professional, and romantic. The
ability to set personal and relationship emotional limits and
boundaries is vital to all relationships.

- This mother teaches her children to trust their instincts,
  internal feelings/beliefs, and thoughts. Over time, these
  habits create self-confidence and a strong sense of self-
  worth. These strengths allow for young adults to venture out
  into the world with courage.
- Sons and daughters of this mother feel loved and understood. The sense of understanding and of their mother's
  ongoing support allows them to take risks, create relationship opportunities, and emotionally connect and bond
  without reservations or fear. Regardless of the profession,
  all business is conducted through secure relationships.
- Daughters and sons of the complete mother are able to
  create, maintain, and foster long-term professional, social,
  and intimate relationships. They don't harbor long-term
  grudges or resentments.
- Daughters and sons of the complete mothering style are able
  to achieve success and completion during the dual separa-
  tion/individuation process. Their mother has the prior life
  experience to allow her children to separate and create their
  own identities.

The inner confidence daughters and sons get from their
mother is transmitted to them every day of their life. They have a
large amount of inner confidence and emotional stability to meet
any crisis or life challenge. What is very striking with this type of
mother compared with the other four types is the lack of unmet
emotional needs, little-to-no unresolved issues, and little-to-no residual anger/resentment. More succinctly, the point is the absence
of "baggage." This keeps all the conflicted emotions that go with
family history from being dragged into the present day. There isn't

a backlog of old problems that keep the present day clouded with despair, anxiety, fear, or hopelessness.

The central problem with an old emotional issue is that it keeps reappearing as a new one in every relationship, conflict, and misunderstanding. Free-floating anger, resentment, emotional insecurity, attention-getting behavior, perfectionism, and approval-seeking behaviors aren't part of this woman's/mother's life or relationships. Instead, she has energy, time, and interest to develop positive, life-affirming qualities, which include, along with the ones listed above, strong self-esteem, empathy, compassion, courage, a forgiving attitude, stability, secure personal and intimate relationships, and a wide circle of friends.

Many would consider the complete mother as the new female role model for women in the twenty-first century. This is a woman who can work outside the home or choose not to with no sense of guilt or social shame. She isn't controlled by arbitrary rules or old social roles that aren't appropriate for her life. The emotional approach of this mother is basic: the world is a safe place. Her personal needs, wants, and desires will be met and understood. There isn't a sense of deprivation, anxiety, or panic that if she doesn't have the right job, the right friends, and the right clothes, she is worthless or "not good enough." These types of fears or insecurities aren't part of her relationships or emotional interactions or connections with people. The children of the complete mothering style are able to grow up to pursue their dreams, regardless of the negative peer pressure to stay a certain way or conform to the norm. These adults already have the approval and support needed to be the person they desire to be.

NURTURING 101—"WHAT IS IT ALL ABOUT?"

When people are asked what a good mother is, their responses are usually along the lines of, "She is loving and nurturing," "She is giving and patient," and "She can be emotionally understanding." These positive answers are all essentially extensions of the same idea and train of thought. It is a fact that motherhood is fundamentally about nurturing. How a mother nurtures is as creative as the woman doing it. There is no particular pattern or way to nurture, but there is a critical component: *empathy*. The principle of nurturing/empathy is as fundamental to mothering as water is to fish. Mothering is all about nurturing, and the two are inseparable and necessary for all daughters and sons, regardless of their age. Nothing feels better than the emotional touch of understanding and acceptance that a mother or mother figure can give to her children.

Nurturing is technically the direct application and use of empathy. Empathy is the ability to focus on, understand, comfort, soothe, listen to, and emotionally connect with a daughter or son. Being empathic is using your emotional ability to take in valuable nonverbal information, body language, and facial expressions, and then responding appropriately. Mothers who are empathically connected to their children know what is upsetting them before they speak a word.

Adults who are empathic can be described as attuned to their environment and the people around them. This means these sons and daughters have an emotional presence of mind and are aware of the emotional climate surrounding them. These daughters and sons have the ability to read someone, understand their current emotional state, and appropriately respond to the need or issue at hand. They were mentored as they grew up and have the capacity to share their knowledge with others. Nurturing creates in the recipients the desire to give back what they have experienced. There is no withholding or emotional scarcity for these daughters and sons. Their behavior is based on their emotional abundance. They have a full reserve of positive emotional experiences and beliefs, as well as a strong sense of self to reach out to the people in their life. These adults had the constant experience of good mothering, which was always empathically attuned and nurturing.

For some adult children, it can be pretty disheartening to read about the complete mothering style. Nevertheless, no one—no mother or adult child—is doomed or sentenced to continue the same frustrating, depressing, and nonproductive behaviors that have compromised their life up to now. We can all change. Regardless of your mothering style, remember that roughly 90 percent of us didn't have this "complete" woman as our mother. Yet we all have potential in our emotional life to create and have these types of secure loving relationships. The key is to better understand how nurturing and empathy can work in your adult life today with your closest friends, family, and partner.

EMPATHIC ATTUNEMENT—HOW IT WORKS

The first step in becoming the parent, adult, partner, colleague, and friend that you've always wanted to be is to understand the role of empathic attunement, which is the key to any successful, high-functioning relationship. Empathetic attunement is one of the primary functions of the complete mother. The complete mother has the intuitive nature and awareness of how to support and emotionally attach to her children, regardless of their age, on a day-to-day basis. This constant secure emotional attachment, bond, and connection allows daughters and sons to develop their own sense of self-love, self-worth, and relationship competence. *It is important to remember that a child's feeling of being loved is more than how he or she is actually loved.* Children, teenagers, and adults will naturally develop secure emotional attachments based on how much they *feel* loved and cared for. Children know this by how their mother consistently took time to really listen to and to empathize with how bad their feelings were hurt in the fourth grade at recess or how scared they were about going on their first job interview after college. Children can tell if they are loved by their mother's nonverbal gestures and nurturing-empathetic behaviors.

Second, the best example of how to be empathically attuned is the ability to share in others' excitement when they get a job promotion, make a marriage announcement, find a new home, or when their child is accepted at a desired school. And you share their exhilaration even though you're feeling depressed or emotionally flat. The ability to join other people wherever they are emotionally is a great ability and gift. The complete mother does this so consistently that her children aren't even aware of her own mood swings or feelings. Children typically don't need to know about their mother's internal struggles or feelings. Mothers who believe that their children should know everything about their life automatically recruit their daughter or son to become their emotional partner. The absence of emotional limit setting isn't empathy but a dependent mother-child relationship. Children of the complete mothering style are very sensitive to others' feelings and emotions. They aren't dependent on their mother to know how and what to feel. Her ability to separate herself emotionally and keep adult personal issues out of their world is good mothering and necessary. Children will learn about their mother's life as they grow up, but they first must learn about their own world and how it works.

The complete mother repeatedly connects on the same level as her children. She communicates the invaluable sense of safety and love to them. We all know what a painful and disappointing experience it is when an important person (mother, partner, friend) in our life does not intuit or empathically share our excitement about a particular event or accomplishment. The emotional "miss" is painful and causes us to rethink whether we should share our excitement with that person ever again. Daughters/sons who repeatedly experience this type of emotional loss and disappointment with their mother will eventually stop experiencing positive feelings toward her. The emotional letdown is so painful that it is avoided at all costs. Over time, these types of emotional injuries cumulate into an angry daughter/son or a self-destructive pattern of behavior. Children of the complete mother don't have these emotional wounds or experiences.

Third, the complete mothering style focuses on the daughter/ son as individuals, not always on their behavior. The core foundation to any healthy relationship, regardless of its context, is the ability to always connect with the person, not the behavior. You see the individual as a complete person who isn't defined by one action. This is especially helpful when a son/daughter is a teenager, a friend disappoints you, or something negative happens. The message that this mother sends to her daughter/son, friends, partners, and colleagues is that they are important to her. The proper consistent focus allows both parties to have an ongoing open line of communication with an uninterrupted emotional connection.

Fourth, let's keep in mind that the complete mother is not without failure, moments of emotional outbursts, or negative feelings. Her children always know that she loves them and cares about them, even if she misunderstands certain situations and their behavior. This is especially true when children are between the ages of thirteen to thirty, when a daughter/son will have mood swings, emotional meltdowns, and unreasonable arguments, which can be very unpredictable. These daughters/sons, whether living at home or three thousand miles away, know that they have their mother's guidance and love to carry them through rough and uncertain times. The inner confidence is the internalization of their mother's nurturance and empathy in their mind and spirit.

The fifth and final point to the complete mothering style is that her children have a positive internalized picture, emotionally empowering experiences, and a constant emotional memory to draw on for support, guidance, understanding, and compassion. These wonderful recurring themes of nurturing and empathy are part of these daughters' and sons' minds, emotions, and hearts. We all have an emotional file system that records positive events, good experiences, and nurturing beliefs. When a challenge or change comes that is stressful or anxiety-producing, a son or daughter who has these supportive beliefs and feelings stored away will automatically use them to get through and cope with the event or situation.

BLENDING THE COMPLETE MOTHERING STYLE INTO YOUR MOTHER FACTOR

The following list contains some of the ideas and behaviors (empathy, compassion, and responsiveness) that you can incorporate into your mother factor legacy. The list is critical to "softening" your edginess, defensiveness, and angry, unresolved issues of rejection, abandonment, and approval seeking. The following qualities are the things that we all want to strive for and develop in every type of relationship we have and will have in years to come. Your life is in front of you, and putting your old, recycled issues to rest is a worthwhile endeavor and a doable project. These qualities of nurturing, empathy, and compassion aren't sugarcoating a hopeless situation. Rather, they will empower your life, emotions, and relationships in ways you have never imagined. Emotional strength and insight means the ability to reach out to others and connect and bond with them. Being isolated, angry, and emotionally closed off is a "living hell" that many children/adults have endured and don't need anymore.

Everyone needs to feel loved, connected, and supported. These core emotional needs are natural, and we should all have our needs met. The following list is composed of some of the highlights of incorporating the complete mother emotional legacy into your life, relationships, and inner feelings.

The Emotional Growth Process—Seven Steps

1. *Emotional Presence of Mind.* This means knowing what to do emotionally before it happens. You aren't a mind reader,

but you aren't sleepwalking through life either. You will draw on your insight to think ahead of a crisis or a person's needs or wants. You will see ahead of the "curve" what might happen and what needs to be done. You aren't surprised or scared about what could happen in a relationship or situation.

2. *Emotional Climate Awareness.* You will be using your emotional feedback loop to read your partner's, children's, or colleague's verbal and nonverbal messages and all the communication messages that people send. Based on your emotional insight and understanding/compassion, you can say or do what is necessary and helpful. You are constantly taking in information about people's emotional state of mind. You aren't acting codependent, because you will do what is necessary and proper, not cater to whims or mood swings. You know that your son wants to go to his teacher and tell her off, but you help him write a constructive letter instead, allowing him to express his frustration in a more appropriate way.

3. *Emotionally Responsive.* You know how to accurately respond to or address a problem, issue, or crisis with emotional empathy. Your ability to respond emotionally is critical to the use of empathy, compassion, and nurturing. This could mean you will be sitting up all night with your son and his first newborn baby or holding the hand of your elderly, sick parent. Whatever the situation, you are now able to respond. You don't have a lack of emotion or understanding for people's pain, frustration, and panic. You can emotionally join them and be supportive. Your daughter comes home from school in tears about her friends. You will listen to her, and thirty minutes later she will be on the computer talking with them again.

4. *Nurturing.* Nurturing is the ability to react to the circumstances at hand and appropriately manage them. Your nur-

turing actions will comfort and empower your son/ daughter, partner, or the Little League team you coach. You don't rescue people or insult them by nurturing them. Your goal is to help the people in your life feel better about themselves and act upon that confidence. Those actions based on support are very empowering and loving.

5. *No Residual Resentments or Accumulation of Anger/Rage.* You no longer will be carrying grudges or long-standing resentments toward the loved ones in your life. You won't emotionally function from a place of anger/rage. Instead, you will choose to be even-tempered with people. You won't allow anger to take you over and you will avoid allowing misunderstandings to develop. You will be emotionally free from old issues. It takes courage to let go of perceived "wrongs." The choice to let go of past emotional injuries is the sign of mental and emotional health. Living in the past created a depressed personality and a sense of hopelessness.

6. *You are a joiner and supporter.* You aren't reluctant to listen to your colleague express his despair about his potential job loss. You aren't emotionally withholding of your empathy, compassion, and support. It is critical to emotionally join someone wherever they are at that moment. This is one of the strongest and most powerful nurturing gestures you can give a person. It is all about going to the emotional place where your child, partner, or friend is at. People will always remember that you were able to reach out to them in their panic and pain. This action is a classic example of your emotional legacy functioning at its full capacity and strength in relationships.

7. *Accepting of Yourself.* You know that the most important opinion about you is your own. You are teaching others by example that accepting your "perfectly imperfect" traits is very powerful and will create emotional security. No one

holds or has the power to make you feel bad, guilty, or shameful. You are the only one who controls your feelings, emotions, and thoughts. This is the most nurturing thing you can ever do for yourself and others.

These seven traits, qualities, actions, beliefs, and applications of your emotional strength are your incorporating the complete mothering style and taking it to the next generation of children, people, family, friends, and co-workers. Even though approximately 90 percent of us didn't have this type of mothering style, it is possible to have these traits in our relationships and life. These seven actions steps are designed to create a step-by-step road map to developing this type of legacy.

TWO TALES ABOUT MOTHERS AND DAUGHTERS AND SONS

The following are two very emotional stories that need to be told. They represent a silent but serious group of children/adults whose numbers are large but overlooked. The mothers in these two stories aren't perfect and in fact, one isn't even living. I have always wondered how children overcome the death of their mother. Some psychological and mental health experts believe that children under the age of twenty-five—and especially under the age of ten—never emotionally recover from the loss of their mother. These children's lives are permeated with this tragic loss. Nonetheless, those narrow beliefs and old psychological limitations about children are grossly inaccurate. People do recover from being motherless. Though they experience horrendous emotional suffering and often have stories that are beyond belief, many find a path to emotional health and well-being.

It isn't correct to assume that children who are actually motherless (have no mother physically in their life) are automatically sentenced to a life of depression, hopelessness, and despair. This isn't true or accurate. Daughters and sons who have had a taste of nurturing from other female role models can be as happy and productive as any other child. The influence of maternal nurturing has the power to reverse any circumstance or situation for a daughter or son. This is a bold statement, but I have seen this happen time and time again. Remember, being cynical is always based on a limited amount of information and thinly veiled bitterness. Regardless of your life circumstances, emotional setbacks, grieving, mother-child conflict, divorce, or death, it is never too late to change. In my professional, personal, and relational experience, it is the sense of hopelessness and the belief that things will never change that are the biggest hurdles to overcome. Writing this book, I have yet to meet a daughter or son who doesn't want to tell his or her story and how they cope with mother factor issues. People want to live their lives more fully, feel healthier mentally, emotionally connect more effectively, and bond securely. If this weren't true, marriage and remarriage wouldn't be so popular, and the notion of love would be dismissed.

Marie and Alexander

Alexander, thirteen years old, was in the seventh grade when his father was murdered during a bank robbery in Westwood Village, near Los Angeles. Alex's father was doing his banking during lunch and was shot dead at point-blank range. Marie, Alex's mother, spent the next two years working and helping her son grieve the loss of his father. Then the unimaginable happened. Marie was killed on the freeway while driving home from work when Alex was in the ninth grade. Alex was an only child.

I met Alex when he was twenty-seven-years old, working for an investment firm based in New York with offices all around the world. Alex, whose father's family lived in South Africa with no relatives in the United States, had lived with his mother's best friend's family after his mother's death. He came to see me because he felt that he was emotionally frozen. He hadn't cried since his father's funeral and had never cried over his mother's death. Going strictly by appearances, Alex was a "superstar." He graduated from college with a business degree and didn't use drugs or alcohol. Alex was sharp looking, behaved perfectly, and had been a perfect son. The problem was, Alex didn't feel perfect and, in fact, he felt absolutely terrified of any more emotional loss or lost connections.

I asked Alex to tell me about his mother. Alex told me his story with a smile on his face.

> My mother was awesome. She loved and adored me. I always knew even before my dad died that my mother would always take care of me and make sure my world was right. I think that is why twelve years later, I am still waiting for her to come home. I guess with all her love and support, I have been able to go on with my life. I remember my doctor telling me that most kids who lose their mother usually end up on drugs or on medication. I am doing well, considering that both my parents are dead. I had a really good relationship with both my parents while growing up. My dad was a hard worker, very patient and loving, who always coached me in sports. My mother was my emotional rock. She always taught me to be generous and giving to less fortunate people. My parents told me to be a good guy and never take life for granted. My aunt, my mother's best friend whom I lived with, is just like my mother. I am really lucky because I have never felt unloved or like an orphan. My aunt calls me twice a day and she is a bit too much, but I understand. She is only doing what she feels I need.

I asked Alex about his present-day life, relationships, his grief, and his plans for the future.

Alex said:

I have had a few girlfriends. I have been dating someone, Cindy, seriously for two years. She would like to get married and I would also. I have a lot of great friends from childhood, who all knew my parents. I have stayed close to my friends throughout the years. Even though my parents are dead, I had a better relationship with them than most of my friends and buddies from college had with their parents. My guy friends can't get along that well with their mother and most of them didn't even know their father. I am lucky because I have a great memory of my mother. She was always emotionally strong and loving. I always felt cared for, with plenty of attention and time from her. I miss my mother terribly but I don't have bad or guilty feelings about our relationship. I feel that I have a lot to use in my marriage. I just can't cry about losing my mother. Losing my father was awful, he was great too. My mother being dead is still too much for me. I carry her in my heart but I really miss her.

Alex came to see me for a period of time to begin his grieving process about his mother's death. He had meanwhile graduated from college, earned a master's degree in business, and was working full-time. He had a very large network of friends, some of whom were older men and women. Alex functioned at such a high level emotionally, it was stunning. He had no resentment, anger, or fear about being intimately involved with his girlfriend. He had such a positive emotional legacy from his mother factor that his life seemed to be on autopilot. Alex did finally grieve the loss of his mother and then became fearful of losing his strong, emotional connections and friends. Alex's aunt, Yvonne, with whom he had lived during high school, came with Alex to meet me one day.

Yvonne was a very charming, warm, nurturing, and sweet woman. She had a positive energy about her that was very calming and relaxing. Yvonne wanted me to know that Alex was the most exceptional human she had ever met.

Alex, in spite of losing both his parents, has never felt sorry for himself or resentful toward life or the universe. When his mother was killed, he almost lost confidence and hope. Alex kept telling me that everything always works out and I could believe his emotional strength and clarity. He never lost focus or forgot what he had learned from his mother. I am telling you that this is a very special boy. His mother did an excellent job raising him and preparing him for life. I just never imagined that after his father was killed that Alex would have to endure another devastating loss. He did, and I know that both his parents would be very pleased with him.

Alex's story is truly exceptional. I am always emotionally moved when I hear how much he has done and overcome. He has the full understanding of his mother factor and has applied it to his life. There isn't anything in his life that doesn't reflect or represent the complete style of his mothering legacy. His mother prepared Alex for life and that life also included her not being in it. Alex will always have a sense of grief and sorrow about losing both of his parents as a teenager. Alex finally allowed himself to cry over his mother's death. It is healthy and very normal. Alex has also learned to be less fearful of losing those around him. His mother's influence didn't die years ago, but is very alive in her son's life today. That is the complete circle of the mother factor legacy—the next generation can either benefit or suffer.

Mandy, Joan, and June

Three generations of women and three different stories. The family was made up of June, the grandmother, Joan, the mother, and Mandy, the granddaughter. In June 1986, Joan and June were driving back from a local bar. Joan was driving drunk and June was in the passenger seat. Unfortunately, Joan hit a tree while going around a corner and killed her mother, June. Joan spent the next six weeks in the hospital recovering from the accident. Mandy had always been a good daughter—well behaved and not emotionally burdened by either her mother or grandmother. Prior to her death, June had taken emotional care of Joan as well as Mandy. After the accident, Mandy found herself with a new mother-daughter dynamic; with Joan, she had no emotional support or female mentor. I met Mandy in 1998 during one of my workshops on the mother factor. Mandy was twenty-eight years old at the time.

The background story of Mandy was that she lived in a duplex with her mother in California. Joan lived in the front unit and Mandy in the back unit. According to Mandy, Joan had always had a drinking problem, and it only worsened after the accident. Joan was/is a paralegal for a large law firm in downtown Los Angeles. She worked from seven in the morning until three thirty every afternoon.

Mandy met with me to discuss how she could separate and individuate without Joan disowning her. I asked Mandy if she was serious about her fear that her mother would reject her if she created her own life apart from her. Mandy said the following,

> I am my mother's whole life. Since grandma's death, my mother has only focused on me. I feel like she is my daughter. I have to give her attention three or four times a day. If I don't call her by 3:00 p.m., then I will get an emergency phone call from her. At night when I come home, I have to go say hello to my mother or she will become very angry with me. I used to have a beer with my mother but not anymore. I don't drink with my mother either. She is drunk every day by 5:00 p.m. I don't see myself ever living away from my mother until she dies. I just can't see her ever emotionally or mentally functioning on her own. Currently, my mother is seeking permanent work disability so she won't have to ever work again. That scares me because I don't know what I will do with her.

I explained to Mandy that her mother wasn't her responsibility, nor was it her full-time job to care for her emotionally or to plan for her entire life. Mandy had become more codependent with Joan. Mandy knew that if she continued to deal with Joan's alcoholism, her unresolved grief from the accident, her emotional dependency, and her passive/aggressive behavior, her own life was going to become more and more difficult to manage. Mandy had been raised by her grandmother, who had many of the traits of the complete mothering style. Mandy possessed those same abilities and emotional strengths. She didn't know how to manage her mother's overwhelming neediness and excessive emotional dependency. Mandy knew that if she didn't change her mother-daughter relationship, she would become emotionally paralyzed and not be able to move forward with her own life. Mandy made a plan that was similar to a mother's getting her fifty-seven-year-old daughter to move out of the house. In this case, however, it was Mandy who was going to move out. Mandy explained the following to her mother at 6:30 a.m., so she would be completely sober and coherent:

Mom, I am taking a job with a land development management company based in Florida. I have two weeks to move and get my belongings to Orlando by the first of the month. This is the career move I have always wanted. I know that if I stay here living next door to you, we are both going to never move on with our lives. I know that you can function without me at your side all the time. I don't want you to keep stalling your life. If I stay here with you, we are both going to only resent each other. Mom, I want to get married, have children, and live a different life than yours. I know we both miss grandma, but she would never want us to live like this. Mom, we can do better. I have to take this job.

Joan pleaded with Mandy not to move and told her it would kill her if she moved away. In the meantime, Mandy made the move. She barely made the transition emotionally, though both she and her mother survived. Mandy, who had wanted to lose weight, lost eight pounds in her first five months away from her mother. In the meantime, Joan met a man and asked him to move into her house within four months of Mandy's departure. Joan didn't call, e-mail, or write Mandy for five months. Mandy had her best girlfriend, Shannon, check on Joan daily to make sure she hadn't killed herself.

Mandy has now lived in Florida for three years, is married, became pregnant, and has lost over one hundred pounds since moving away from her mother. Joan didn't come to the wedding, nor has she ever come to Florida for a visit. Mandy accepts her mother's emotional limitations and her sense of abandonment. Mandy knew that the most loving, nurturing, lifesaving act she could perform was to pursue her own life. Joan has never spoken to or asked Mandy about her new husband or baby girl (her granddaughter). Mandy openly acknowledges that if it wasn't for her grandmother's positive female role model and loving, supportive, nurturing influence, she would never have been able to move on with her life.

SUMMARY

Alex and Mandy represent parts of all of us. We all have fears, sadness, anger, resentments, issues, hope, and courage. These two people found a way to make their life work and succeed despite severely unfavorable circumstances. It is the internal, emotional connection they had to a positive and complete mother legacy that they drew on to overcome extreme hardships. Alex and Mandy illustrate that the power of mothering is never limited to any one place, situation, or life circumstance. These two young adults had to find something in their hearts that had been planted there by their nurturing mother, grandmother, or aunt. They both found the emotional courage to take the necessary developmental steps. It is always amazing how some people take these incredible steps and others don't. The underlying strength for them was having a complete mother figure their life.

Whether or not you had a complete mother figure in your life, you, too, can succeed, or you wouldn't be reading this book. In the next section, we are going to consider how to put your mother factor legacy into full gear. Before we go to the next section, consider the following questions.

- Who was/is my mother?
- How do I act toward my mother today?
- Who do I want to be in my intimate relationships, in my personal life, and with my friends, family, and children?
- What was the mothering style I experienced while growing up?
- Do I know the strengths and weaknesses of the mother-child relationship?

Now let us reconsider your mother factor and put it to work

Section III

MOTHER FACTOR POTENTIAL
Creating Your Life

Chapter 8

CHANGING YOUR SCRIPT
Starting with Your Mother's Rules
Rewriting Your Book

If I listened to my mother's rule book or script for my life, I would be a stripper, married four times, and have had children with each different husband. I stopped listening to my mother at about age eleven. If I didn't, my life would be a wreck.

—Shannon, age thirty-three

WHAT'S MY RULE BOOK?

The concept of discovering your rule book has become very popular in recent years. Many celebrities, infomercial hosts, and self-improvement experts are all talking about rewriting your life script. It is the positive thing to do, encouraging people to reconsider their lives. Never forget, all life scripts follow strict guidelines, protocols, and prescribed outlines, and they even cover your relationship choices. No one can accurately or thoroughly rewrite his life script without becoming very familiar with his inner rule book. The most powerful rules, guidelines, oaths, emotional commitments, and choices are the unconscious ones. It is these intrinsic rules, emotions, and feelings deriving from our mothers that shape and form us much more than any of us know or would like to believe.

As any good daughter or son knows implicitly, following rules is like breathing: *it is something we do automatically and don't even know we do it until there is a violation.* The problem is that when we break or don't follow one of our inner rules, we often feel guilt or shame for it. For instance, you may experience an uneasy feeling if you decide to skip your weekly Sunday dinner at Mom's, or if you're dating someone who isn't on your mother's "wish list" for you. These sensations can cause any adult children to alter their life in order to avoid those uncomfortable feelings or tension with their internal mother figure. It is these uncomfortable feelings and emotions that cause all of us to alter our behavior, choices, and decisions. Confronting the underlying issue (old rules vs. new rules) is the key to taking full control of your life and relationships.

A very good example of the power of a mother's rule book is that of my client, Julie, and her boyfriend, John. They had been dating for nine months, and Julie hadn't met John's mother or been invited to a family dinner or holiday celebration. Julie wanted to discuss her concern about John's fear of violating his mother's wishes as well as her control over his life. John, thirty years old, came to therapy with Julie and explained the following, "My mother only wants me to date the women she picks out for me. She has never liked or accepted any other girlfriend. I am really hesitant to introduce Julie to my mother, then our relationship becomes my mother's."

Julie ultimately broke off her intimate relationship with John because he was unwilling to challenge or rewrite his mother's script for his life. John didn't have control of his life and hadn't confronted his avoidance of mother-son emotional separation. Julie was devastated by John's fear of going against his mother's rules and wishes. When it comes to recreating your rule book, it requires much more than love. You need to make a deliberate life choice to take full control of your life and relationships. Julie had been writing her script and living by her own rule book since college. John's inability to confront his mother made no sense to Julie, because for her, such changes were an automatic process and very natural. When relationships are terminated because of rule violations, it isn't about love or caring for the other person. It is about unresolved issues emanating from the mother factor—they obstruct the emotional progress and complete bonding of the couple. It is imperative to examine and thoroughly understand the unspoken, unconscious rules, guidelines, values, ethics, and choices that control your life. It is essential to know these things and draw on your emotional insight so you can create a productive relationship model. Your pathway to emotional freedom is knowing and writing your own rule book.

Rules distinguish each of the mothering styles. All five mothering styles (perfectionist, unpredictable, "me first," best friend, and complete) have their own distinct sets of rules, beliefs, and particular expectations—spoken and unspoken requirements. Rules are like the furniture in the living room of your life—every piece has its proper place and purpose. It is important to understand the function of each piece of furniture and its placement and purpose within the scheme of the entire room. The same analogy can be used for your mother factor rule book. Each rule, guideline, boundary, and expectation has its exact purpose, place, and specific role in your life. Your mother-child rules are in your life regardless of whether or not they make sense. You have to know which rules of yours or of your mother cause you relationship problems, emotional conflict, and fear of separating from your mother. These feelings, actions, and experiences that cause you anxiety and waves of shame are emotional responses to an unconscious rule violation. People discount those emotional experiences as a mere feeling of discomfort. They are correct insofar as rule violations are emotionally uncomfortable. But why are these feelings of guilt or shame so strong? The answers are written in your rule book! Have your ever taken time to consider what rules—both conscious and unconscious—are written in your book?

MOTHER'S RULE BOOK

Every mothering style has its own rules that all the family members live by, including your father, regardless of his relationship status with your mother. Whenever I mention the rule book concept to daughters or sons who've had a turbulent relationship with their mother, they immediately look panicked and scared. It is without question that these sons and daughters carry an extensive amount of fear, guilt, and shame about not living up to what they think their mother wants or demands. The more conflicted that mother-daughter/mother-son relationship was or is, the more rigid the mother's rule book will be for her children. The rigidity is directly correlated to the level of emotional clarity and emotional freedom within the relationship. In short: *the level of emotional disturbance within the mother will create an equally disturbed set of rules for a daughter or son to follow.* Therefore, if your mother gets "crazy" about certain things, it is safe to assume that her unspoken/spoken rules about nearly everything will be equally as strict, crazy, and problematic for you. If your mother has a mental illness or severe emotional/psychological issues, you need to be extra careful with the rule book that you use. Even though it might be common knowledge that your mother has emotional issues, she still handed you a rule book. However, just because your mother believes it's wrong to live with your boyfriend/girlfriend or that homosexuality is right or wrong doesn't make her a "psycho."

Such values, which you and others may consider to be misguided, are not out of the mainstream of social debate. The rules such as "never eat wheat products on Tuesdays because you will develop cancer"; "never have sex prior to dinner"; or "spanking children will keep evil spirits out of them" are extremely questionable. These types of irrational rules have to be amended in your life for you to develop high-functioning adult relationships and strong emotional connections. Rules that are developed from or based in fear, anxiety, religious mythology (evil spirits possess people), family abuse, family secrets/shame, sexual inappropriateness, and anti-intellectualism have to be questioned. These types of rules never help personal growth or emotional independence but are rather a form of mother-child relationship dysfunction.

One example of such dysfunction is Helen, age thirty-three, the only one of six children in her family who is currently divorced. Helen got married right after college to her longtime hometown boyfriend, Mike. Over the next eight years, Helen and Mike grew emotionally, mentally, and physically (no sex life) apart. Mike had an affair with his co-worker and left Helen for her. Helen's mother, Dorothy, became clinically depressed and enraged about Helen's divorce. Helen came to therapy to discuss why her mother's chronic irritability and moodiness was causing her to be highly anxious. Helen went back home for the Christmas holidays and asked her mother what was really the problem between them. Dorothy told Helen, "You got divorced and I am upset that you let your husband slip away. Women in our family don't divorce. What did you do wrong? I raised you to be a good wife and partner. I didn't raise you to be a career woman and neglect your husband and children [Helen had no children]." After many hours and weeks of talking on the phone after that initial conversation, Helen finally accepted that her mother resented her for not following her rules/beliefs about marriage and love. Helen worked in therapy on accepting that her life was her own, not her mother's, and that her mother's emotional problems were her mother's and not hers. Helen did remarry three years after that mother-daughter argument/ confrontation. Dorothy didn't come to Helen's wedding because she didn't believe Helen should remarry after a divorce.

This example is very typical of mothers and their disappointment when their children don't follow their rules and life script.

Helen knew that her exact point of entering adulthood was when she decided not to remain single for the rest of her adult life, despite her mother's thinking it was best for her. Helen rewrote her rule book and emotionally moved forward with her life. This process initially was very anxiety-provoking for Helen. She never wanted to disappoint or upset her mother, but the time had come for Helen to take full control of her life. Once Helen realized that she was really living out Dorothy's life, she found personal changes were much easier and less painful to make. Helen also accepted that Dorothy wasn't able to be emotionally open to any changes or perceived challenges to her rule book. Dorothy firmly believed that she had failed as mother because Helen got divorced. Prior to this entire discussion on marriage, divorce, and women's roles in a family, Helen had never challenged or questioned her mother's rules/beliefs/script. It is amazing that Helen's and Dorothy's lives and viewpoints had meshed so well and so perfectly for so long. They didn't have any typical mother-daughter conflict or misunderstanding until Helen was thirty-one years old. This overdue mother-daughter crisis pushed Helen to establish herself and her personal identity as separate from her mother. Helen had to decide whose life she was going to live: hers or her mother's.

When you consider Helen's story, you have to ask yourself: what are five rules, beliefs, or script changes you would like to make in your life? Don't argue with yourself that the changes aren't practical or realistic, just acknowledge the potential for a rule modification. These changes, ideas, beliefs, emotional adjustments, relationship shifts, career moves, and relationship transformations all start with taking a complete look at the inside of your mother's rule book for living your life. You have to read and discover what her rule book contains for your life today. This isn't meant to sound negative or critical. Your complete exploration of your mother factor is necessary if anything of personal value is going to continue to transpire in your life. Please go ahead and write in this book. Use ink pen, not a pencil. Put your changes down in permanent ink. It might be a rule violation to write in a book, but it is your book! Besides, if you write it in ink, you can't erase what you need to do.

Five Changes?

1.

2.

3.

4.

5.

How did it feel to put those unconscious/conscious desires and new rules down on paper? Did it seem like it was scary, wishful thinking, anxiety-provoking, hopeless, or exciting? Did you feel it is time to move your relationships forward? Don't minimize the power of what you wrote and thought about. Many times, the mere acknowledgment of a deep desire can be enough of an impetus to begin a very powerful emotional shift. You have to be honest and courageous to start the wheels of change moving in your life and relationships. *Remember that unless you are willing to try something new, nothing new is going to happen in your life.* You can't expect big emotional or relationship changes if you continue your old patterns of behavior and thinking and keeping the old rules. Rewriting your rule book is a metaphor for redirecting your life, relationships, and emotional connections.

UNSPOKEN AND SPOKEN RULES: WHAT'S THE DIFFERENCE?

It might seem obvious that there is a communication style, influence, degree of importance, and difference between unspoken and spoken rules. Which rules—spoken or unspoken within the mother-child relationship—have the most influence and impact on a son's or daughter's life?

Well, the first time I heard the theory of unspoken versus spoken rules, I guessed wrong. The correct answer is *unspoken rules*. There is a huge difference in the types of unspoken rules learned, observed, and internalized within the mother-child relationship for all sons and daughters.

Unspoken rules are the rules that aren't even considered rules. They are your automatic actions, values, behaviors, emotional reactions, and belief system. Spoken rules pale in comparison to unspoken rules, which exist in the hearts, automatic behaviors, and minds of people. There isn't a single thought or behavior that isn't driven by your unspoken rules. Many people refer to these unconscious, unspoken rules as personal values, ethics, or morals. But they all, in fact, fall under the category of the unspoken rules of the mother factor. Unspoken rules are by far the most powerful rules in your daily life and relationships. Even though unspoken rules have enormous influence in how you work, handle conflict, communicate, and emotionally bond, they tend to be out of your conscious awareness. These rules are very influential in forming part of your core self and relationship template for adulthood. Everyone has a rule book that they follow, live by, and use to navigate their relationships. No matter how absent, emotionally distant, or enmeshed your mother was or wasn't, she handed you a rule book to follow.

In contrast, spoken rules can be state laws, social norms (e.g., don't telephone people after 10 p.m. at night, don't call your boss on Sunday), company policies, and basic codes of conduct. These are the concrete behaviors that we all know about and understand. We learn these rules at school, home, in the community, and with our friends. For instance, all adults know that getting in a physical altercation at work, at your children's sporting event, or at family gatherings isn't right and in most cases is not legal. No one can say that they didn't know getting in a fistfight wasn't legal and appropriate behavior. Yet, there are people who want to sell that excuse—that they didn't know it was wrong.

Another example is underage drinking. Every year, I have two or three teenage clients who get arrested for being drunk in public. They all plead to me and their parents that they didn't know that drinking in public was illegal or that falling facedown drunk is criminally offensive. And it is absolutely absurd to argue that you didn't know what the legal drinking age is. In contrast, an unspoken rule, although quite questionable, might be that, if you drink your daily three glasses of high-quality Scotch on the rocks after 4 p.m., you aren't a problem drinker. In actuality, you probably are. Unspoken rules are very private, individual guidelines for how you operate in your family, love relationships, social support system, as well as spiritually, professionally, and personally. There isn't an area of your life that falls outside the guidelines of your or your mother's rule book. The key is knowing whose rules you are following. Do you know?

One of the goals here is for you to become aware of your set of unspoken rules. These rules create an integral part of your fundamental core belief system and emotional state. You began learning your unspoken rules from the time you can first remember crying, being fed, and getting your mother's emotional attention. All these childhood experiences and observations of your mother go into creating your core emotional belief system: *your unspoken rules*. Adults will many times become very upset, angry, or outraged when one of their core emotional beliefs is violated or dismissed. The anger is a result of your core emotional sense of self being dismissed. The reason it is vital to understand and explore your emotional beliefs, unspoken rules, and values is so you can avoid becoming irrational, judgmental, and/or prejudicial against people when they unknowingly violate one of your beliefs or rules of life. The more you acknowledge your predisposed beliefs— unspoken rules—the more you can take control and redirect your relationships. Your individuality is further formed with your new insightful ability to know your own rules and desires.

Your particular mothering style had a certain set of rules, beliefs, values, and emotional guidelines for relationships. For instance, if your mother was constantly needing your attention and/or seeking your approval and support, you might have learned never to say no to a friend. You may have learned that you always help someone regardless of your circumstances. The idea of being supportive is great. The problem is that violating your internal rule book and saying no to someone might cause you a high degree of stress and anxiety. Your internal/unconscious, unspoken rule book tells you to always say yes, to avoid those extremely uncomfortable feelings. Another example of how your mothering style affects your rule book is the unpredictable mothering style, which is always finding and creating ways to start a conflict, avoid responsibility, or prevent an intimate emotional connection. You learned that unless there is a certain degree of drama in your life and relationships, you are boring or in the wrong relationship. (Your belief is that drama equals love, which is based on your mothering style and chaotic childhood.) These are the types of beliefs that you rarely question or challenge. They just seem to be business as usual and how your world operates.

MOM'S UNSPOKEN RULES

All mothers live by their own unspoken rules. The problem is everyone else in the family either lives by these rules or a family conflict ensues. It is a given fact, regardless of your mother's emotional or mental health, that her rules shape the emotional life of the family. Think of some rules that your mother still lives by (or lived by, if she has passed away) and how they reflect her personality, mothering style, and relationship model. For example, Shannon, who was quoted in the beginning of the chapter, knows that her mother wants her to live by her script. Shannon's mother, Yvonne, believes and tells her four daughters that using drugs isn't a problem but rather a gift of life. Shannon, because of her mother's addiction to prescription pain relievers (Valium), has been the parent in the relationship since about age eight. Shannon married a man, Keith, who had had a prior drug abuse history. Ultimately, Shannon ended up playing out the role of strict rule enforcer in both relationships. Shannon kept her mother's unspoken rule of always being the caretaker—nurturing people in her life. Shannon also took emotional responsibility for two of her younger sisters, who were both struggling with illegal drug use and abuse. Unfortunately, Keith was killed in a motorcycle accident, and eventually Yvonne was placed in drug rehabilitation center by Shannon. During the first year of grieving over her husband's death, Shannon completely rewrote her own rule book—spoken/unspoken.

Earlier in the book, we discussed the power of emotional pain to motivate us to change our mother factor. Shannon finally had enough grief, emotional pain, and years of frustration attempting to manage her mother's and husband's drug abuse. Now was the time to make the changes she had always want to make but didn't, since she couldn't manage her anxiety. The combination of the death of her husband and her mother's chronic use of prescription drugs were the final straw. All her attempts to stop their drug use in the past were to no avail. One of the things that Shannon discussed was: what were four unspoken rules she had learned from her mother? These four unspoken rules, scripts, or emotional guidelines had shaped how Shannon approached adulthood, parenting, career, and marriage. The four rules from Yvonne to Shannon were:

1. You are the parent, the responsible one.
2. Never leave me—emotionally, physically, or mentally.
3. Always be my emotional support system.
4. Always have a man in your life [Yvonne had been married four times and had a daughter with each husband].

It took Shannon several weeks to finally articulate this list and realize the power of each rule. Shannon began to see why she married at age nineteen, lived with her mother for the first four years of her marriage, and then moved next door. Shannon never took a full-time job, so she could always be around the house to care for her mother and children. She helped her mother and stepfather manage their money and loaned them money. Shannon began to understand that most of her major life decisions were based on Yvonne's four unspoken rules. Shannon followed those rules perfectly and therefore was the "perfect" daughter for her unpredictable mother.

Shannon's example isn't extreme, but rather a very common scenario despite its being a complicated emotional conflict. Evan's situation demonstrates the other example of following a mother's rule book to one's own detriment. He has struggled with how to keep his mother happy, less anxious, and not lose his identity in the process. Evan, much like Shannon, had to rewrite his own rule book or he wouldn't have been able to have a relationship with a woman on any level: professional, social, or romantic. Evan's four basic unspoken rules were very similar to Shannon's. They both had an unpredictable mother-adult/child relationship. Evan never realized that his unconscious rules were paralyzing him and causing him tremendous guilt, shame, and fear. He didn't make the connection that his intimacy problems with women were based in his mother's rule book. Upon further exploration in therapy, Evan began to see that the majority of his issues with women were really with his mother's code of conduct for him.

Evan knew that if he wanted to have adult romantic relationships, he had to stop treating every woman as a *mother replace-ment*. He had a strong sense of guilt that no matter what a woman was feeling, it was his problem and his responsibility to fix. Evan's rules were:

1. Always fix any problem your mother (or any woman) has.
2. Never upset or anger your mother—if you do, you are an awful man.
3. A woman's happiness is your (Evan's) responsibility.
4. Never leave or do anything to emotionally separate from your mother.

When Evan finally came to terms with the unnecessary emotional burden he was carrying for his mother and any women he'd meet, he began to discover his own feelings. He had never considered his own feelings or thoughts in connection with women. His automatic response was, what does she want, need, or expect? He found himself in a constant state of emotional and physical exhaustion, attempting to always keep his mother happy. His "perfect" son relationship model transmitted into his seeking the approval of whatever woman he was dating. When Evan started to pragmatically explore his mother-son relationship, he discovered that he had repressed and forgotten all the emotional terror of his childhood. Evan had been emotionally traumatized by his chaotic, unpredictable mother-son relationship while growing up. Evan was emotionally and mentally abused by his mother's constant mood swings, rage-fueled outbursts, screaming tantrums, and threats of sending him to a military boarding school. He had never considered that his childhood was different from the norm or that it was extreme. Evan unconsciously equated his mother's irritability with his emotional lack of safety. That reaction was unconscious and the basis for his mother's rule book: Always take care of me.

TWELVE HOT TOPICS

Now that you are starting to feel the momentum of change and understand that alterations need to be made to your rule book, we need to address several topics. Evan and Shannon had to explore the twelve topics below in order to fully complete their rewrites for their rule book. You'll find some of the significant areas for change to your relationships among the following "hot topics." There are at least two or three topics below that need to be amended in your rule book. These topics are sticking points between you and your mother. It is essential to know what your mother told you verbally and nonverbally in regard to these topics and relationship issues. Let's focus on your mother's rules—what they are and how they affect your life today. Next to each particular subject, write the first thing that comes to mind when you see it and think of your mother's rule regarding it. Don't edit yourself or over think your answer. If you have difficulty coming up with an answer for a particular topic, move on to the next one. There is no doubt that your mother had an opinion about all twelve of these topics and many more. The goal is to focus on your life themes and choices and how they are currently affecting your functioning in relationships.

Each of these areas can trigger a great deal of emotion when combined with your life experience. What would it take for you to change any of these areas in your life and in your current relationships? *Read this list with the idea, intention, and purpose of expanding your rule book and enlarging your life script to include more of the things you want in your life.* The rationale behind discovering your mother's unspoken rules is to find which rules impede your life and which ones empower it.

Sexuality (orientation, sexual activity, female/male roles)—

Money—

Communication (verbal/nonverbal)—

Relationships (social, family, work, intimate)—

Spirituality (you, me, and a higher power)—

Emotional Expression (anger, love, openness)—

Your Father—

Parenting/Children (abortion, adoption, pregnancy, in vitro)—

Ethics—

Career (full-time mothering and work, career, and family)—

Marriage/Divorce—

Separation/Individuation—

What did your mother tell you both nonverbally and through her actions concerning these twelve very basic life issues? After all, you learned about these critical elements of relationships from her. The twelve areas cover all the various aspects of relationships: friends, intimacy, career, society, family, children, and you. It is often because of these particular areas that the mother-child relationship gets stuck and derailed over a value, rule, or personal ethical belief. The emotional power struggle between you and your mother causes the issue to become a nonnegotiable point. These are the various issues that separate families, terminate friendships, end marriages, and divide personal relationships. This is why knowing where you personally stand on your core issues is essential.

The primary issue is, what do you think and feel about your ability to form intimate relationships? All these rule book elements go into the making of your individuality. You can't emotionally separate from your mother until you understand your feelings—not hers—on these twelve topics. This list is about you and taking more control of your life, relationships, and future. You can tailor this list to your life, but don't skip the different areas of your life in order to keep the peace with your mother. Ultimately, like Helen, Shannon, and Evan, you will discover it really doesn't work.

Chapter 9

YOUR MOTHER AND FOOD

Learning to Feed Yourself
The Nurturing Secret

My entire life has been consumed with food, my mother, and eating too much. My mother has forced food on me all of my life—now I am fat. I never felt loved by my mother's making me eat all the time. My mother is super skinny.

—Brianna, age seventeen

I have a problem remembering to eat. My food issue is my inability to take care of myself so I become starved. I was so anxious as a child that I would not eat for two or three days at a time. Now I have to force myself to eat, otherwise I won't do it. I am out of touch with my body.

—Mark, age fifty-three

MOTHERS AND FOOD

My experience in writing this book has been extremely enlightening for hundreds of reasons. One of the most interesting things that occurred to me was the emotionally charged discussion between mothers and their adult children about their relationship with food. It was stunning how many conflicts in mother-child relationships dealt with food and nurturing and how they were/are handled (mishandled) in their childhood and in the present day. When this book project was originally created, this chapter wasn't even in the outline. Over the next twelve months, it became very apparent that more and more mothers, daughters, and sons were as opinionated about their relationship with food as they were about their other emotional issues. It became glaringly obvious that any comprehensive discussion about the emotional legacy of the mother factor had to include the food factor. The power of food in the mother-child relationship was something that I personally and professionally had underestimated. It is a force that has to be reckoned with for all daughters and sons. Food and nurturing are extensions of each other and have a direct reflection on your emotional status and core self-image.

Over the last ten years, the eating disorder epidemic has become increasingly more public. Prior to this, food and the shameful secrets associated with this obsession were kept in the mother-child closet. No one is neutral on the topic of food. We will be discussing the emotional component of food. There are hundreds of wonderful books about the medical and physical issues of food, dieting, portion control, body image, eating disorders, body mass index scale (fat vs. muscle), and nutrition (see bibliography for some great references). *This chapter is about you, your mother, nurturing, and food.* The goal is to further uncover your emotional relationship with food and its connection to your mother-child relationship. The weight loss industry knows that emotions and food are one and the same and are not to be treated separately.[1] Weight Watchers International uses the group therapy concept for group/peer support of its members who have weight loss goals. More and more people are starting to acknowledge that emotions are the driving force in everything we choose to eat and the feelings that go with these decisions. If this chapter was omitted, our discussion of your mother factor would be incomplete and missing a critical piece of valuable information about food and you. There is an old saying—we are what we eat. Let's add, but *why, when, and how do I eat*?

When the topic of mothers comes up, it isn't very long before the issue of food is brought into the discussion. Symbolically, motherhood throughout literature has always been equated with love, support, and nurturing qualities. *Mothering* is another word for nurturing. We have discussed in the mothering styles section that motherhood and nurturing are critical emotional elements in your personal development and your adult relationships. One of the most tangible and logical ways to show concern or love or to take care of someone is to feed them. Babies learn to emotionally express themselves (crying) when hungry and having their needs satiated by their mother (breast-feeding). This dynamic of requesting to have your physical needs of hunger met and experiencing that pleasure is a very powerful bond between a mother and a child. The emotional bond between the mother and child is developed partially through the dynamic of food/nurturing. This starts at day one of your life and continues until the day you leave this life. This nurturing bond is too powerful to ignore if you want to understand your life and relationships. We were all raised to learn to express our needs by asking for breakfast, lunch, a chocolate chip cookie, or our favorite birthday cake with dark chocolate filling. When these requests are fulfilled repeatedly over time, we begin a process of a lifelong emotional pattern of fulfillment, contentment, and emotional trust. All children learn from this nurturing gesture. This relationship is a very powerful emotional connection between pleasure and our sense of emotional happiness. When our physical needs are repeatedly satisfied, then our sense of frustration, deprivation, and anger isn't a driving force in the formation of our inner sense of self. Rather, our sense of trust, well-being, empathy, compassion, and emotional stability is developed.

Food and motherhood are almost as closely related as nurturing and motherhood. Food is a direct physical demonstration of nurturing. This strong emotional connection between feeling nurtured, loved, and listened to is played out with how we learned to eat. The psychology of food is a complete book unto itself, but for our purposes, let's take a hard look into the mother-child aspect of the subject.

PICTURES OF YOUR EMOTIONS— FIVE SHORT STORIES

If you are going to have emotional clarity about your unresolved issues with your mother, one of the areas that will always show up is your relationship to food. The anxiety and the displacement of it and how you calm yourself down are critical elements to understand. Many times, we use food as a drug, so to speak, in order to keep our sense of hopelessness and panic under control. The idea of feeling and resolving our emotions without the use of food can be a very powerful life-changing behavior. Now is the time to begin to see the many emotional connections that surround your relationship to food and your mother. These timeless connections can become very clear in your ability to manage and nurture yourself with food. The feelings of neglect, shame, guilt, low self-esteem, self-loathing, anger, and emotional well-being all show up in your relationship to food. How we feel at a given moment and our ability to nurture ourselves are all learned behaviors.

Nurturing has many different manifestations, and food is one of the primary examples of how we care for ourselves. *This is why your relationship with your mother is so intertwined with your relationship to food.* The first place you learned and experienced that someone cared for you was with your mother. One of the primary ways your mother bonded with you was to feed you. Now, that emotional legacy is passed onto you in how you handle food and how you feed yourself, and how these both connect to your various emotional states. Your sense of abundance, emotional well-being, and trust are all part and parcel of the mother-child relationship. How you handle these particular emotions is closely related to how you handle your own cravings, longings, impulses, and desires. These feelings are natural responses to everyday experiences and relationship issues.

The following five scenarios are typical of everyday experiences, difficulties, and frustrations. How we emotionally respond to them is very informative and valuable for our own emotional development and growth. No one wants to be emotionally, mentally, or psychologically controlled by food.[2] Yet, because of the nature and source of nurturing and our emotional development, there is a connection between food and our feelings. The problems of focusing obsessively on food, dieting, body image, and chronic exercising points to the underlying issue of your unresolved mother factor legacy. If you had to focus on one issue that seems unsettled between you and your mother—regardless if she is living or not—what would it be? Consider the following five scenarios and how you would emotionally respond. Each scenario is representative of a particular mother-child relationship that is now an adult model for nurturing relationships. Next, consider how, what, and why food would be an issue in these particular situations for you. What scenario seems most on target in describing your emotional/nurturing reaction? Consider all five styles and how you react to disappointing and stressful news.

FOOD CRITICS INVENTORY

Scenario One: After a long day of school, work, or mothering, your house is completely empty. No one is home except you. The phone rings, and you receive some very frustrating, disappointing news about something you had set your hopes on. This was something you really wanted and desired. You are instantly upset and feel many uncomfortable feelings. You immediately walk into the kitchen and go directly for your favorite comfort food. You see it and start eating it. You are completely numb emotionally, mentally, and physically. You're detached from the major disappointment you suffered five minutes earlier and are now completely zoned out. You are on automatic pilot and putting food in your mouth to offset the horrible feelings inside of you. Instead of tolerating these feelings, you've chosen instead to eat your favorite, unhealthy, mind-numbing food. Before you are even consciously aware of it, you have consumed three times more than you intended. You feel better for about thirty minutes, but the underlying frustration, deprivation, panic, and disappointment is only minimized, not resolved.

The deeper level of uneasiness in your emotions is not only unresolved but further agitated. You spend the rest of the night and part of the next day in a self-loathing state of mind. You promise yourself the next time you get upset you will not eat three packages of cookies, an entire frozen cake, one jar of crunchy peanut butter, or bags of barbeque potato chips. You soothed yourself this way, despite the fact that you may have realized that this pattern of self-soothing through food began when you and your mother would get into an argument about your friends, your clothes, your weight, or the people you dated. You found your mother was often very critical of you and your life choices. It didn't matter what you did, it was never right or good enough. And now, it is difficult to deal with anyone who is unhappy or upset with you. You have trouble in any type of relationship receiving feedback, because it all feels like criticism and rejection to you.

Scenario Two: You hang up the phone, but rather than devour comfort food, you skip the next three meals. You are so upset that you begin to pace around the house. Unconsciously, you feel that you don't deserve to nurture or take care of yourself. The bad news is typical of your life and luck. You aren't even aware that you haven't eaten since Monday afternoon and it is now Wednesday morning. Your frustration, anxiety, and emotional emptiness are like a sore tooth pain that isn't going away. You can't sleep, eat, or focus. In fact, you become even more anxious, to the point that you are beginning to have panic attacks. You typically shut down emotionally, physically, and mentally when something distressing happens. This particular event is very upsetting, and you feel absolutely panicked by it.

The emotional and physical pattern of neglect is a familiar, long-standing pattern for you. Avoiding your emotions and body is something that you do whenever you are stressed or anxious. In fact, unless someone reminded you to eat, you typically don't think of it or choose to do it. You are very distracted by your feelings and emotional fears on almost a daily basis. You have the habit of being out of your body whenever you feel anxious or scared. You first noticed this habit after your parents divorced. Your mother would complain that she couldn't handle her life and wanted to run away. You tended to overreact to any disappointment or frustration and not eat. Your avoidance of eating has created wanted and unwanted attention from people. *You feel emotionally in control when you are not eating.*

When you don't "leave" your body, you will pick a fight with your partner, co-workers, your mother, or other family members. These fights are very problematic and upsetting for you. The aftermath of your emotional crisis is that your family and close friends are upset with you because you became so angry with them. You feel that no one understands or supports you. Your response to emotional situations always varies depending on your mood and feelings on any given day. You are surprised sometimes by how angry and "out of control" you feel over minor issues. Not eating is one of the few times you feel in control.

Scenario Three: You hang up the phone and instantly walk out of your house without consciously thinking. You drive to the store and proceed to buy four boxes of chocolate brownie mix. You come home and, over the next two days, make and eat all four boxes of brownies. You eat all the brownies by yourself, and no one knows about it. After baking each batch of brownies, you eat the entire portion alone in your bedroom, car, or office. Then approximately twenty minutes later, you self-induce violent vomiting. You do this four times in two days. After each episode of vomiting, you feel remotely better for a few hours. No one knows about your secret vomiting and emotional food cycle.

The panic, anxiety, depression, and hopelessness feel overwhelming, so you decide to overeat again. You decide to stop inducing vomiting after the fourth time because you notice that you are now vomiting up blood. You feel absolutely inconsolable about your life and this current relationship problem. You don't tell anyone about your brownie overeating/vomiting cycle. In fact, no one in your life, including your intimate partner, knows about your closeted habit of binge eating sweets and vomiting. You have been doing this for approximately fifteen years, every time you feel emotionally upset or scared of being abandoned. You noticed that this habit started when you moved away from your mother and started college.

Your mother always wanted you to look perfect, so vomiting keeps you looking lean and healthy. You feel physically sick and emotionally guilty about your very private secret after each episode. You feel that there is a big emotional hole in your heart and nothing ever seems to fill it up, especially food. You have felt for a long time that you can never get enough love, attention, or emotional support. You and your mother have never had a very close supportive relationship. The emotional strain between you and your mother impacts all of your feelings and sense of self. Nearly all your friends, male and female, share anger and resentment toward their mothers. One of your strongest emotional bonds with your friends is your angry relationship with your mother. Your friends have the same food behavior as you do or some other type of food-related problem. The reactions to food, your mother, staying thin, and emotional neediness all seem very common among your friends and family.

Scenario Four: You walk into the house and answer the phone. You are so upset about the news that you can't talk or express your emotions. You immediately think of your mother and how this news would impact her. Two hours later, you meet your mother for dinner but don't tell her anything about this incident or the negative consequences it is causing in your life. Rather, you focus on your mother's summer plans and her irritation with your younger sister for missing her birthday. You don't feel that you can express your emotional upheaval with your mother; she wouldn't understand or couldn't emotionally handle it. Instead, you skip dinner and drink four vodka lemonades. Whenever you are upset, you will drink large amounts of alcohol and not eat anything. Your partner is concerned that maybe you have an eating disorder or alcohol abuse issue. You feel even worse, because you are your mother's emotional support system and you can't lean on her. You are your mother's best friend and confidante. Your relationship excludes the rest of your family, including your father.

When you become emotionally upset, you don't have a network of friends to lean on for support. Your siblings resent you because of your "special" relationship with your mother. All your relationships are based on your ability to be the "fixer" or "supporter." You sometimes overeat, or don't eat at all, because of your mother's need for you to look good and her constant complaining that you don't eat right or watch your weight. Your mother is more concerned with your looks and appearance than she is with how you think or feel. You have felt like a "motherless" child because your relationship with your mother isn't normal or right. You are the parent and your mother is the child. All you and your mother discuss is food, your sister, your brother, and shopping. You are a man and your mother treats you like a husband or special friend. Food and alcohol have always been an emotional escape from your mother's endless emotional need for your attention.

Being a son and having a very dependent mother has caused you to resist forming an intimate, exclusive relationship with a woman. You have a fear of being stuck with a needy woman who will take control of your life. You have never completely committed to any woman you have loved or dated. You have a fear of intimacy because of always feeling emotionally suffocated by your mother. Your mother has never approved of any woman whom you have dated, lived with, or considered a life partner. Further, when you ignore or emotionally pull away from your mother, you tend to stop eating and start drinking heavily. You have found that drinking and not eating has always been a great emotional escape from the constant pressure you feel (guilt, anger, shame) from your mother-son relationship. Your current girlfriend wants to get married and you are very fearful of making that emotional commitment.

Scenario Five: You get off the phone and, rather than avoid your feelings, you sit down and write about your emotional distress. You decide to call a friend and explain your anxiety. You meet your friend for dinner, watch a sporting event, and have a pleasant evening, sharing and bonding together. You don't use or avoid food as an emotional tool, punishment, or comfort. You choose to address the issue and not overreact to the bad news. You know that things will work out however the problem gets resolved. The next morning you get up and feel better after having spent time with a close friend and confidante. You have been keeping an ongoing journal for over thirty years, since high school, and find writing a very helpful tool. You've learned that the best way to handle your feelings, emotions, thoughts, or upsetting events is to write them down. You have a network of friends who share your concerns and are very supportive of you and your relationships. You share your feelings with your partner, who is very supportive of your course of action to resolve this particular conflict.

You find that many of your friends don't take the positive action to nurture themselves, but rather they make choices that cause them more emotional pain and disappointment. You have always found that taking time for yourself keeps you emotionally centered and balanced with people. You have to have quiet time to process, understand, and respond to typical relationship challenges. When you take time to understand your feelings, you find that the situation is never as bad as it first appeared. You have moments of feeling overwhelmed and angry. Your automatic response is to make choices that will keep you emotionally centered and connected to yourself as well as the significant people in your life. Food, alcohol, and excessive behaviors aren't part of your emotional response to stress and disappointment.

These five short scenarios are likely reflective of the particular mothering style you grew up with and the type of emotional bonding that occurs in your relationships. With the exception of the complete style of mothering, all the rest cause emotional and nurturing problems. The other four styles (perfectionist, unpredictable, "me first," and best friend) all have the potential of creating in the son/daughter emotional deprivation that drives all these different types of excessive behaviors. Excessive food behaviors such as overeating, binging, anorexia, bulimia, starvation, chronic dieting, along with body image issues, bodybuilding, and extreme exercising are usually all motivated by a lack of nurturing. Throughout this book, we have seen that nurturing is the ability to be empathic and compassionate and accepting of yourself and your actions.

NO MORE EMOTIONAL HUNGER

The most important point of nurturing is your continuing to develop your ability to like and take care of yourself emotionally, physically, mentally, and psychologically. This might sound a bit elementary, but it is one of the biggest secrets in the weight loss industry. Weight loss experts know that if people feel good about themselves, they will eat less, exercise, make better food choices, and lose unnecessary weight. Adults are so accustomed to feeling a certain way about themselves that it is a challenge to consider other options and behaviors. Taking care of yourself in all areas of your life is your adult style of nurturing your life and all your various relationships. Nurturing is your ability to make choices that make you feel empowered and emotionally attached to the important people and things in your life. The nurturing behaviors that create a sense of empowerment within relationships are as different as the daughters and sons doing it. Consider the following list and your emotional food triggers. The more you are aware of your emotional panic switches, the more control you will have over food. Eating behaviors, emotional responses, nurturing behaviors, and your relationship style all make up the inner fabric (sense of self) of your life.

What are the things, events, relationship issues, and work/family interactions that make me sad, depressed, anxious, and/or scared?

1.

2.

3.

4.

Write your answers in this book. Answer these questions candidly and without editing—put down your first thought as your answer.

When I feel these things, how do I use food to comfort myself?

After I have had an emotional eating encounter, how do I feel?

If I didn't emotionally eat, what would I do instead?

What is something I could do rather than eating to relieve my anxiety, panic, or feelings of hopelessness?

What are a couple of nurturing behaviors that I could choose instead of using food as an emotional comfort?

Imagine how you feel when you reach for a certain food. Food doesn't need to be a negative force in your nurturing behavior. It depends on how you use it. If you don't make positive nurturing choices in your private/personal life, you won't do it in other parts of your life. Our discussion could very easily be about alcohol, sex, smoking, gambling, ultra-marathons, or any type of addictive/excessive behavior. Most other addictive behaviors involve things we can live without and don't need on a daily basis to survive. Food is an addiction issue that is very unique, because your life depends on how and what you eat. No matter how or what you do with food, you will always have to eat. The underlying question is: *Can I eat and not use food as an emotional release—as an escape for my feelings?* Your life isn't dependent on whether or not you have five glasses of wine a night or smoke only one pack of cigarettes a day. In fact, your life would probably benefit from not drinking, not smoking, or doing any excessive behaviors that are anxiety-driven.

It is common mainstream psychological knowledge that any type of excessive behavior is rooted in unresolved anxiety, shame, or guilt. The need to avoid the feelings of discomfort cause intelligent adults to become compulsive, addictive, and reckless in their actions and choices. The emotional connection of your mother-child relationship is the starting point to understanding your response to food and your emotions. Nurturing will always produce a sense of comfort, ease, confidence, emotional perspective, insight, and willingness to connect with and reach out to others. Excessive self-destructive behaviors don't create the emotional clarity and stability that are necessary for your growth and development.

Food is a comfort. Feeling loved is a comfort. Feeling appreciated, understood, emotionally supported, and achieving your goals are comforting. Spending time doing what you like is a comfort. Watching your favorite movie, taking vacations/trips, attending sporting events are all relaxing, pleasurable, and energizing experiences. Talking with your girlfriends, meeting your buddies for a round of golf are comforts too. The list is endless and important to know. What are some of the things, activities, events, and situations that make you feel comforted, loved, and cared for, aside from food?

1.

2.

3.

4.

This list is the core foundation to understanding the emotional, mental, physical, and psychological factors that make you feel nurtured, safe, and comforted. This list is something you have had in your mind for years. If you find it difficult to come up with four activities, habits, or ideas, don't panic. Nurturing yourself is something that people do to varying levels of self-acceptance. All your nurturing behaviors are based on your ability to accept, like, and empower yourself. Men and women who have a strong dislike and disdain for themselves will tend to be more addictive, excessive, and less nurturing of their personal needs. Addictive and excessive behaviors are all in degrees of self-loathing, self-destruction, self-defeat, and can even lead to suicide. Nurturing is the opposite belief and emotional state of self-loathing. You can't resent yourself and simultaneously take care of yourself. The two emotions and beliefs are completely incompatible. *Your mother factor and your manner of nurturing yourself will reflect on how you accept and like yourself and what kind of relationships you choose in your life.*

In many cases, a turbulent mother-child relationship can create a natural pattern of self-neglect and self-loathing. The emotional issues between you and your mother don't need to be the only nurturing elements in your life. You have to become the person who actively examines your own unconscious needs, wants, and hopes as separate from your mother. Regardless of your childhood history, you have the power to change and create a different life for yourself. Your life starts with your ability to know what you need and want: nurturing. It is never too late or too early to begin to change your personal emotional legacy and how you feel about yourself. The entire theme of this book can be summarized in your new ability to effectively nurture yourself emotionally and in all the different types of relationships in your life. If these are the two things you begin to change in your life after reading this book, then you have done an outstanding job in creating a very positive future for yourself and all the people connected with you.

SUMMARY

It is important to understand that one of the important aspects of your life is how you eat and your emotional relationship to food. For some of you, food isn't an issue or a problem. For others, food is an ongoing struggle, constant emotional problem, and a recurring basis of shame.

Most holidays, birthday celebrations, family dinners, and fine dining include the element of eating, sharing, and being with friends. These positive sides of food are also very powerful and often get lost in the shame-based behavior/addictions of food. Another issue with food is how your mother related to food. Many of the nurturing issues of adults today have their beginnings in how your mother viewed food. The more you understand how you were raised with food, the more you will be able to unlock your potential in other areas of your life.

In the next three chapters of the book, we are going to discuss how to mend your attachment bonds, heal your emotional wounds, create a new emotional legacy, separate and individuate, and use the positive aspects of your mother factor in your adult relationships. All these approaches are related to the nurturing style you grew up with.

Chapter 10

Functioning at
YOUR FULL
EMOTIONAL POTENTIAL
The Power of Your Legacy

I have always lacked self-confidence. I remember in the first grade wondering why I wasn't in the better reading group. I hate to see the same insecurities in my son. He is only nine and he already questions himself and his ability to try new things. I know my mother wanted me to be brave, but I have never been.

—Edwin, age fifty-two

My mother has always been a great support and encourager. I know that though she had a lot of issues with my father, she has always loved me. I have my own struggles that hold me back and cause me to be anxious. I wonder what my life would be like if I wasn't so anxious?

—Lindsay, age thirty

OPENING YOUR MOTHER'S DOOR

Every boy growing up was told to open the door for his mother as a sign of respect. Daughters were told by their mothers to allow someone to open the door for them. Both sons and daughters know from childhood that opening doors and entering a room are very important, regardless of the circumstances or the occasion. It doesn't matter who is holding the door open, you have to walk through it. Respect and courtesy means allowing someone the chance to be gracious by opening a door for you literally and metaphorically. These symbolic acts are all emotional transactions. Now it is time to open your mother's door. Many of us have been told never to open certain doors, raise certain subjects, or discuss certain aspects of our mother-child relationship. We have been told not to open certain doors metaphorically and literally concerning our mother. Now is the time to start opening all the doors and ask the difficult questions about yourself and your adult relationships. Start asking the hard questions about your life and how you feel about it. You can no longer allow your strained internal relationship with your mother to hold you back from your full emotional and relationship potential. We have discussed, examined, and explained the various ways your internal mother factor has developed and shaped your current-day relationships and your sense of self. Your entire emotional life has been influenced, directed, and developed by years of interactions between you and your mother. No matter how difficult, painful, splendid, or uneventful your relationship with your mother has been—or could be, it is now time to remove some of your personal concerns from it. This process isn't about blaming your mother. Those types of reactions only make the underlying issues more problematic.

Regardless of the current status of your mother-daughter/son relationship, the tension holds valuable information for your future. If we had to summarize all our discussions, insights, theories, styles, rules, and wisdom thus far in two words, they would be *mothers matter*. No one argues about the importance of mothers, but we may ask how and why mothers are so critical to your adult life. Your mother matters in ways that you might not expect or even want to consider. One of the goals of this book is to open up the discussion (your doors) now that you are an adult, to examine your emotional life and see how it affects all of your relationship patterns and bonds. Your style of connecting, forming, and maintaining relationships is all related to your emotional legacy: *your mother factor.*

Insight coupled with new behaviors creates movement in the directions and pathways that you have always wanted to travel. We aren't talking about new vacation spots, but rather the quality and content of your evolving life. You are in the process of fully uncovering the mystery buried within your heart about your mother and her remarkable influence upon your life—past, present, and future. The issues, conflicts, and recurring frustrations with your mother can no longer be a ball and chain around your life. You have to move beyond the emotional issues of your mother-daughter/son relationship. Your movement and changed emotional behavior may be met with resistance from your mother, but your life isn't hers to control. Your personal issues, relationship style, and approach to life are all yours now.

The rest of this book isn't about self-help, but rather the deep psychological, emotional, mental, physical, and personal changes that you have anticipated making for years but haven't quite known how to begin. Fully understanding your mother factor legacy will allow for the emotional shifts and relationship paradigm changes to occur and to take root in your life.

The key is to identify the issues, feelings, beliefs, and experiences that have created emotional roadblocks in your adult relationships. There isn't anything that you do that doesn't have some kind of relationship or attachment to you. All your relationships start with you, people in your community, colleagues, family, children, friends, neighbors, employees, social circle, managers, and animals/pets. Additionally, we have a relationship/bond with the objects in our life, such as our house, apartment, cars, favorite dress, shirt, sports teams, boats, favorite food. The list of objects, people, and places with which we all have relationships is endless and purposeful. Couples will go to the same restaurant or honeymoon spot every year to celebrate that special occasion. The importance of our relationships gives our life meaning, purpose, and direction. These attachments to relationships and objects are the substance and texture of our life. This is not to suggest that we should be materialistic but that certain objects have special meanings for us. We all learned from our first relationship how emotions, feelings, beliefs, disagreements, communication, nurturing, and attachments shape our life. The goal is to redirect self-defeating habits, learn new nurturing connections, and implement our positive emotional spectrum of choices and relationships.

REMOVING YOUR EMOTIONAL/RELATIONAL ROADBLOCKS

When you read the previous section on the five styles of mothering, which one of those styles best describes your mother-child relationship? Consider the five styles—perfectionist, unpredictable, "me first," "best friend," and complete mother. You might want to refer back to the chapter that most accurately depicts your mother-child relationship. Consider the following questions, and see how your answers can provide you with even more valuable information about your relationships and your feelings about them and yourself. Let's fully explore your mother's style and its long-term effects on your relationship pattern and your style of connecting. It is worth mentioning again that each mothering style provides certain strengths as well as weaknesses. The point of this chapter is to uncover and bolster your strengths and lessen your weaknesses in all the different types of relationships that touch your life. Now ask yourself the following questions:

- What was your mother's primary style of mothering while you were growing up?

- How do your various relationships reflect your mother's style in terms of conflict resolution, confrontations, and communication?
- Which one of the five major roadblocks—*shame, deprivation, codependence, anger, and abandonment*—is the most apparent in your present-day life?
- How do you cope with and/or avoid your personal and emotional roadblock(s)?
- Do you find it difficult to acknowledge your emotional and personal relationship issues to your partner?
- What would you consider your personal strength in relationships?
- What is your primary weakness in your intimate relationships?
- What rules do you keep that emotionally connect you to your mother?
- What is a common theme that you share with your mother in how you handle stress and conflicts?
- What is your attachment style (intermittent, avoidant, depressed, or secure/stable) in your primary relationships?
- Do you have different attachment styles for different areas of your life (family, kids, parents, career, social, and friends)?
- What is a recurring theme in your life that you would like to change?
- What self-defeating, self-loathing, and/or self-neglecting behaviors do you have?
- What is your primary nurturing behavior?
- What are your feelings about your emotional connection to food?
- What is one of your relationship issues that you would like to change?
- What mothering style would best describe how you relate in your intimate relationships?
- What is one emotional pattern between you and your mother

(positive or negative) that is common in other areas of your life?

These questions merely scratch the surface of your mother factor legacy. The questions were designed to illuminate the common threads and themes that run throughout your world of relationships. Each mothering style carries a tremendous amount of influence on how you function in all levels of your life. Many sons and daughters weren't allowed to develop an emotional life, language, or understanding while growing up. Those same limitations, restrictions, and/or emotional straitjackets are no longer appropriate or acceptable today. Your emotional life is as significant as your physical health. There is nothing that you will do, say, or achieve that doesn't require your emotional investment and wisdom. Your mother's style set the tempo for your emotional life and development. It is essential that you now fully embrace the different aspects of your emotional life in daily interactions. But to do that, you need to first appreciate both the strengths and the weaknesses of each mothering style.

MOTHER FACTOR STRENGTHS AND STYLE

Let us first explore the strengths, insights, and liabilities that derive from each mothering style.

The Perfectionist Mother

This mothering style emphasizes the importance of perfection. The drive is toward always becoming a perfect daughter/son and never arriving, which results in a never-ending cycle of shame. Perfectionist thinking and acting is a brutal taskmaster for children, teenagers, and adults. No one escapes the collateral damage of the constant pursuit of perfection, which is an impossible task and impossible personal goal. It leaves a son or daughter in a constant emotional state of guilt, shame, and never feeling "good enough." There is very little room for natural human mistakes or naturally occurring imperfections. The end result of a perfectionist son/daughter is that all emotional and internal feelings are avoided and dismissed as secondary. The relationship's emphasis is on appearance and outward behavior. If the exterior of your life is in place, then the rest will follow suit.

The pressure to achieve for either the daughter or son is incredible and relentless. Your mother had an invisible undercurrent that made you strive to measure up to her standard, or you would feel her powerful disappointment. No child, regardless of his many talents and gifts, can withstand his mother's constant disapproval and emotional letdown over a lack of perfection. The result of this performance/perfection-based relationship is the development and implementation of a shame-based personality in a young son or daughter. Shame is considered by many psychologists—myself included—as the most negative emotional force in a person's life. Shameful feelings can immediately paralyze anyone at any time and for any reason. Shame doesn't respect education, wealth, gender, or family position. Shameful feelings are persistent and extremely toxic to the carrier (you) and the relationships in your life. Shame can be summarized as never feeling "good enough" or never allowing for feelings of being "perfectly imperfect."

Changing Shame into Perfectly Imperfect Emotional Insight

The active removal of shameful feelings, thoughts, and behaviors starts with your viewing your perfectionist behavior as a major cause of your personal and relationship struggles.[1] The added belief of never feeling "good enough," "lovable enough," or "acceptable enough," are all from the same toxic source: *your shame.* The nuclear fallout from the perfectionist style of mothering is the deep-seated level of inadequacy and chronic incompetence that you feel permeates your entire life. The insight necessary to shift from an emotional failure to emotional insight and an understanding of your life is accepting your "perfectly imperfect" nature. In chapter 4, we discussed five steps to resolve your shame-based emotions and beliefs. Now we want to expand on some of the inherent strengths that are part of this type of perfectionist mother-child relationship. These strengths go along with your accepting the positive side of this kind of relationship. It takes new understanding and deeper insight into appreciating how you have benefited from your mother's legacy. This list of strengths and inherent talents of your mother's style are important to consider and value. Don't dismiss or discount your mother's positive influence entirely because of the shame factor and issues of perfection.

The following list is composed of some of the common strengths and character qualities separate from the toxic feelings of inadequacy and never feeling good enough that this style of mother produces. We want to focus on both ends of the perfection continuum. Shame is at one end and insight and emotional understanding are at the other end. The goal is to move you closer to the positive side and farther away from shame and self-doubt/loathing. This positive view entails viewing your mother as more than just a taskmaster or a chronic perfectionist. Your mother embodies a combination of many traits, strengths, and weaknesses. It is your responsibility to figure out which strengths that derive from her are helpful in your adult relationships and which aren't. It is very safe to assume that any feelings of shame and self-hatred will always leave the holder (you) in a constant emotional state of fear and panic. Your emotional legacy from your mother, however, is more than the experience of shame. It also contains many positive traits and qualities. Your job is to uncover these strengths and fully recognize your own emotional and relationship potential in connection with them.

Strengths of the Perfectionist Mother

- You have a strong sense of commitment in your relationships.
- You are very responsible and reliable in everything you do.
- You highly value hard work and persistence as core character qualities.
- Your relationships are based on "never giving up" during an emotional hardship.
- You have an innate understanding of social rules and appropriate behavior in all types of settings.
- You never abuse drugs, food, or other substances. You have excellent emotional and psychological boundaries.
- You aren't emotionally excessive.
- You know how unspoken rules for your career, family, and friendships operate and what is expected of you.
- You have the ability to accomplish and complete tasks, projects, and objectives without being directed.
- You are very faithful and a commitment-oriented type of person in your relationships, family, and career.
- You have courage and insight to attempt new things, start new relationships, and confront old problems.
- You aren't scared or avoidant of hard work in a relationship or with your family.
- You are a very loyal person.
- You are an excellent emotional support to friends and family during a crisis. You know what to do and how to get it done.
- People respect your work ethic and practical approach to problems, relationships, and business.

This list of strengths is for you to expand and use in your personal life and relationships. The ability to move beyond your shame is to replace those nagging feelings of self-doubt with insight and understanding of your "perfectly imperfect" life and relationships. You have many skills and talents that were formed by the need for perfection but that can still be very useful with your new sense of balance and self-acceptance.

The Unpredictable Mother

This mothering style is very chaotic and crisis-orientated. Your childhood was an ongoing series of crises, dramas, and unpredictable behavior from your mother. You quickly learned that her mood swings, overreactions, and emotional meltdowns were daily occurrences. The emotionally unstable home environment taught you by the age of five how to read your mother's body language and emotional state without her saying a word to you. You knew when things were going bad or when nothing was going to happen. You were traumatized by the constant instability of your mother's mood swings and perceived problems. Your innate people skills helped you survive your chaotic childhood, teen years, and adult life. You often feel that you are a survivor of a screaming mother. Unfortunately, you endured many kinds of abuse, two of the worst being emotional and psychological. As a result of your chaotic childhood, you currently struggle with varying degrees of anxiety, excessive self-defeating choices, avoidant behaviors, and fear of the future.

You have excellent people skills and know how to defuse any interpersonal situation without having to think. Your ability to read, understand, and take care of people is automatic. In fact, you are so competent that you forget to consider your own opinions and actions before reacting. The idea that someone is upset or angry with you is extremely troubling to you. Your childhood safety was based on keeping your mother happy and in control. You can't tolerate anyone being upset or angry with you, including your partner and children. You have personal issues with being codependent because your self-worth is based on other peoples' opinion of you. You feel valuable or lovable only if you are helping or saving someone. Your childhood was always about taking care of your mother emotionally and mentally. Your inner feelings, thoughts, and desires were never developed or given your mother's attention. Now it is difficult to know or understand what you want for yourself without fixing a crisis or creating one.

Your mother always became fearful or upset by some type of crisis or impending doom. Ultimately, all the different types of crises and horrible events weren't as serious or as life threatening as you were first told or even thought. Everything in childhood felt excessive and overly dramatic. There wasn't any calmness or peace in your life. Now when you get upset, anxious, or panicked, you reactions can also be very excessive. You tend to displace your anxiety onto food, alcohol, and emotional exaggeration. You will automatically attempt to rescue people or become overly involved in a crisis, regardless of your responsibility in the matter. It is difficult as an adult to find an emotional balance and a moderate response to your emotions and feelings. Everything seems very urgent and in need of your immediate attention. Your mother was able to shift your focus onto her problems and gain the attention and concern that she was secretly craving. Much of her drama and crisis attention-seeking behavior was unconscious and an attempt to gain the love and concern of the people in her life. Her unpredictability was an emotional tool for seeking and getting her emotional needs met.

Emotional Codependence to Emotional Independence

You have spent most of your adult life worrying about other people's opinions of you. You have a difficult time saying no to people and not becoming overly involved in their problems. Your emotional life feels like a series of crises that are never ending and unresolvable. The driving force behind codependence is the fear of being rejected or abandoned. The ongoing dependent behavior creates a lack of emotional clarity in your life. You have difficulty in not overidentifying with and becoming absorbed in other people's dramas and life. You feel purposeful when you are thinking about and anticipating what someone else is doing or feeling. This emotional style of behavior is extremely problematic in romantic or marital relationships. This pattern of attachment doesn't work and will always result in a failed relationship. Adults don't want someone to control their thoughts, feelings, or reactions. Therefore, to avoid a replay of your mother-daughter/son relationship, you must become a predictable, stable, and consistent friend, partner, and employee.

Tennis Court Analogy and Codependent Behavior

Betsy is a thirty-two-year-old single professional woman. She was raised by an unpredictable mother who had extreme emotional reactions to everyday life and regular daily events (flat tires, poor weather, sick child, traffic, crowds). Betsy was in a perpetual state of anxiety as a young girl. She was always waiting for Brenda to become upset and start screaming about something that was wrong or that had happened that day. Betsy became very skilled by the age of eight at being able to emotionally defuse her mother when she became upset or started having a meltdown. Betsy spent most of her time growing up thinking about what her mother might be thinking or feeling. Based on her accurate read of her mother, she could keep the peace for her and her younger sister. Betsy never considered that this type of mind reading (making assumptions about others' thoughts) wasn't a normal mother-child relationship function and duty. Betsy related the following story of her boyfriend's complaint:

> My boyfriend says I am always guessing what he might say, think, or feel. He feels that I am always more aware of his feelings than my own. I think he is right. I am always concerned about what Frank is thinking and feeling. I always think of his

response or feelings before I express or say anything. I never stop and think about my own thoughts and just share them. I always think about what the other person will say or feel, and then I think about what I should say or do. I don't want to hurt anyone.

Betsy was playing a metaphorical game of tennis: hitting the ball over the net, then running over to the other side of the court and hitting the ball back for her partner, friends, and colleagues. Her behavior was consistent in this regard and not limited to her intimate relationship or any one person in her life professionally, personally, or socially. Betsy was always playing both sides of the court and never able to stop and consider her own thoughts, feelings, and emotions. She couldn't allow her boyfriend to have his own responses, thoughts, feelings, or opinions. She had to direct and control everything. Her codependence was an unconscious way of attempting to make herself feel safe and emotionally secure. Betsy's codependence was her attempt to control her boyfriends' emotions and actions. But the opposite would happen, because her behavior would drive her intimate partners away and make the people in her life angry. She couldn't allow or tolerate anyone to have his own feelings, thoughts, or reactions because she felt so emotionally traumatized by her mother's unpredictable responses. Therefore, Betsy unconsciously would attempt to script everyone's life as a form of safety for her own emotional well-being. Eventually, she began to realize that as long as she was creating and controlling peoples' responses and behavior, she was still acting like a traumatized girl/woman. Nevertheless, having an unpredictable mother has its benefits.

Strengths of the Unpredictable Mother

- You have excellent people skills and the ability to be very empathic.
- You are an excellent motivator and emotional support to your colleagues, friends, children, and partner.

- You understand relationship needs and what is necessary for people to manage a conflict.
- You know the value and importance of clear, unemotional communication.
- You know how to defuse a volatile situation.
- You are very diplomatic and aware of social rules and behaviors in the workplace.
- You avoid using anger as a form of communication.
- You understand the value of a safe, consistent, stable relationship for a secure emotional bond.
- You have excellent human resource skills and talents.
- You know how to be empathically attuned and emotionally connected to people.
- You are a very loyal and supportive friend, partner, employee, and parent.
- You know and understand the value of acting appropriately and respectfully in any type of relationship or social setting.
- You are very intuitive, perceptive, and insightful with people in all types of relationships.
- You understand the emotional struggle of not being codependent and always fixing people's problems.
- You are excellent at solving problems and supporting your friends emotionally.

This is a very short list of some of the positive traits, talents, and interpersonal skills that you developed within the context of your mother-child relationship. You know the value of not being overly dramatic or catastrophizing everything that happens to you or in your relationships. You have strong interpersonal strengths that are valuable and necessary in your career, your different relationships, and any personal endeavor you enjoy. You know the value of being able to express your feelings without having to fix or solve someone else's problems.

The Me First Mother

This mothering style is a very common and complex style of mothering. It is a self-absorbed, self-directed mothering style that focuses primarily on the mother, not the child. The mother is concerned with her well-being and has a difficult time being emotionally attached to or understanding of her children. This is a mother who knows what she wants but isn't aware of the emotional concerns, wants, and nurturing needs of her daughter or son. Much of the daughter's/son's childhood is centered on making the mother happy. Seeking her approval is one of the child's primary tasks growing up. The problem with this mother-child relationship is that the child (you) doesn't get the support to develop his own sense of self. If you were brought up with the "me first" mothering style, your internal needs and natural emotional development were shaped by your mother's own needs and wants. Your life was a series of maneuvers to keep her happy and not angry at you.

The harsh attitude your mother had toward other people who upset her was something you didn't want to experience. The constant need of your mother to make herself better than others, more important, and more special than others, was never ending. Your mother had positive mothering qualities despite her narcissism, but her narcissism ruled her life. The need to be the center of attention, the one with the most important opinion, the one with the smartest children was a constant pressure and compulsion for your mother. Because of her unmet emotional needs and low self-esteem, your mother had to make everyone else less than her. You feared that this could happen to your relationship with your mother. If you didn't understand your mother's needs and wants, then you would be ignored, dismissed, or the object of her anger. You experienced many emotional letdowns because you weren't viewed as important enough. The long-term effect of this emotional neglect created a sense of deprivation in your life. You began to feel that your life was, in fact, not important. The lack of interest and concern for your fears, challenges, and accomplishments caused you to doubt your self-worth and value. In order to compensate for these feelings, you either became self-centered or became very insecure about your place in relationships and the world around you.

Deprivation → Emotional Strength → "Good Enough"

The goal of coming out of a narcissistic mother-child relationship is to resolve, heal, and understand your sense of emotional deprivation. All degrees of self-centeredness and "me first" behavior of a parent toward a child have the collateral effect of creating emotional holes in the child's life. Having a narcissistic mother leaves a child feeling emotionally deprived with unmet needs. The "me first" style of mothering creates huge emotional deficits that lead the daughter or son to create a defensive personality that will protect his or her vulnerability and neediness. This psychological process is the creation and definition of a "me first" son or daughter. The pathway toward healing and going beyond the defensive shell of emotional protection is through empathy, courage/self-confidence, and self-acceptance. These three traits create a sense of being "good enough" and begin to fill the emotional holes in your heart, life, and soul. The ability to accept that being "good enough" is what is important—not being "number one"—is your personal power in action.

Sons and daughters struggle with the legacy of a self-absorbed mother and all her critical beliefs, rejections, and anger. Narcissistic mothers have large amounts of resentment and anger for the misunderstandings, emotional wounds, and lack of appreciation they have experienced. The "good enough" rules are listed below because you have learned a great deal from having a narcissistic mother. These lessons are nine insights you have gained by having a "me first" mother.

"Me First" Mothering Insights

Good Enough Rule #1—You can change your beliefs, actions, and unmet emotional needs. You don't have to live in isolation, hoping someone can break through your emotional defensiveness. Acknowledging the possibility for change is the opportunity to start your change. You, better than anyone, know this needs to be done.

Good Enough Rule #2—Become fully aware of your automatic responses, behaviors, and feelings. You can be more than self-centered and create emotional fulfillment within your relationships. Automatic responses allow you not to be conscious of your behavior or feelings. Consider this an option, not a wish. You know more than anyone else that you need to be attuned to your own needs and desires.

Good Enough Rule #3—Develop a feedback loop of information in your relationships. You can tolerate feedback, even if it doesn't make you look or feel good. Feedback gives you an ongoing perspective of your life and emotional connections to people. You have a great need to hear from others and you know this is the time to get the feedback you need.

Good Enough Rule #4—Develop understanding into your behavior and defensiveness. Look below the surface of your feelings, actions, and emotions. Examine the root, which is your need to feel loved and cared for. You, more than anyone, know that defensive behavior is off-putting and you don't want to act that way anymore.

Good Enough Rule #5—Being right isn't always right. Your unconscious need to always be right is about your mother-child relationship and seeking your mother's evasive approval. Insisting on being right is never about the topic at hand but your need to appear special and brilliant.

Good Enough Rule #6—It is an inside job. You can meet, understand, and learn to satisfy your own emotional needs. The things you truly want are within you and are worth developing. Your life is internal not external; it is an inside job and you have direct access to it.

Good Enough Rule #7—Learn to say no to your mother and develop tolerance for fear of rejection in all your relationships. You don't have to be loved and accepted by everyone. Rejection is an inevitable fact of life and relationships.

Good Enough Rule #8—Stop telling the world that you are great. The people in your world are sick and tired of hearing you brag and pump yourself up. Remember your mother's constant bragging and emotional insecurity—how did you like it? Allow the world to discover and experience your uniqueness; it will be more meaningful and substantial to you.

Good Enough Rule #9—Your greatest strength and asset is your humility. Never forget this truth; it will change your life and everyone that you emotionally connect with. Your entire life is a composite of relationships, and humility is the glue that connects them all. Humility will serve you well in all aspects of your life. There is nothing in your life that will not benefit from your humility and empathy for others. The people in your life will jump over buildings to help you because of your compassion, empathy, and humility toward them.

These nine "good enough" insights emphasize that there isn't anything in your emotional legacy that doesn't require your internal sense of self-acceptance and feeling "good enough" in your relationships. Everyone can benefit from applying these self-acceptance builders and emotional roadblock removers. Feeling and believing that you are "good enough" allows you to experience people and in a much deeper, more meaningful manner. You aren't spending your emotional energy trying to convince everyone that you are great, special, or in need of extra attention. You will find an enormous amount of strength and personal confidence in not being the focus of attention or the monopolizer of everyone's emotional energy. These old behaviors never worked for you or your mother anyway. Don't forget that you were unable to meet or adequately address your emotional and psychological needs of belonging and feeling loved by being "me first" or emotionally desperate.

The Best Friend Mother

This style of mothering is also very common and extremely problematic for a son or daughter. The conflict is that a relationship is either a mother-child relationship or friend-child relationship. It can't be both and it isn't. Daughters and sons growing up in this context know the difference and always prefer the mother-child dynamic. We discussed at length the numerous emotional issues (anger, abandonment, neglect) that this mothering style creates. All three of these emotional wounds can be very problematic in all your adult relationships and connections. Anger is the most toxic and dangerous of the three. It covers up the much deeper wounds of abandonment and neglect. Anger is a natural response to the long-term experience of neglect and/or abandonment, both of which have to be resolved in the child's life. Best friend mothers often cause their daughter/son to feel "motherless," even though the mother is physically present. The lack of appropriate mothering triggers the feeling of being unimportant, neglected, and emotionally abandoned.

"I don't understand it, my mother is great but she isn't a mother," is the common frustrated statement that comes out when discussing the best friend mother. Anger is the natural response to this deep mother-child wound that hasn't been resolved or fully understood. These neglected daughters/sons carry their pain and resentment into adult relationships, careers, marriages, and their parenting. Feeling motherless and paradoxically having a good relationship with your mother is a very confusing and complex psychological issue. The fact that the friendship element supersedes the mother role is the ongoing dilemma for the daughter/son. You love your mother; she is a wonderful woman, friendly, sweet, and understanding, but she doesn't act like a mother or want to be one. She doesn't want to be anyone's mother. It is this quandary of confusion that creates feelings of abandonment, neglect, and anger. Then you feel extremely guilty for these conflicted feelings toward your mother—after all, she did pay for your college education, new sports car, your MBA at an Ivy League school, and your wedding. Your mother is very generous and sweet, but she isn't emotionally supportive of you. You want a mother, not a friend who competes with you. Your mother doesn't like being put in the role of being a mother; she resents it and even gets mad. She doesn't like your questioning and your emotional requests for her wisdom, support, and guidance. Your mother ignores these requests for mothering and maternal love.

Motherless/Best Friend Mothering Strengths

The ongoing issues of resolving your sense of neglect, abandonment, and anger are healed by first changing your perspective and approach to the relationship. You have the opportunity to relate to your mother differently. It is critical to accept the fact that your mother is available as much as she can be. Your role now is to stop going to the motherhood well and becoming angry that it is bone dry. The intangible things, unspoken support, and motherly love that you crave will not be found there. Your responsibility is to find other nurturing, supportive, and wise women in your life. You probably already have supportive women and friends in your life; this applies to both sons and daughters. Accepting that your mother isn't the complete mother is a huge step toward your emotional stability and will allow your anger to diminish. When we accept and stop trying to fit a square peg (your mother) into the perfect round hole of motherhood, we are the ones who benefit. Anger can only exist when we keep insisting on certain things that aren't going to happen. Once we discover the source of the anger, we can deal with it.

A common question is: What do I replace my anger with in my life? The answers can vary, but essentially what you put in place of your moodiness, anger, and resentment is empathy, self-acceptance, and compassion. These three emotional choices benefit you, the child, the way water refreshes a dying plant. These emotional choices allow you to accept the limitations of your mother-child relationship and emotionally move beyond resenting and hating her for her lack of maternal qualities. Another issue is not constantly arguing with her about being a better mother or more of an adult rather than a girlfriend or buddy. That type of behavior only connects us to our emotional pain and perpetuates our sense of neglect and abandonment. Choosing to be empathic, accepting, and loving toward your mother will only benefit you. Lets us look at the insights you've gained from having a best friend mother.

Best Friend Mothering Insights

- You understand the power and destructive nature of anger in relationships.
- You are able to defuse and redirect colleagues, friends, family, and your children's disappointments toward a positive perspective.
- You are very faithful and emotionally connected to all the people in your life.
- You have emotional insight, understanding, and personal life experience in how conflicts need to be settled without anger.
- You are aware of the limited value of resentment, anger, and rejection as personal motivators.
- You understand the importance of being emotionally present for people on a daily basis.
- You understand the importance of boundaries between parents, children, colleagues, and family.
- You have the ability and courage to stand up for yourself and others.

- You know the value and importance of being a leader, parent, and good friend.
- You have leadership qualities. Because of your sense of "motherlessness," you are very aware of leading people and taking responsibility as an adult.
- You know the value of being committed and consistent with your family, friends, children, and co-workers.
- You have a demeanor of compassion, empathy, and insight that is necessary for any task that you undertake.
- You aren't willing to quit a relationship, partnership, or business deal for a trivial reason.
- You will be the mother or father to your children, friends, and family that you have always wanted.

We are all guilty at times of not focusing on or remembering the positive deeds or good values we received from our mothers growing up. What is one value that you received from your mother that stands out the most to you? Mandy (chapter 7) told me, "My mother always told me to work hard and be very responsible. Those two things have always guided my life in school and now in my career." Evan (chapter 8) told me, "Steve, my mother was unpredictable but she always emphasized that I do well in school, go to college, and develop a professional life. I have done it and she was right." Regardless of how problematic, volatile, and crazy your mother-daughter/son relationship was or still is, don't lose sight of what benefit you received. What are some of the other hidden emotional, interpersonal, and professional strengths that you gleaned from your mother? Looking at your mother as a valuable resource in your life is a very positive way to move beyond any long-term conflicts. It also affords you a different perspective in which to see her.

SUMMARY—MOTHER FACTOR MOVEMENT

Regardless of how strained, troubled, disappointing, unsupportive, and/or painful the relationship with your mother was or still is, there is in almost every situation some degree of benefit and strength to be gleaned. Don't buy into the very common social fad of "mother bashing"; it is a misdirected approach to your anger and unresolved emotional pain. There is another old adage about hate and anger: *If you hate someone, it is like drinking poison and hoping it kills the other person.* The analogy works beautifully, because it is all about you and your emotional disposition, feelings, and beliefs. It is solely your adult choices that will direct the growth or decline of your mental health. What is your primary mother-child strength that you use today? Whatever it is, it is important to recall that you probably have many more strengths than weaknesses from your mother. Consider the four mothering styles below. (The complete mothering style isn't included, because it is the subject of the next two chapters):

- Perfectionist Style of Mothering—shame becoming insight, understanding, being "perfectly imperfect."
- Unpredictable Style of Mothering—codependence becoming independence and emotional stability.
- "Me First" Style of Mothering—emotional deprivation becoming feeling "good enough" and having self-acceptance.
- Best Friend Style of Mothering—anger, neglect, and abandonment becoming compassion, empathy, and self-acceptance.

As we've seen, despite your relationship with your mother, or, in some extreme cases, because of it, you have acquired strengths and insights that have served you well in your relationships—professionally, socially, and intimately. Let's further explore how we can continue to bolster those strengths and add even more insights, and new emotional capacities, to expand your relationship connections.

Chapter 11

THE BIG SEPARATION

Getting beyond Your Mother

Separation/Individuation

The hardest thing I have ever done is to emotionally separate from my mother. I had to literally leave home or I wasn't ever going to make a break into adulthood. My mother didn't talk to me for six months, she was so mad that I moved out before I was married. I didn't even have a boyfriend.

—Heather, age thirty-four

I never expected my mother to be so mean and angry about moving away to college on the West Coast. My mother suggested going to school away from home, but she meant within driving distance of our home in upstate New York. I feel that my mother never got over the pain of my leaving. I was the youngest of four. It wasn't like she hadn't done it before, but it felt like a betrayal.

—Brett, age forty-five

THE SEPARATION PROCESS—WHAT IS IT?

T he reality and importance of the separation and individuation process is something that intuitively has always made sense. The cultural myth of "go West, young man" meant that at some point, you had to leave home. Men have always been defined by their ability to emotionally separate from their mothers and to create their own life/home/family. Daughters today have the same mandate to leave home. Both genders are faced with a monumental task of completing their emotional development by creating their own identity and a life that is separate from their mother's. The major problem is the mother usually hasn't successfully completed her own emotional separation process from her mother (your grandmother). The incomplete emotional separation and identity formation become the next generation's problem and emotional weight.

We are going to discuss the most important developmental task that you will ever encounter. Your ability to navigate the waters of separation and identity formation are critical to everything you will do for the rest of your adult life. All the problems, strengths, mothering style issues, emotional intelligence, shameful feelings, success, emotional roadblocks, lack of confidence, personal empowerment, constant relationship failures, and sense of uneasiness within yourself all start and finish with this task: *separation and individuation*. There is nothing in your life that is not influenced by this critical, naturally occurring process. Ultimately, we all have to move out of our mother's house—literally and figuratively.

What is this process really all about? The clinical definition of separation and individuation is *the emotional ability to form your own sense of self, with your own opinions, thoughts, and feelings. It is also the ability to keep emotional boundaries in the context of relationships and not become the other person, or allow the other person to control and direct your choices, life, and emotions.*

What matters here is in the application of creating your own feelings and thoughts without asking for permission or others' opinions. Creating and acting on your own dreams, hopes, and desires is part of the American dream. Yet so many intelligent, gifted, professional, educated, loving, empathic, and compassionate women and men get emotionally stuck someplace in the separation/individuation process. Many of these daughters and sons leave home reluctantly and never arrive at their desired destination of becoming an independent, high-functioning adult. The majority of adults have never fully completed the process of individuation or separating from their mother.

Oftentimes, sons or daughters will get married, move away, have children, live with their partner, and become overly involved in their career just to avoid their mother's rage about separating and creating their own life. All these milestones are wonderful if you aren't using them as a defense mechanism to avoid disappointing and upsetting your mother. It is a twofold process. First, you have to take steps, regardless of your mother's support, to find your own opinion, "voice," and place in life. Second, your mother needs to support you and guide you in this individuation process and creation. Many sons and daughters can't complete this process because they don't have their mother's support or cooperation. In order to fully understand each of these processes, let's break down their function:

Separation is the process of experiencing yourself as a woman or man distinct from your mother. This does not imply that in order to feel separate you must physically move to another zip code or around the world, yet that does happen frequently. Rather, it means that you feel comfortable about having your own feelings, thoughts, opinions, and emotions, and making your own choices. You take responsibility for making your own life decisions in every area and relationship. The separation process reaches a leveled plateau when you are able to emotionally withstand the pressure, criticism, and anger from your mother for being in conflict with her. Many times, the potential conflict will cause high-functioning daughters and sons to stop their separation process for fear of losing their mother's love.

Individuation is the emotional process of creating an internalized picture of yourself as an independent daughter or son. This independence includes feeling frustration and joy in your ability to create and do the things that you want in your life without your parents' emotional and financial support or their permission. You have the emotional strength to know and state your own values, preferences, and behaviors. This can range from career choices, lifestyle choices, religious/spiritual beliefs, sexuality orientation, finances, and parenting. You view yourself as a complete person, making your own life decisions.

MOVING OUT

These necessary developmental processes are a lifelong task and continue to occur and evolve over the course of your life and through your many different relationships. Sometimes a marriage, a painful third divorce, career loss, a death of a loved one, bankruptcy, or sudden wealth will cause you to reexamine your life and beliefs. Grieving or celebrating life transitions are pieces of the separation/individuation process and your personal growth. The goal of creating your own emotional, physical, and spiritual life is to basically relinquish primary dependence on your mother. You can't make or develop other significant emotional connections with the people in your life if you are still in your mother's orbit. It is essential to be your own "planet" and have your own orbit, sun, and universe. There is nothing wrong with sharing information and content about your universe with your mother, but it has to be yours. You can't be the moon reflecting back your mother's wishes, demands, and opinions. The analogy is powerful because many adults never leave their mother's orbit and in fact remain on her planet. *Have you left your mother's orbit?* If you have, how do you know? The power and pull to stay within your mother's orbit/sphere of influence and control is something every child/teen/adult must face and resolve in order to attain future success. Until you have created your own functional orbit and life, your level of emotional satisfaction and functioning isn't fully realized.

MIKE AND LEE—SEPARATION ANXIETY

The floor fell from under me in disbelief during my first internship, in September 1991, in California. A high school junior, Mike, and his mother, Lee, came to see me. Mike had been arrested for his second DUI (driving under the influence of alcohol) while riding his bicycle. The only reason they came to therapy was that the juvenile court judge ordered mandatory counseling for Mike for his chronic drinking.

The background story was that Mike had been arrested when he was fifteen and sixteen years old for riding his bike "drunk." The story seemed very odd; there had to be something missing from it. First I met Lee for the initial parent interview. Lee, a divorced single mother, said the following, "I don't believe in therapy and I think most psychologists are weird." I remember looking at Lee and thinking, this woman has a major crisis and is more worried about maintaining her control over her son than about his severe drinking problem, which was out of control. Lee was convinced that I was going to disturb the relationship between her and her son. She was correct, the goal was to give both of them emotional breathing room and a new perspective on their relationship. Lee had been divorced for ten years, was not dating anyone, and was currently unemployed. I understood her defensiveness and anger about being ordered to mandatory therapy. Lee didn't want anyone to interfere with her emotional bond with her son.

When I met Mike, he told me the following, "My mother is

always in my room, my space, and anywhere I go. I can't seem to get away from her unless I drink with my friends. When I am drunk, my mother doesn't bother me and has no control over me. I hate that my mother is always following me around and talking to all my friends." Mike's complaints didn't seem that uncommon or unusual for a rebellious teenage boy. But Mike was different: he was a sweet, well-mannered boy, a smart, good student, athletic and polite. Mike wasn't angry or trying to ruin his life. He felt emotionally suffocated by his mother. He firmly believed that his only emotional separation from his mother was drinking. Mike's older brother, Sean, had gone to college in Wisconsin to play baseball and came home only three times a year. Mike felt trapped by and emotionally enmeshed with his mother. He lived alone with his mother and was the sole focus of her attention and energy.

Over the next two years, Mike was arrested three more times for alcohol-related infractions (drunk in public, drinking at school, and having an open container of alcohol in a vehicle). His behavior was fueled by his mother's attempt to control and manage her son's potential alcoholism. Lee told me once on the phone that "Mike is the only man in my life. My older son, Sean, and my ex-husband don't want anything to do with me. Mike is the only man who pays attention to me. I would die if Mike wasn't in my life. I really need his help and support." After Lee told me this, she said, "You know of course that I was referring to a mother and son relationship." My heart dropped, hearing Lee's motivation and explanation of her excessive controlling behavior with her son. It had been recommended several times by other professionals that Mike go live with his father in Florida and get away from his high school drinking buddies. But Lee needed and wanted Mike, and no one was going to interfere with the relationship. Her emotional need for a man and using her son as a substitute lover, partner, and emotional object was very problematic for both of them.

Lee was an attractive woman, intelligent, humorous, and very capable of having adult relationships with men. She had never emotionally separated from her mother. Mike, after high school graduation, left California and moved to Florida with his father. When Mike left his mother's house, he stopped drinking, entered college, and graduated five years later. Lee unfortunately didn't understand why both of her sons moved away and never came to see her. Lee lost her job as a fund-raiser and had her eighty-year-old mother move into her house. She decided that since she liked being a mother, she would open a child day care center. Lee died from a stroke a few years later. Mike had never fully separated and individuated from his mother because he was angry about her controlling behavior and her constant emotional need for his attention and time. Even though Lee died, Mike struggled with her voice, criticism, and harsh opinions in his head. He still had to emotionally separate and individuate from her. Many times, sons and daughters assume that because their mother has passed away, the process of separation is complete, but this is absolutely wrong.

HELEN AND ANNE—CRITICAL PARTNERSHIP

When I met Helen, she was thirty-nine years old. Helen came to see me regarding her avoidance issues and her problems with men. In a matter of a few months, it was clear that Helen had been gay since she was a teenager and had never accepted her sexual orientation. Helen had secretly had a crush on numerous women throughout her life and career as a nurse. Each time she had romantic feelings for a woman, she dismissed them as nothing more than those of friendship. Once she finally knew what her sexual preference was, she didn't want to upset her orthodox religious family.

Helen decided not to tell her mother, Anne, about her romantic life. Helen had her then girlfriend, Lisa, move in with her after Helen accepted her sexual orientation. Helen lived with her girlfriend for almost four years in an exclusive relationship. When Helen's father died, however, she felt a sudden need to take care of her mother. Helen insisted that her mother come and live with her in Los Angeles.

Helen and Lisa came to see me about Helen's mother issue. Helen said the following, "I have to have my mother live with me. I would die if something ever happened to my mother. I am responsible for my mother, she is my best friend." Lisa ultimately broke up with Helen when her mother, Anne, moved in with them. Helen didn't see the problem or why Lisa was threatened by her mother. Over the next six months, Helen revealed that she had wanted to live with her mother since she moved out at age eighteen. Helen always felt emotionally connected to her mother and didn't want to lose that connection.

Anne moved to Los Angeles and bought a new house with Helen in Malibu (an exclusive beach community north of Los Angeles). Neither Anne nor Helen ever considered the option of being separate and not living together in the same town. At first Helen didn't miss Lisa, her girlfriend of four years. Helen told me the following during one of our sessions, "I have always been very close to my mother. I didn't want to lose out on the chance to live with my mother again. Since my father is gone, it is my responsibility to live with her. My mother needs me and I can help her." Helen didn't view her separation or individuation from her mother as something worth pursuing, valuable, or necessary. Helen soon learned that if she was ever going to have another relationship again, she would have to create some emotional distance from her mother.

Helen and Anne still live together three years later. Since Anne moved in with her daughter, Helen hasn't had any romantic relationships, connections, or a single date. Helen and Anne spend a lot of time together and both enjoy the mother-daughter bond.

Helen came back to therapy recently to discuss her issues with her mother. Anne now completely controls Helen's life, her eating habits, and her friendships. Helen admitted the following:

I always considered the need to separate from your mother as psychobabble and just a bunch of new age jargon. It isn't and I am miserable. What was I thinking? I have an eighty-three-year woman living with me, who still treats me like I am eight years old and needs her constant help. This was a huge mistake living with my mother. My mother was fine in Chicago. She had all her friends in the neighborhood, the temple, and lived there for forty-five years. I don't know what to do with her. My mother listens to all my phone calls. She wants to know where I am at all times and is completely helpless to get anything done.

Helen began to create emotional distance with her mother by starting to live her own life again and not allowing Anne to make decisions for her. She began to date Lisa again and decided to move out of her mother's house. Helen knew that if she didn't take some action to create emotional and mental boundaries from her mother, her adult development and life weren't going to move forward. She felt that her entire life came to a four-wheel skidding stop when she invited her mother out to California.

THE EXPERIENCE OF BEING SEPARATE BUT CONNECTED

In order to make the transition from a dependent son/daughter to an autonomous adult, you need to experience yourself as an individual, separate from your mother. For this process to take place smoothly, you and your mother must feel good about this change. The reality is that roughly 90 percent of mothers and children struggle with this process. This number is based on the fact that only about 10 percent of all mothers have the complete style of mothering. The complete mother encourages and supports her daughter/son to move forward and make the necessary life changes to create a sense of self and have an individual life. The other four mothering styles all have the potential and ability to do the same for their children.

The separation process that we discussed in chapter 2 starts and ends with the emotional bond that daughters or sons have with their mother. Each of the four styles of attachment (intermittent, avoidant, depressed, and secure) play an important role in your ability to move forward in your life and relationships. The stronger and more secure the emotional bond is with your mother, the easier time you will have with the process. So for your emotional separation to take place without tremendous conflict, a daughter/son must truly believe that the mother not only supports the separation but approves of it. As we see from the two stories above, a daughter's and son's move toward independence can be very anxiety-provoking for all parties involved. The higher the anxiety, anger, and tension, the less successful your mother likely was in attempting to separate from her mother, your grandmother. If your mother's attempts to separate were met with frustration and threats, it is understandable that your mother might be very clingy and hold on tight to you as you move forward. It is always a worthwhile effort to ask your mother how her mother (grand-mother) handled her independence. You might be very surprised by the story and the struggle.

There are five very common ways most sons and daughters separate from their mother. Each style is connected to the style of emotional bonding they had with their mother. If you feel that your mother is intermittent in her attention, support, concern, and love, then you will wonder if you can leave home and if she will even notice. If the style of attachment was depressed, you might have to generate a lot of drama and fighting to create your own emotional space. Families function on an emotional continuum. One end is the enmeshed family and the other end is the disengaged family.

The Enmeshment Emotional Family. This a very tight emotional family group led by your mother and her mothering style. In this type of family, it is an unspoken rule that no one should have secret thoughts, his own feelings, independent ideas, actions, or relationships. All things must be considered the family domain and open to family opinion (your mother's). The emotional glue is closeness, full disclosure, and no privacy. Everything that happens in the family is discussed with the mother as the mediator. If this sounds familiar, your mother is overly involved in your public and private life and your friendships. You don't have any emotional or psychological privacy. Your life is an open book for your mother's own emotional needs and wants. During the separation process, this mother-child relationship can seem to the child like a form of emotional suffocation. Conformity and compliance are emotionally rewarded. Any movement away from the family/mother is viewed as a violation and will be punished. Many times, the punishment is the withdrawal of emotional support, approval, and connection. Sons and daughters from this mother/family style assume that everyone knows their thoughts, feelings, and actions without explaining them. Adults raised with enmeshed mothers have problems keeping proper emotional boundaries and maintaining personal limits in relationships. There are no individuals in this family. Everyone is one group surrounding your mother.

The Disengaged Emotional Family. In this type of family, the mother is very distant, cold, and emotionally negligent. It is as if there were cement barriers between you, your mother, and other family members. Your home is like a hotel, where everyone comes and goes without any emotional connection or acknowledgment of each other. The unspoken mother's rule is to keep all strong emotions and feelings undercover and out of conscious awareness. Your mother is likely caring, but she doesn't demonstrate or express it to you. All loving feelings, support, and concern are assumed, not spoken or expressed. This mother-child emotional relationship/bond feels very insecure, distant, and full of resentments. The daughters/sons always wonder, does anyone notice them? Home is just a place where you sleep at night and leave in the morning. These sons and daughters will tend to wonder in their intimate and personal relationships if they are noticed, wanted, valuable, and important to their lover/partner. Feeling ignored or lonely is very common for these sons and daughters.

These two types of mothers/families are on opposite ends of a continuum. And every mothering style and mother-daughter and mother-son emotional attachment operates somewhere on this spectrum. The goal is be toward the middle of the emotional spectrum—where the optimal balance of emotional freedom and closeness fosters daughters' and sons' individual growth and personal development. Being on either polar end is extremely problematic for any son or daughter. If a mother is on the far end of emotional enmeshment, then her daughters or sons will feel like they have on cement boots attempting to separate from their mother. All the mothering styles have elements of both the enmeshed and disengaged styles, which are part of the overall mother-child emotional relationship, though each clearly has different proportions.

Look at the diagram below. Take a pen (not a pencil) and put an "X" on the spot that marks your emotional place with your mother and all the various elements of your relationship with her. Don't worry about the past or present or future; mark your emotional spot. Roughly 80 percent of us are someplace between the extremes of emotional enmeshment and emotional disengagement. This number is based on the statistical principle of the 80/20 rule. Ten percent of any group is on each polar end and the other 80 percent are someplace between these two extremes.[1] It has been my professional and personal experience that this is a very accurate barometer of the mother-child emotional relationship legacy. Where are you today with your mother (regardless of her physical status)? Where would you like to be on this emotional attachment scale in six months? The answer is yours, not your mother's.

Disengaged _____ **Optimal** _____ **Enmeshed**

FIVE STYLES OF SEPARATION

Now, let's go to the heart of the mother-child relationship and discuss how we actually do separate from each other. Separation in any type of relationship is challenging and requires emotional, mental, and psychological clarity. How does this process really work? What does separation/individuation look like and feel like for the mother, daughter, and son? The stories above about Mike and Helen both represent a particular style of separating. Each of these adults were/are strongly influenced by the composite of the following mother factor variables, which we've discussed throughout this entire book:

- Your mother-daughter/son style of attachment.
- The mother's degree of emotional enmeshment vs. emotional disengagement.
- The application and enforcement of the mother's rule book in the child's life.
- The style of separation used throughout your relationship history.

These four variables make up the substance and texture of your mother factor legacy. We have discussed each variable and element at length. It is important to remember that everyone comes from a family, a mother-child relationship with its own particular style of relating, bonding, and attaching. Every adult daughter and son has approached the style of separating from a unique perspective. The list below is to further elaborate on some of the more common approaches to separating that many daughters and sons have used to achieve a certain level of fulfillment and completion. Consider the five styles and which one fits and describes yours the best.

The five styles are explained in detail. Look for your emotional patterns, feelings, anxiety tolerance, triggers, resentments, and desires to move forward in your life. Your story of separation is in these styles, because we all have to go past our mother on the way out of her house. No one can metaphorically separate, unless he or she walks past the mother and out the front door. Some of us will run out the back door, some of us will go into the night and sneak out, some of us will start a fight and then leave in anger, some of us will blame our mother for helping us leave, some of us will act like the mother and be responsible and never leave, and a few of us will simply walk out the front door with our mother's support and love. How have you gone out of your mother's house?

- submissive daughter/son style
- rebellious teenager/adult/passive-aggressive style
- the frustrated son/daughter style
- the parentified daughter/son style
- secure adult style

The Submissive Daughter/Son. These sons and daughters are the "good" girls and boys who never questioned or broke their mother's rules. These aren't the teenagers who came home drunk, stayed out all night at some unknown destination, or drove their mother's car into the neighbor's pool (true story). This son and daughter were taking all their cues from their mother about how to navigate adolescence and early adulthood. These children grew up to be passive in their approach to their lives, dreams, goals, education, sports, and relationships. They are like reeds on a river bank, bending whichever direction their mother wants them to go. These are passive, unassertive daughters and sons. Many times, these children grow up to become depressed or extremely anxious. They tend to be codependent in all their different types of relationships. These daughters/sons will be fully dependent on other people's support and approval for their inner self-esteem and sense of belonging. These adults have relationships based on their ability to fix, serve, and take care of their mother, partner, and/or friends. The submissive adult will always feel loved if he or she is able to save or help someone.

The emotional separation necessary for the natural adult development is unconsciously avoided and redirected toward being supportive of other people (the mother). These daughters and sons will attempt to enter adulthood without having to address these issues and any other potential conflict. Submissive adults will skip any type of conflict that could lead to an emotional separation between them and their mother. Unless life circumstances force the emotional break—conflict—the role of being perfect and good is the driving force in their life. They find it emotionally terrifying to anticipate the idea of possibly losing their mother's love and support by creating their own life.

If the above rings true for you, the fear of losing your mother's love has caused you to avoid any challenges that would create an emotional gap or long-term tension with her. Your unconscious choices to avoid certain careers, to stay at home after college, to live within a few minutes of your mother, to date/marry the partner your mother selects are all the choices you've made. Your role of being the "perfect" child is a very tough identity to abandon when contemplating the possibility of following your own desires. You have spent years of your adult life avoiding and denying certain emotions, thoughts, and actions.

If you are the submissive daughter/son, how can you become more assertive and empowered with your mother and the other people in your life? In chapter 5, we met Julie, who couldn't allow herself and her husband to buy a house unless her mother approved of it. Julie then had to have her mother's approval to keep her enmeshed relationship intact. Julie's husband, Stan, went ahead with the purchase of the house without Julie's mother's approval. Julie had a sudden panic attack about doing this without her mother's approval. Julie's mother ultimately didn't really care about the house or the finances. Her sole agenda was just to have her daughter close to her. Julie was emotionally enmeshed with her mother, which caused her marriage to be cold and distant. She always placed her mother's opinion ahead of her husband's. She was in a constant anxious state regarding her mother's happiness and approval. Finally she was confronted with having to create her own identity separate and apart from her mother's desires when her husband filed for divorce. She didn't fight the divorce and moved back in with her mother. She left her children with her husband.

Rebellious Daughter or Son. The rebellious daughter or son is a lost child, regardless of age, who is looking for attention and love. Such daughters or sons are the teenagers sitting in the coffee shop, the mall, or around the neighborhood with a lost and angry look in their eyes. These are the kids that grow up to become adults who wonder if anyone (mother) really cares about them or notices them. Unfortunately, these sons and daughters can end up as high school drop-outs (even though they might be extremely smart) or "A-plus" students who get arrested for drug sales. These kids might cut their bodies, use body paint (tattoos), and engage in any behavior that can be self-destructive and personally dangerous. The goal is to hurt themselves to gain some degree of nurturing, empathy, and compassion from their mother. All the rebellion is directed toward becoming noticed, loved, and cared for. If these unmet emotional needs aren't resolved, the rebellious teen grows into the passive-aggressive adult.

This son/daughter has never been able to successfully separate and is still fighting with the mother for attention and love thirty years after high school graduation. For instance, the passive-aggressive adult will slowly kill himself by binge drinking half a bottle of vodka and then driving home from a family party. He then wonders why his partner, mother, or friends are upset with him. Rebellion, acting out, anger, and passive-aggressive behavior are all preseparation behaviors. Many times, a son or daughter will spend an entire life in this phase and never metaphorically leave the mother's home and become emotionally whole and content. These sons'/daughters' lives are an ongoing series of failed relationships, legal problems, employment concerns, anger issues, and attention-seeking behaviors.

The process of separation and the psychological purpose of individuation are lost in this son's or daughter's life. The emotional pain of feeling neglected, rejected, and/or abandoned results in an angry approach to life. The years of pain and conflict between the mother-daughter/son prevent separation from occurring. The relationship is so severely fractured that emotional bonding, nurturing, and normal mother-child interactions are never developed. There isn't enough emotional clarity, strength, insight, or purpose to separate from the mother. The natural process of separation is never fully embraced or understood by the daughter or son. The constant rebellion, contention, conflict, and anger are the central behaviors covering up the underlying need for emotional closeness and empathy.

When these rebellious adults do finally create some productive separation from their mother, the damage and self-defeating life choices are severe. The use of anger as a defensive tool to create separation has only stalled the emotional development of the daughter/son. Anger is a very strong emotional bond and creates no separation, no insight, or emotionally appropriate mother-child distance. Rather, all the rebellious actions only reinforce the attachment and bond to the conflicted relationship between the mother-son/daughter. This is the biggest irony for rebellious daughters or sons; their behavior accomplishes the very thing they didn't want: more conflict and emotional hostility.

Many times, the teenager will be an "A" student and then suddenly develop academic problems. The college-age daughter will get married and pregnant and refuse to involve the mother. The twenty-eight-year-old son will continue to force his mother to financially support him. The forty-two-year-old son will suddenly divorce his wife, stop talking to his mother, abandon his children, and marry a twenty-two-year-old intern. The thirty-nine-year-old daughter will decide to have a baby out of wedlock and conceal her pregnancy from her mother. All these examples demonstrate real people attempting to create their own functional identity and life. Unfortunately, they've not successfully separated from their mother's home. They got stuck in the middle of the process.

The Frustrated Daughter/Son. These are the daughters or sons who know they need to be emotionally and mentally separate from their mother but haven't been able to accomplish it. The reasons seem as varied as the people involved. The separation hasn't happened or been completed for one primary reason: *emotional deprivation.* These are the daughters and sons of mothers who were unpredictable, inconsistent, self-absorbed, needy, and emotionally ambivalent. These children learned that one day Mom was great and two weeks later, Mom was upset, unavailable, and emotionally distant. The inconsistent maternal bond creates an ongoing personal sense of frustration and emotional longing for security and approval. These daughters/sons began to develop individual feelings of insecurity and anxiety about their place in the world. These emotions hindered their ability to create a solid sense of self and life purpose. Their adult relationships reflect an insecure attachment pattern and underlying excessive behavior.

The common question that these children, teenagers, mother-daughters, mother-sons, and adults ask is: *How do I leave home or separate when I have never received the emotional support and approval I need?* The answer is very complex and difficult. It is very challenging to separate when you don't have the emotional support, approval, and empathy you need to finish the process. How can you start the separation movement when you never felt attached in the first place? This ongoing mother-child dilemma becomes the frustrated adult's source of anxiety and depression. Your sense of loneliness, emotional emptiness, and anxiety is fueled by your emotional deprivation. The way deprivation functions is in your emotional sense of never having enough or believing you will ever get enough. The deep craving to have your primary emotional developmental needs met and fulfilled is constant. Therefore, the challenge of leaving the only possible source of nurturing—your mother—seems very frightening and terminally frustrating. The fact that you are discouraged about separating is a very positive sign and part of the maturation process. Regardless of your frustration, anxiety, and fear of failure and rejection at the prospect of separating from your mother, you are beginning to create your own life in pieces, one at a time.

Once the adult daughter/son actively begins the separation process, they will vacillate between intense love and intense anger toward the unpredictable, distant, cool, "drama queen" mother. Your frustration can be a cement block around your legs in your attempts to move forward. The frustrated daughter/son is consumed with various degrees of emotional deprivation, worrying about where the next emotional meal will come from or if it will come at all. Even if the metaphorical meal is bread crumbs, it is still better than starving—or is it? It might feel too risky to leave home, walk past your mother, and worry about your next emotional meal. How do you leave home if you spent your life dining on crumbs? It is this cycle of deprivation that creates frustration, excessive behaviors (e.g., alcoholism, gambling, addictive shopping, eating issues), anxiety, and long-term depression. The more you understand this pattern of deprivation and fear, the easier it will be to create the foundation to move forward, individuate, and emotionally separate from your mother. Regardless of if your mother is living, if you haven't spoken to her in years, or if she lives three thousand miles away, everyone needs to create his or her own emotional life and individuality. You need to try out your "wings" and move forward in your life.

The Parentified Style of Separating. "I think I was born an adult." This is what Madeline, age twenty-six, said to me on our first meeting. Appearing competent and mature, she continued, "I can't remember a time when I wasn't making sure my mother was happy or at least okay and that everything in our house was running smoothly." Madeline's feelings of being the parent aren't particular to her but rather are very common. Daughters and sons of this style grow up feeling and knowing that they are the emotional and psychological mental health caretakers of their mother. This is the job of these daughters and sons, and it is for life.

Madeline, like many other daughters/sons, finds it incredibly hard to leave her mother's metaphorical home and separate from her emotionally. It is difficult for so many children/adults to leave home when they didn't get what they needed growing up. Remember, in order for sons or daughters to successfully separate, they need to feel that what they are doing is the right and appropriate thing for them to do. Doing what feels developmentally appropriate is easier said than done. It is very complicated for a daughter who for many years has played the caretaker, "best friend," and/or emotional partner with her mother and family to suddenly abandon that role. The daughter/son is going to feel very guilty and shameful for giving up the role of "parent." This is one of the toughest things that parentified children have to emotionally understand. Many times, the family pressure from the mother and siblings is too much—the daughter/son will unconsciously never approach the opportunities, relationships, or careers that would create emotional distance from the mother. The caretaker role for a child is underestimated in its pull and long-term residual impact on the adult daughter and adult son.

The process of emotionally separating and forming a cohesive sense of self is the neverending challenge of this mother-child relationship. Madeline—and Nicole and David from chapter 6 ("The Best Friend Mother")—never had a normal childhood. These three adult children felt responsible for their mothers' needs and wants. Madeline not only had to help take care of her brothers and sisters, she also had the job of reassuring her mother that she was a wonderful mother. All three adults were constantly reassuring their mother that she was special, needed, loved, and the best. There was and still is no emotional or psychological room for Madeline's, Nicole's, or David's developmental needs to be addressed: *their mothers' unmet emotional needs are still first and foremost*. Their mothers' lives are the primary force in everything they did past and present. These types of loving, mature, and wonderful children/adults never fully understand their own role in life. It is only when the natural process of separation/individuation starts to become an issue that these adults even begin considering other ways of relating to their mothers.

Children of all ages gain a sense of who they are by seeing themselves reflected back in their mother's approval and support. When that motherly feedback says that they are doing fine, that they are loved and valued, a child internalizes it. Supportive reflection allows them to develop a secure sense of themselves. When Madeline, Nicole, and David looked to their mothers for validation, emotional support, guidance, and love, all they saw was their mothers' unmet emotional needs. These three adults entered adulthood feeling inadequate, guilty, and personally flawed (they couldn't fix their mother). There was no affirming mirror or maternal support available to them. It was all about taking care of their mother and all the aspects of her life. Parentified children grow up with a skewed view of the world. The pseudo-maturity among these children, teenagers, and adults is really an artificial covering for their developmental need for support, guidance, and confidence in the world.

We first met David and Dana in chapter 6 ("The Best Friend Mother"), and the following events have occurred since their story began. David was clearly the parentified son and Dana the extremely needy but sweet mother. David's sense of guilt and anger toward his mother didn't dissipate or evaporate when he suddenly moved to Wyoming (eighteen hundred miles away) to get out of his mother's house, literally and metaphorically. He decided that the only way he could successfully separate from his mother was to do the following. He discussed in therapy how he was going to fly his mother up to his house for the weekend and have the following discussion with her (per Dave's memory):

Mom, I have felt for years the pressure and need to take care of you. This is something that has evolved between the two of us for as long as I can remember. I love you, but I am not responsible for your life and your choices. The more I help you, the worse I feel. It is non-stop complaining by you for what I don't do. You are right. I am not that son, who does it all anymore. I will never have a successful marriage, father my children, or become the person I desire with this parent/child caretaking of you. I care about you, but I can't get emotionally involved in all of your daily tasks, crises, and personal issues anymore. It isn't my place and job, I resent and feel guilty for not always taking care of you. Please understand if I am not doing more for you, I simply can't be codependent with you.

David did have this discussion with Dana in an attempt to set clear boundaries with her. Dana then left David's house and went to the airport to change her flight home to leave three days earlier than planned. Dave and Dana didn't speak for five months. During that time, Dave felt enormous relief but also fear that his mother might do something drastic to herself. He called his mother on Mother's Day and wished her well. Dana spoke to Dave, and they began to discuss how they both could continue in a relationship without resenting each other. Dave never imagined that he could represent himself clearly to his mother without feeling emotionally enmeshed, paralyzed, and overwhelmed with fear.

Secure Adult Style. This is the style that represents approximately 10 percent of mother-daughter/son relationships. This is the mother who clearly was able to successfully achieve her own emotional separation and sense of individuality from her mother (your grandmother). This mother found her pathway to her own goals, feelings, values, opinions, and choices. This mother was supported by her mother for her continued development and growth. Regardless of the circumstances surrounding your mother's evolution, she was able to accomplish her own emotional separation and growth. Your mother's ability to have her own life—separate and apart from her mother's—allowed many of her psychological, emotional, spiritual, and physical needs to be realized and met.

When this process of separation has been successfully achieved, it allows the next generation of daughters and sons to do the same. The absence of unresolved emotional and enmeshment/disengagement issues creates psychological room for the daughter/son to explore his/her own inner life. Residual emotional concerns are nonexistent, enabling a positive mother-child connection. This style of mothering, bonding, problem solving, and communication empowers the daughter/son. The relationship between the mother and child is centered on the child preparing for adulthood so he can function at his full potential and emotional capacity.

This mother understands that her sole purpose in being a mother is to prepare her daughter/son for adulthood. Mothering is all about creating, developing, and nurturing full functional productivity in daughters and sons. Emotional separation and individuation are on the highway to those goals. This mother has helped to equip her children with emotional insight, understanding of relationships, psychological tools, self-esteem, emotional strength, and courage. These daughters and sons are the children that go out into the world and make great contributions. It has nothing to do with economic status, ethnicity, or education—it has to do with healthy emotions and functioning relationships. The mother who displays the secure separating style knows that her children don't exist for the sole purpose of meeting her needs. Children can't be used to fulfill a parent's unmet emotional issues from childhood. It never works, and the side effects of this type of emotional connection are very problematic. The daughters/sons of the complete mother have the pleasure of not being a replacement part in their mother's life or history. Unfortunately, many children feel like they are the substitution pieces in their mother's life, which causes all sorts of emotional issues and concerns. As noted earlier, the degree of difficulty in separating for a daughter/son from the mother is directly correlated to the level of separation she never completed.

All daughters or sons can develop a secure style of separating and individuating and pass that on to their children and/or other people in their life. The list below of the nine fundamental steps on how to successfully complete the formation of your identity is your next life task. The rest of your life—your relationships, your achievements, your setbacks, the deaths, the births, your marriage, the divorces, and all the other momentous things in your life will all continue to form and define your individuality. Your goal is to get out of your mother's house and build your own house.

YOU HOLD AND OWN YOUR SET OF DOOR KEYS

Do you remember the first time you received the keys to your first car, first apartment, first office door? It felt so good. Your sense of empowerment, success, excitement, and level of satisfaction in holding your own set of keys is life changing. You *have* your own set of keys to your life in your hands, though you might not even believe it or know what to do with them. We could spend more time discussing the importance of separating and individuating, but now it is time to actually do it. The nine keys for successfully separating/individuating from and moving out of your mother's orbit are for you to use. You have already begun launching yourself; now keep going forward with a goal in mind: you! It is all about your legacy, your choices.

NINE SEPARATION-INDIVIDUATION ACTION STEPS

1. *Stop the blame game.* Blaming your mother is like drinking poison and hoping it kills her. Blame, resentment, bitterness,

regret, and fear only halt your life. Blaming your mother is often a substitution for not taking action, making choices, and doing what is necessary in your life. Daughters and sons from enmeshed, disengaged, chaotic, and codependent mothers can successfully separate and create their own life.

Regardless of your mother's emotional state or mental health, you can make different choices—decisions that will empower your life. If you still blame, resent, or hate your mother, consider the problem as a way not to move forward. Blame is the number one reason for daughters/sons to have an underdeveloped life and unmet dreams. When you are fifty-six years old, it isn't your mother's fault for how your life has turned out. Your life is all yours and that is what you want.

2. *Accepting your mother.* Viewing your mother more accurately is good for both of you. Your mother isn't perfect, and you aren't either. What you can do is allow your mother to be who she really is, not what you always wanted her to be. Hoping your mother will be someone she isn't capable of being only keeps you in a perpetual state of frustration. Many times, a daughter/son is fearful of separating, so hoping that the mother will change only stalls the process. Your mother doesn't need to be ideal for you to move forward with your life.

3. *You aren't responsible for your mother's life.* This is one of the toughest sticking points when you have been raised, conditioned, and trained to be your mother's keeper. Taking full responsibility for your own life isn't an unloving behavior or disrespectful act. Many daughters and sons will get caught in the emotional trap of showing respect and "doing what is right." Carrying your mother emotionally and psychologically isn't good for either of you. This step addresses the underlying codependent issues, ties, and hidden enmeshment between you and your mother. *Loving your mother and being her emotional caretaker are two entirely different behaviors.* Learn the difference, because it will decide your future.

It is your duty to separate, not your mother's. Your mother doesn't need to separate from you or develop her own individuality. It is your developmental task and option. Many times, sons/daughters will wait for their mother to initiate the separation process. Waiting or asking for permission to move forward with your life is very risky. In either case, you are giving away your personal power to your mother and allowing her to dictate your behavior. Individuality is your ability to create your own feelings, increase your frustration tolerance, and metaphorically walk out of your mother's house. Your mother separated from her mother to whatever degree she did, and it is now your turn to do it.

4. *You have all the tools necessary to create your own life.* Your personal development is an inside job. You know what to do in order to further push your life forward. Many daughters and sons will rightfully complain that they didn't get the needed emotional support, self-confidence, or love to leave home. The answers to all these questions about your life are all within your reach. When you stop and consider what you want, should do, or will do, you know what action to take. Ignorance isn't an excuse to stall your development and personal growth. You already know what to do. You don't need your mother's direction or her approval. If you didn't know what to do, you wouldn't be considering the process.

5. *Change emotional deprivation to emotional abundance and excitement.* Daughters/sons who come from very emotionally distant, neglected, disengaged, cold, and abandoned childhoods have a difficult time valuing their life. Creating your own life is a form of nurturing and self-empathy. Feeling unimportant, unloved, or unnoticed are things that can be changed from the inside of your life outward. Knowing what you always wanted and pursuing it is the separation from an emotionally empty life to an emotionally enriched life. Deprivation needn't be the emotional condition of a lifetime. It can be resolved and changed to a sense of abundance and fulfillment on your terms. If you feel deprived in your adult relationships, it is something that you can address and change.

6. *You separate and create your own identity one step at a time*. Don't be discouraged that the things you want in your life aren't coming to you as fast as you would like. The rest of your life will be a series of steps in the continuation of forming your identity and a secure sense of self. Panic, impatience, and irritability about your life not unfolding as quickly or in the exact way you imagined can be a form of your deprivation/fear of never getting what you want. It takes time and patience for certain things to happen. Other events will occur rapidly and without much effort. Either way, write down the things you want in a partner, your career, your relationships, your children, your finances, and for yourself. Then make a vision board. This is a poster board with pictures out of magazines (or any source), sayings, and other visual images of what you want your life to be like. These exercises are very powerful because they show you consciously what you desire unconsciously. They also allow you to take your life one step at a time and not rush into circumstances for fear of losing the opportunity. *You are the opportunity*

7. *You can't fix your mother*. Her life is her sole responsibility. You aren't your mother's keeper, psychologist, or life partner. Commit yourself to learning and better understanding yourself first and foremost. Learn about what happened to you and your mother when you were growing up. Develop emotional tolerance for your mother's upsets and disappointments, becoming less emotionally enmeshed in her life. Your clear emotional boundaries will allow both you and your mother to develop a more functional and productive relationship. Both issues will make your life easier and more productive. The idea of fixing your mother's emotional pain and unmet needs is like taking a cup and trying to empty out Lake Michigan.

8. *Know what you always wanted from your mother and put that on your list for your life and relationships*. Allow your interpersonal needs to be the guideline for what you want in your life. There are many secrets, as well as valuable information, waiting

to be tapped into about your emotional legacy and life. Your unmet needs and wants with your mother are a great jumping-off point to begin addressing those issues in your relationships. The more you understand your emotional legacy, the more chances you will have to create the emotional life and relationships you want.

9. *Courage, empathy, and your internal instincts are very powerful.* Don't dismiss your life. Regardless of your prior personal history, this is your turn, your life to make the most of. The people in your world are waiting for you to step out and make everything come together in your life. All your relationships—social, professional, famial, intimate, and with yourself—are a reflection of you and your emotional legacy. *You are in full control of your life.* You wouldn't be reading this book if you weren't well on your way to having the type of relationships you have always wanted and craved. Your life is a combination of hundreds of relationships, and your emotional legacy holds them all together. You have the power, courage, empathy, and insight to continue with the needed separation/individuation steps in your life. Remember, it is very difficult to go out in the world if you stay inside your mother's house; the two directions aren't compatible or consistent. You can make the move and have the relationships and emotional connections you desire.

Chapter 12

Perfectly Imperfect
YOUR EMOTIONAL LEGACY
Lose the Baggage

I have always tried to move away from my mother. My mother
is very clingy and wants me to stay home. I resent her for not
letting me go to college. It is tough being my mother's best
friend and moving away.

—Nicole, age twenty-four

It took me forever to get over the burden of being resentful and
angry with my mother. I dated women for years that were like
mother substitutes and kind of like fill in, for the approval I was
seeking. Now I finally let go of my wish for my mother and me
getting along. It doesn't work and I have to move forward.

—Todd, age forty-three

NICOLE AND KERRI

We met Nicole and Kerri in chapter 6. Kerri displays the
best friend style of mothering, and her daughter,
Nicole, is her best friend. Nicole is now a twenty-five-year-old
single woman. Stan, Nicole's father, intervened between Nicole

and her mother and moved Nicole to New York City. The goal was for Nicole to get her master's degree in education. She told me the following when she came home during spring break,

> I have always been my mother's best friend. My mother is very depressed about my leaving home and moving three thousand miles away. My mother doesn't understand why my father pushed me to move and she wants to divorce him, but she won't. I have never felt so relieved and relaxed. Because of the three hour time difference, I am not always accessible to my mother and it is great. For the first time since the tenth grade, I have a serious boyfriend. I have never considered my life separate and apart from my mother's. I know that I will live near her at some point, but not right now, it is a relief to be single and not being my mother's keeper.

Nicole developed enough courage and emotional strength to physically and emotionally separate from her mother. Nicole told me that she asked her father to help her find a way to separate from her mother without hurting her feelings. Stan told Nicole that this was her fight and something she had to confront and resolve. She ultimately spoke to her mother and related the following story to me, "I told my mother that if I didn't move away I would never move. My mother only stared at me and had tears in her eyes. I felt like I was killing her." Nicole now lives in New York City and is attending school there. Her story is very special, because she found the emotional clarity and her own personal strength to separate from her mother and pursue her own individual goals and dreams. She had always struggled with low self-esteem and feeling inadequate to pursue her own dreams. She still calls her mother about twice a week, which is a 2,000 percent decline in contact between the two. Kerri feels very resentful that her husband and daughter made her out to be a "bad" mother for being too emotionally close to her daughter. Kerri and Stan are currently in marriage therapy to discuss their lack of intimacy and communication difficulties.

Like Nicole, many of you have to make a clear, nonnegotiable emotional boundary with your mother. This psychological boundary becomes the starting point of many more things you will do with your life and the separation/individuation process that is necessary. This is one of the biggest steps that daughters or sons can take to create the emotional space and distance to develop and grow their own dreams and life. Unless you begin to move toward creating your own opinions, thoughts, and tolerance for maternal disapproval, your self-esteem, individuation and separate life, and adult relationships will be very limited. Your self-limiting behavior will be your unconscious replay of your mother-child relationship.

STEPHAN'S STORY

I never intended to discuss or go much into my own mother factor legacy story, but I couldn't end this book without discussing some my own struggles. I wasn't raised with the complete style of mothering or anything remotely resembling that type of balanced mother-child relationship. I grew up with an emotionally enmeshed mother who employed a best friend style of mothering. I had no room to breathe while growing up. My mother was completely focused on me when she needed my support and extremely forgetful when she had something else on her mind. I learned to read her face and mood by the age of five. My mother factor has been an issue for me for as long as I can remember. I think I have always been an adult in a young boy's body. I was raised and groomed to be my mother's confidante, friend, and emotional caretaker. I wasn't raised to understand or know my own feelings, thoughts, and sense of self. I knew more about my mother's internal feelings than I did about my own. My mother never understood my natural need or desire to be independent and emotionally separate.

There were two seminal events that had a tremendous effect

on me as a child growing up. The first incident was when I was twelve years old. I was entering the seventh grade and needed money for a new ten-speed Schwinn bicycle—which was like four Porsches or a designer wardrobe at the time. A retired neighbor, Don—whose nickname "Shot Gun" came from his World War II duty riding shotgun with the troops in Europe—had broken his hip. My mother thought it would be great if I volunteered to be his helper, gardener, and friend for the summer. My mother wanted me to be a good neighbor, and this made sense to me. I got paid to watch reruns of the original *Candid Camera* TV show every afternoon. Life seemed pretty good until Don asked me if I had ever seen my mother naked. I remember thinking, this guy is a freak and why is he asking me that question? The answer was NO, though I pretended not to hear the question.

Well, the summer came and went but something really weird was happening. I had never considered my mother sexy, good-looking, or a "hottie." Don was always commenting on my mother's appearance. My mother looked like a mother and that was how I always viewed her. This was my mother, for goodness sake, and I didn't view my mother as any kind of sex object. My mother wasn't inappropriate in how she dressed or how she related to men. My father later told me that no normal guy views their mother as "hot." I felt normal after his sound fatherly advice, yet I didn't tell him about the inappropriate comments that Don was making on a regular basis. I always kept my mother's secrets and her opinions to myself. That was one of her rules, don't tell anything to anyone, even my dad.

Don played the "sick" patient long enough to make a sexual pass at my mother. He wanted her to come over at night and check out his hip alignment. One day, I walked into the living room of Don's house and caught him trying to touch my mother's breasts. They both yelled at me for walking in without knocking first. My mother came home, and we never discussed the incident and we never went over to Don's house again. He would flip me off with his middle finger whenever he was driving down the street or mouth, "f_ _k you." One time I threw the baseball I was holding and it hit his car. He stopped, got out, and I said in my meanest thirteen-year-old voice, "Go ahead, hit me and I will tell my dad the whole story." He got back in the car and never looked my way again. Don ultimately moved less than a year after sexually molesting my mother.

The second incident was two years later, in August of 1974. I was fifteen, and my father announced on a Friday afternoon that the following Sunday was the last day he would be living with us. I felt my stomach drop to the floor. The amount of sadness that overcame me was enormous. That Monday afternoon, my mother went in the backyard and couldn't stop crying. I never felt so scared, protective, overwhelmed, and numb. My dad was gone, and I now felt absolute and full responsibility for my mother's well-being. What a burden my mother became for the next ten years. I had saved her from that creepy neighbor and now my father had left her. I never felt that my father left me. We had a solid relationship and a good understanding between us. It was a very long ten years between my father's leaving and eventual return. My parents reconciled their marriage after a ten-year separation. I understand now, as an adult, why my father left. I never blamed him. My mother didn't want him around. She had me as her best friend and male support.

These two events, along with another two thousand daily occurrences of being my mother's rescuer, perfect son, perfect husband, protector, savior, and buffer against the world, were overwhelming. I never even considered that it was my mother's responsibility to handle the neighbor and the impending divorce, and that my older sister and I did not have to feel guilty about either event. Everything in my mother's life was always someone else's fault, their problem, or they were "bad." My mother and I were so emotionally enmeshed that I didn't really have a serious girlfriend until my junior year of college, and then my mother didn't like Kim (my girlfriend) or her mother. I truly felt like I carried my mother's entire emotional, mental, and psychological life. My mother would always complain to me what a "jerk" my father was for what he didn't do or say. I was always in conflict with her resentment and anger toward my father. The problem was that I was a man, and 50 percent of me came from my father. This fact always seemed to be missed by my mother when she ranted on about my father.

My sister, who was five years older, didn't experience my mother's emotional enmeshment and dependency the way I did. My teen years into my mid-twenties were emotionally frustrating and at times very lonely and hopeless. My mother didn't believe in spending money or expending her energy on me. Fortunately, I received an academic/financial aid scholarship for tuition. Even while attending college, however, I had to move home and continue taking emotional care of my mother. I felt this incredible responsibility to help and care for her. I never even considered the possibility that I was enmeshed with her. It was like breathing, I just did it. My mother is a wonderful woman, sweet, smart, intuitive, who had numerous unresolved emotional needs that tapped right into me and shaped me into the "perfect son." My mother had emotional concerns that I had no way of resolving. It wasn't until I was in my early thirties when that realization finally hit me.

My big emotional break came in several small pieces. Each time a life transition would happen, I would take another emotional step away from being enmeshed toward what I now know is the middle of the optimal emotional functioning scale. Even today, I still have to be very clear about not being codependent, feeling deprived, or "rescuing" people in my relationships, including my children. I had to apply every tool, step, insight, and idea in this book to create enough emotional breathing room in my own life. Separation and individuation from an emotionally enmeshed mother is like having your right arm removed one cell at a time. It is a very painful process. I have heard numerous women say how needy and demanding their mother is and that men have it easy. The mother factor legacy isn't a gender issue, nor does one side have it tougher than the other. It isn't a male/female problem but a universally occurring process. The dilemma of the mother factor legacy has to be resolved by every child/teen/adult. We all eventually have to separate/individuate from our first love. We all have a first love, and it isn't the cute guy in the second grade or the unbelievable girl in your third-period English class. It's your mother.

OWNERSHIP OF THE MOTHER FACTOR

After all of our discussions, we need to think about what the mother factor really is. And how can a man write about a woman's issue—or is it? We all are sons and daughters. Well, I need to say that we all have a mother, an emotional relationship with her, and her emotional legacy. We are all sons and daughters, and mother-child issues are universal. Your mother-child relationship isn't defined by your gender. It is defined by your emotional functioning, connections, and style of relationship. Mothers, daughters, and sons are struggling to make sense of their relationship, which many times make no sense at all. So who does the mother factor affect? It is people with very strong emotional bonds, unresolved conflicts, enmeshment issues, disengagement issues, and one of five different styles of mothering, all trying to move forward with their lives.

The mother factor then is *the conscious understanding and emotional awareness of the significant role your mother had in forming your relationship style, your template for emotionally relating to everyone in your life, your emotional style of connecting, as well as the unconscious and conscious rules you live by, your ability to nurture yourself, and your capacity for empathy, compassion, and emotional insight.* These qualities make up the fabric of your mother factor legacy and the quality of your present-day relationships. Your comprehension of these traits isn't just for your intimate relationships but for everything in your life that you emotionally attach to and connect with. There isn't any area of your life that hasn't been impacted by your mother's influence. Regardless of the degree of enmeshment, disengagement, and/or emotional balance, you can gain an enormous amount of insight into your life today from an understanding of your mother. Nothing is wasted. Look and think about all the stories in this book and all the ones you personally have. No matter what happened between you and your mother, you can use it to move your life forward in a positive direction. There is no time or room in your life for blame, resentment, or fear of leaving home. It is time to move forward to the level of intimacy and the depth of relationships that you crave.

The most productive style of mothering—the complete style—is the emotional model we want to move toward in all our relationships. This style of relating is a very high-functioning and nurturing model for all areas of your life. The fundamental emotional, mental, and psychological strengths of the complete mother factor are:

1. emotional insight and psychological understanding
2. self-confidence and emotional security/strong attachments
3. emotional/mental stability—balanced attachments (optimal)
4. courage, as in the separation/individuation process
5. high emotional functioning—being empathic, emotionally attuned, compassionate, emotionally responsive, and emotionally present

TIME TO UNPACK YOUR SUITCASES— NO CARRY-ON BAGGAGE

There isn't a quality, behavior, or emotional strength listed above that all of us haven't had or used at times with our mothers, partners, friends, and ourselves. This list is the heart of your emotional life and every relationship you will ever form and attach to. This is the bottom line of what spurs, accompanies, and follows separation and individuation. People ask all the time, what is emotional health? The list above is your new pocket edition of what we all desire.

You have nearly finished reading and experiencing this book. You now feel change is in the air and in your immediate future. You know the most common emotional roadblocks that create severe emotional pain and heartbreak. You have experienced these feelings, thoughts, and emotions in your professional, personal, and family relationships. These emotional blocks can cause all of your potential and natural abilities in relationships to be wasted and undeveloped. We've seen that the emotional side effects of the different mothering styles are:

- Shame—never being "good enough"
- Excessive/Addictive Behaviors—emotional instability
- Codependence and Dependent Personality
- Fear of Abandonment/Intimacy—emotional neglect
- Anger—rage/resentment

These aren't the qualities, reactions, connections, or feelings that you want emotionally or relationally. We all have to leave home, and many times our emotional suitcases are jam-packed with these emotional bricks. *They leave no room for the positive emotions, secure feelings, and optimistic beliefs that strengthen our life and everything we attach to and love.* This entire book has been dedicated to showing you how to lose your emotional baggage from your mother and your childhood and to rethink your choices. No one wants to perpetually carry around two large eighty-five-pound suitcases of emotional baggage. Your life can consist of no baggage or only a small carry-on bag. We all agree less emotional baggage from your mother is better than more. Recall the classic Buddhist saying "Less is more." The "less" translates into less emotional conflict, pain, and anger. The "more" becomes more freedom, choices, and secure relationships.

Losing your emotional baggage and becoming "perfectly imperfect" is in your hands now. It is all up to you. No one can hold you back or tell you that you don't have enough information for your journey into adulthood. You know that self-acceptance is the royal highway out of the valley of despair and self-hatred. You now understand that excessive behavior is related to your childhood and the unresolved anxiety from it. Remember that our mothers aren't responsible for our life now—it's all ours. Your mother was clearly a huge influence on your life, but she isn't your life. Many of us (me included) lived a great deal of our early adult years as if our mother was our be all and end all. Now it is time for you to take over your life. One of the core messages of this book is that the mother blame game or emotional ignorance isn't an option any more.

Finally, don't allow another day to go by that you carry some residual problem, issue, or painful emotion from your mother-child relationship without doing something about it. Don't allow the biggest emotional cancer—shame—to eat away at your inner fabric and core strength. Your life isn't about being perfect. We all have experienced emotional disappointments and worse, such as divorce, career failure, parenting issues, poor financial choices, poor intimate selections, eating disorders, sexual abuse, and even a criminal record. Your life is full of people who will tell you to give up on your mother-child relationship issues, that all that stuff is "psychobabble." Make no mistake, this is your key to optimal emotional health and fulfilling relationships. If you don't act in your best regard and interest, there aren't enough medication, drugs, alcohol, or money that will take away the sense of failure and regret and depression that you may carry into your future relationships and attachments. I urge you to seriously reconsider your life and how to unload the emotional baggage. A timeless psychological truism is that *there is no substitution for action.* Insight without action is love with no emotional attachment. You have the keys, the wisdom, the insight, and the personal power. I know it takes courage to open the "mother" door and all the other doors that you will face in your life. Your legacy is in every page of this book and played out in every minute of your life. You can open all the doors you want and close the ones you want. What do you choose to do?

ENDNOTES

INTRODUCTION

1. Howard Gardner, *Developmental Psychology*, 2nd ed. (Glenview, IL: Scott Foresman, 1988), pp. 93–131.

2. Jess Feist, *Theories of Personality*, 2nd ed. (Fort Worth, TX: Holt, Rinehart, and Winston, 1990), pp. 154–90.

3. Stephan B. Poulter, *The Father Factor: How Your Father's Legacy Impacts Your Career* (Amherst, NY: Prometheus Books, 2006), pp. 19–38.

4. Judith Rich Harris, *The Nurture Assumption—Why Children Turn Out the Way They Do* (New York: Free Press, 1998), pp. 35–54.

CHAPTER 1

1. Alicia F. Lieberman, *The Emotional Life of the Toddler* (New York: Free Press, 1994), pp. 1–7.

2. John Bowlby, *Attachment and Loss* (New York: Basic Books, 1969), pp. 156–75.

3. Bowlby, *A Secure Base: Parent-Child Attachment and Healthy Human Development* (New York: Basic Books, 1988), pp. 87–99.

4. Howard Gardner, *Developmental Psychology*, 2nd ed. (Glenview, IL: Scott Foresman, 1988), pp. 38–49.

CHAPTER 2

1. Helen Schucman, *A Course in Miracles*, 2nd ed., combined vol. (Mill Valley, CA: Foundation, 1992), pp. 112–36.
2. Ronald Potter-Efron and Patricia Potter-Efron, *The Secret Message of Shame* (Oakland, CA: New Harbinger, 1999), pp. 7–24.
3. Ibid., pp. 59–73.

CHAPTER 5

1. Marion F. Solomon, *Narcissism and Intimacy: Love and Marriage in an Age of Confusion* (New York: W.W. Norton Professional Books, 1999), pp. 63–79.
2. Stephan B. Poulter, *The Father Factor: How Your Father's Legacy Impacts Your Career* (Amherst, NY: Prometheus Books, 2006), pp. 20–39.
3. Jess Feist, *Theories of Personality*, 2nd ed. (Fort Worth, TX: Holt, Rinehart, and Winston, 1990), pp. 648–75.

CHAPTER 9

1. Bob Greene, *Total Body Make Over* (New York: Simon & Schuster Books, 2006), pp. 22–62.
2. David Zinczenko, *Men's Health Training Guide—How to Get Started* (New York: Men's Health, 2007), pp. 52–110.

CHAPTER 10

1. Ronald Potter-Efron and Patricia Potter-Efron, *The Secret Message of Shame* (Oakland, CA: New Harbinger, 1999), pp. 60–74.

CHAPTER 11

1. E. Wachtel, *The Family Psyche over Three Generations: The Geneogram Revisited* (New York: Journal of Marital and Family Therapy, 1992), pp. 335–43.

BIBLIOGRAPHY

Blumenthal, Noah. *You're Addicted to You*. San Francisco, CA: Berrett-Koehler, 2007.

Bourne, Edmund J., PhD. *The Anxiety & Phobia Workbook*. 4th ed. Oakland, CA: New Harbinger, 2005.

Bourne, Edmund J., PhD, Arlen Brownstein, ND, and Lorna Garano. *Natural Relief for Anxiety*. Oakland, CA: New Harbinger, 2004.

Bourne, Edmund, PhD, and Lorna Garano. *Coping with Anxiety: 10 Simple Ways to Relieve Anxiety, Fear & Worry*. Oakland, CA: New Harbinger, 2003.

Brazelton, T. Berry. *Working and Caring*. Reading, MA: Addison-Wesley, 1992.

Brown, Byron. *Soul without Shame. A Guide to Liberating Yourself from the Judge Within*. Boston: Shambhala, 1999.

Craighead, Linda W., PhD. *The Appetite Awareness Workbook*. Oakland, CA: New Harbinger, 2006.

Dacey, John S., and Lisa B. Fiore. *Your Anxious Child: How Parents and Teachers Can Relieve Anxiety in Children*. San Francisco: Jossey-Bass, 2002.

Davidson, Jonathan, MD, and Henry Dreher. *The Anxiety Book: Developing Strength in the Face of Fear*. New York: Riverhead Books, 2003.

Deak, Joann, PhD, with Teresa Barker. *Girls Will Be Girls: Raising Confident and Courageous Daughters*. New York: Hyperion, 2002.

DeRosis, Helen, PhD. *Women & Anxiety: A Step-by-Step Program for Managing Anxiety and Depression*. New York: Hatherleigh Press, 1998.

Eliot, John, PhD. *Overachievement: The New Model for Exceptional Performance*. New York: Penguin Group, 2004.

Estes, Clarissa P., PhD. *Women Who Run with the Wolves*. New York: Random House, 1992.

Farber, Steve. *The Radical Leap: A Personal Lesson in Extreme Leadership*. Chicago: Dearborn Trade, 2004.

Garbarino, James, PhD. *And Words Can Hurt Forever: How to Protect Adolescents from Bullying, Harassment, and Emotional Violence*. New York: Free Press, 2002.

———. *Parents Under Siege: Why You Are the Solution, Not the Problem in Your Child's Life*. New York: Free Press, 2001.

Gottman, John. *Raising an Emotionally Intelligent Child*. New York: Simon & Schuster, 1997.

Harrison, Harry H., Jr. *Father to Daughter: Life Lessons on Raising a Girl*. New York: Workman Publishing, 2003.

Helgoe, Laurie A., PhD, Laura R. Wilhelm, PhD, and Martin J. Kommor, MD. *The Anxiety Answer Book*. Naperville, IL: Sourcebooks, 2005.

Kelly, Joe. *Dads & Daughters: How to Inspire, Understand, and Support Your Daughter*. New York: Broadway Books, 2005.

Kindlon, Dan. *Too Much of a Good Thing: Raising Children of Character in an Indulgent Age*. New York: Hyperion, 2001.

Lang, Gregory E. *Why a Daughter Needs a Dad: 100 Reasons*. Nashville, TN: Cumberland House, 2002.

Levine, Mel, MD. *Ready or Not, Here Life Comes*. New York: Simon & Schuster, 2005.

Lock, James, MD, PhD, and Daniel Le Grange, PhD. *Help Your Teenager Beat an Eating Disorder*. New York: Guilford Press, 2005.

Lofas, Jeannette, CSW, and Dawn B. Sova. *Stepparenting: The Family Challenge of the Nineties*. New York: Kensington Books, 1985.

MacKenzie, Robert J. *Setting Limits: How to Raise Responsible, Independent Children by Providing Reasonable Boundaries*. Rocklin, CA: Prima Publishing, 1993.

Maxwell, John C. *Winning with People: Discover the People Principles that Work for You Every Time*. Nashville, TN: Nelson Books, 2004.

McCabe, Randie, PhD, and Traci L. McFarlane, PhD. *The Overcoming Bulimia Workbook*. Oakland, CA: New Harbinger, 2003.

McQuillan, Susan, MS, RD. *Psychology Today Here to Help: Breaking the Bonds of Food Addiction*. New York: Alpha Books, 2004.

Mellody, Pia. *Facing Love Addiction: Giving Yourself the Power to Change the Way You Love*. New York: HarperCollins, 2003.

Moore, John D. *Confusing Love with Obsession*. 3rd ed. Center City, MN: Hazelden, 2006.

Nash, Joyce D., PhD. *Binge No More: Your Guide to Overcoming Disordered Eating*. Oakland, CA: New Harbinger, 1999.

Navratilova, Martina. *Shape Your Self*. Emmaus, PA: Rodale, 2006.

Osherson, Samuel, PhD. *Wrestling with Love: How Men Struggle with Intimacy, with Women, Children, Parents, and Each Other*. New York: Random House, 1992.

Peabody, Susan. *Addiction to Love: Overcoming Obsession and Dependency in Relationships*. Berkeley, CA: Celestial Arts, 2005.

Peurifoy, Reneau Z., MA, MFCC. *Overcoming Anxiety: From Short-Term Fixes to Long-Term Recovery*. New York: Henry Holt, 1997.

Phillips, Bill. *Success Journal: Body for Life*. New York: HarperCollins, 2002.

Poulter, Stephan B., PhD. *The Father Factor: How Your Father's Legacy Impacts Your Career*. Amherst, NY: Prometheus Books, 2006.

———. *Father Your Son: Becoming the Father You Have Always Wanted to Be*. New York: McGraw-Hill, 2004.

Poulter, Stephan B., PhD, and Barbara Zax, PhD. *Mending the Broken Bough—Restoring the Promise of the Mother-Daughter Relationship*. New York: Berkley Publishers, 1998.

Raskin, Donna. *The Everything Easy Fitness Book*. 2nd ed. Avon, MA: F + W Publications, 2007.

Real, T. *I Don't Want to Talk about It: Overcoming the Secret Legacy of Male Depression*. New York: Scribner, 1997.

Roizen, Michael F., MD, Tracy Hafen, MS, and Laurence A. Armour. *The Real Age Workout*. New York: HarperCollins, 2006.

Rolfe, Randy. *The 7 Secrets of Successful Parents*. Chicago: Contemporary Books, 1997.

Roth, Geneen. *Feeding the Hungry Heart: The Experience of Emotional Eating*. New York: Macmillan, 2002.

———. *When Food Is Love: Exploring the Relationship between Eating and Intimacy*. New York: Penguin Group, 1991.

Saxen, Ron. *The Good Eater*. Oakland, CA: New Harbinger, 2007.

Shaffer, Susan M., and Linda P. Gordon. *Why Girls Talk and What They're Really Saying: A Parent's Guide to Connecting with Your Teen*. New York: McGraw-Hill, 2005.

Sheehan, David V., MD. *The Anxiety Disease*. New York: Scribner, 1983.

Siegel, Michelle, PhD, Judith Brisman, PhD, and Margot Weinshell, MSW. *Surviving an Eating Disorder*. New York: HarperCollins, 1998.

Simon, Sidney B., and Suzanne Simon. *Forgiveness: How to Make Peace with your Past and Get on with Your Life*. New York: Warner Books, 1990.

Smith, Chelsea Browning. *Diary of an Eating Disorder*. Lanham, MD: Taylor Trade, 1998.

Twerski, Abraham J., MD. *Addictive Thinking: Understanding Self-Deception*. 2nd ed. Center City, MN: Hazelden, 1999.

Zieghan, Suzen J., PhD. *The Stepparent's Survival Guide: A Workbook for Creating a Happy Blended Family*. Oakland, CA: New Harbinger, 2002.